CELEBRATING PASSAGES
IN THE CHURCH

CELEBRATING PASSAGES IN THE CHURCH

REFLECTIONS AND RESOURCES

EDITED BY

HUGH W. SANBORN

Chalice Press

St. Louis, Missouri

Biblical quotations, unless otherwise noted, are from the *New Revised Standard Version Bible,* copyright 1989, Division of Christian Education of the National Council of Churches of Christ in the USA. Used by permission.

Those quotations marked RSV are from the *Revised Standard Version* of the Bible, copyright 1952, [2nd edition, 1971] by the Division of Christian Education of the National Council of the Churches of Christ in the United States of America. Used by permission. All rights reserved.

Reprinted by permission of Simon & Schuster, from *The New Testament in Modern English,* revised edition, translated by J. B. Phillips. © 1958, 1960, 1972 by J. B. Phillips.

Scripture quotations marked REB are from the *Revised English Bible,* copyright © Oxford University Press and Cambridge University Press, 1989.

Portions of chapter 4 were first published in *Modern Liturgy,* "Coming of Age: A Celebration of Passage," 14 (Summer '87), 12–14.

Art by Wendy Aldwyn on p. ix is used by permission of the artist.

Cover design: Cecil King, Dreamtek

Interior design: Elizabeth Wright

Art direction: Michael Domínguez

This book is printed on acid-free, recycled paper.

Visit Chalice Press on the World Wide Web at

www.chalicepress.com

10 9 8 7 6 5 4 3 2 1   99 00 01 02 03 04

Library of Congress Cataloging–in–Publication Data

Celebrating passages in the church / edited by Hugh W. Sanborn.

    p. cm.

   ISBN 0-8272-0472-8

   1. Occasional services. 2. Rites and ceremonies. 3. Life cycle, Human—Religious aspects—Christianity. 4. Life change events—Religious aspects—Christianity. I. Sanborn, Hugh Wiedman, 1939– .

BV199.03C45 1998   97–49690

265'.9—dc21   CIP

Contents

Preface

It was an incredibly brilliant, cool, sunlit day as Barbara and I, together with our children, Beth (17) and Dan (13), drove into the city of Palo Alto to begin our joint sabbatical in northern California. Barbara, a biochemistry professor and researcher, had a semester appointment as visiting scholar at Stanford, and I, a campus minister, professor, and pastoral therapist, would be serving as a visiting scholar at the Graduate Theological Union at Berkeley. Our children were registered for the spring term in the Palo Alto public school system. Excitement and expectation as well as uneasiness, travel weariness, and the anxiety of change formed an unsettling mix of emotions influencing our thoughts as we arrived at the small house that would serve as our home for the next six months.

Change seems more often than not to be accompanied by ambivalent feelings. When change, such as taking a prolonged trip, beginning an important new relationship, or experiencing the onset of an illness—experiences referred to as major transitional events in this book—is connected in some way to one or more of life's major stage transitions or passages in self and/or significant others, ambivalent feelings are inevitable. As we began our California experience, Barbara and I, and to some extent our children, were keenly aware that our sabbatical afforded a special time for family sharing during our son's entry into puberty and just prior to our daughter's final year of high school and departure for college.

In preparation for my sabbatical, I had devoted considerable thought to a project that I knew had as much personal as professional interest: a study of how the church might recognize, understand, and celebrate the passage from adolescence to young adulthood. The idea had been spawned years earlier from reflection on a bar mitzvah service I had attended. With our daughter's high school graduation fast approaching, Barbara and I were attempting to prepare ourselves for the reality that Beth would soon be a college student living away from home. Having hardly assimilated the fact that our little girl had passed through the transition our son was now beginning to experience, from childhood to adolescence, it was becoming increasingly clear to us that the next transition marked a major change in our family that would be even more difficult to incorporate into our lives. Just thinking about that passage, which at times of teenage confrontation we wished would take place *tout de suite*, elicited so many ambivalent feelings related to past parental successes and failures, our daughter's development and growth needs, and our own developmental stages, that we usually preferred to imagine it as ahead in the distant future. In my usual approach to such stressful personal concerns, I had determined to tackle the issue on theoretical grounds in order to prepare myself, and hopefully to some extent my wife, to move onto the more sacred ground of offering parental blessing to our blooming young adult daughter.

Thus, the very personal and theoretical idea that had been germinating in my mind for several years took on urgency during our California sabbatical. Soon after I had completed the coming of age essays that appear here as chapter 4, the time arrived for Barbara and me to join Beth in preparing to celebrate the beginning of her passage to young adulthood. It was the power of that liturgical celebration, a meaningful spiritual experience for our family members as well as the members of our extended church family in attendance—few eyes were dry—that convinced me of the potential significance of celebrating such passages and major transitional events in the church. Reflecting on the process that led up to the service and the liturgical celebration itself, in brief, gave birth to the underlying premise of this book, which will be discussed at length in the Introduction. Suffice it to state here that it is the editor's intent to treat all of life's major passages but just a few of life's major transitional events. I hope the latter will suggest how these important life experiences may be celebrated and/or constructively affirmed through liturgy.

The format of the book consists predominantly of a series of coupled chapters that begin with theory/theology and end with practice or suggested liturgies. This format is intended to make the book more readable, both for those interested in turning to selected passages or transitional events, and for those interested in reading the book from cover to cover. The latter will find that the book is organized chronologically on the developmental basis of life's passages from birth to death. Major transitional events, many of which could take place at more than one stage, are somewhat arbitrarily positioned within this developmental framework.

The authors participating in this study have intended to be both theologically provocative and liturgically creative. Few readers, as well as few of the authors themselves, will concur with all the theological assumptions and assertions expressed in the chapters of this book. But few who journey through its pages will escape being drawn into theological discussion on one issue or another, or fail to find fertile possibilities in one or another of the suggested liturgies. The sincere hope of the authors, in other words, is that this study will promote constructive theological dialogue that will contribute to the expansion and vitality of the liturgical life of Christian communities.

The editor is indebted to numerous persons who provided advice and encouragement throughout the lengthy process of this project's formation, especially my clergy colleagues in campus ministry, the Presbyterian Clergy Theological Study Group, and the United Church of Christ Clergy Growth Group, as well as university colleagues, students, and members of the United Campus Ministry Board. All of these colleagues have demonstrated extraordinary patience with me as I have persistently pushed my particular perspective on celebrating passages in the church. Most of all the editor is deeply grateful to Howard Clinebell, who has written such an enticing Foreword, and to the authors who, through their enduring commitment to the project and labor of love, have given this book its unique character. I also express appreciation to my secretary, Martha Brooke, who labored long hours at the computer to put the entire manuscript on disks, and especially to my friend and favorite artist, Wendy Aldwyn, whose artistic interpretation of the theme and character of this book appears below.

One final note of gratitude to the authors is in order, for it truly has been a labor of love. The authors have all agreed to designate United Campus Ministry of Greater Houston, the ecumenical ministry to higher education in the Houston vicinity to which this book is dedicated, as the recipient of all royalties derived from the sale of the book. Thanks to the authors, your purchase has resulted in a contribution to this important ecumenical mission.

Hugh W. Sanborn

Foreword

Howard Clinebell

In the modern period of pastoral ministry, an unfortunate chasm has opened up between the pastoral functions of ministry and priestly functions, including leading sacred rituals. The chasm has been particularly wide and deep in the area of pastoral care. This was because the contemporary renaissance in pastoral care and counseling grew out of the CPE movement that began as a needed critique of hollow moralism and oppressive theology in some traditional Protestant circles. It is good now, indeed, that the chasm has begun to be bridged in recent years, and that this book makes significant contributions to the bridge-building task.

The outstanding group of twelve authors demonstrates repeatedly how rituals and liturgies, rooted in wholeness-nurturing theological and psychological understandings, can be open channels of healing and spiritual growth. They bring fresh illumination to many perplexing life crises and passages by joining in-depth head knowledge with the spiritual wisdom of their hearts. The liturgies they propose are key ingredients in educational processes aimed at facilitating meaningful growth during these periods of stressful transition.

Hugh Sanborn is to be commended wholeheartedly for providing the opportunity for the authors to generate the many bridge-building insights and programs with which this volume is replete. He also models what he asked other authors to write by producing a refreshing pair of chapters on celebrating the passage to young adulthood, triggered by reflections surrounding his daughter's making this important transition. His strenuous efforts and persistence certainly have paid off well with the publication of this book. (As you may know, editing a multi-authored symposium that has a coherent message consumes more creative time and energy than writing a book solo from scratch.) How fortunate we are that Hugh's vision inspired and motivated the well-equipped participants in this project, through all its ups and downs.

What is the guiding vision that provides the book's unifying motif? It is the convincing proposition that traditional sacred ceremonies of Christian churches must now be augmented and enriched drastically by creating new rituals, as well as by contemporizing traditional liturgical practices. By doing this, the authors help bring the healing energies of spiritually empowered rituals to many of life's transitional events in fresh ways. They do the same for the *new* life passages that lengthening longevity—twenty-nine years in the United States since 1900—has given to millions of people in this century. Many of the common life crises and life passages covered in these pages had been virtually ignored in the traditional liturgical dramas of churches.

Sanborn's hope-filled intent was that the book would be "both theologically provocative and liturgically creative." This hope is fulfilled again and again by the innovative authors. The intellectual rigor, fresh insights, and innovative spirit that they frequently bring to its pages are impressive, to say the least. Let me illustrate what I mean by sharing a few personal responses. Having experienced most of the developmental crises and many of the transitional events, I read certain chapters with a blend of personal and professional interest. During this reading, I now and again felt unexpected twinges of sadness. As I reflected on these feelings, their source became clear. They came from my awareness that meaningful spiritual rites of passage were not readily available to help celebrate many of our children's major growth transitions, to help me negotiate some of my own less-than-smooth times of passage. For example, as I reflected on my male midlife struggles, I could affirm William O. Roberts' suggestion that "the church should seize the opportunity to address the need for men to know why they become middle-aged crazy." I read with special interest Marie Johnson's life-affirming, feminist discussion of the theme, "We can celebrate so many things" in women's mid-years. As I did, I recalled some of the depressed, mid-years women with whom I had the privilege of counseling through the years. I wish now that I had had the advantage of some of Marie's insights during those sessions. Furthermore, as I read Marie's and Cricket Harrison's chapters, I found myself wishing that there were more than two women among the book's distinguished authors.

The book is strengthened by the way that many of the authors share from the inner richness of their experience and wisdom as seasoned religious professionals. I knew Paul Maves and found that the wisdom in his chapters spoke to my condition as he reflected on "The Transitions of Later Maturity." You will also be touched, I believe, by this heartfelt tribute by his daughter: "In writing about the process of change that occurs throughout life, my father drew on his own rich experience. He was open to change, including his own death in September 1994. In his 81 years he made major moves in location, ranging from Vermont to California, and also made significant changes in career. He faced change with perception of the challenges and costs, determined to be involved as an active, committed participant in the process." I have a hunch that the adult children of other authors could write comparable affirmations.

As you will soon see, the authors who were invited (and, I suspect, persuaded in some cases by a little gentle arm-twisting) to contribute chapters represent a rich variety of faith traditions, ministerial backgrounds, academic disciplines, and theological perspectives. This is as it had to be. Only thus could the book stimulate readers from many backgrounds to create or adapt their own rituals so that they are relevant to their own professional context. A helpful aspect of the book is the format in which each of the theory-generating chapters is followed by a chapter presenting sample liturgies by which the authors illustrate and illuminate solid theoretical formulations. It is fortunate that the theoretical models have their theological foundations spelled out clearly and that many have been tested and refined in the authors' own ministries.

Like any literary symposium, it is likely that some chapters will be considerably more appealing to you than others. You may decide that certain innovative rituals will not fly in the circles where you do ministry. Several of the models described seem to demand much more time than most busy clergy can commit, however important the objectives. But among these diverse chapters, you can expect to find many that stimulate the creative juices to flow where this matters most—in your own thinking, creating, and planning of resources for ministry.

Let me reflect briefly on why we humans are a ritual-creating species and why empowering, spiritual rituals are so vital to our spiritual and ethical wellness today and tomorrow. Some key findings of the classical cross-cultural studies by two sociologists—Emile Durkheim and Max Weber—are relevant to these issues. They observed that the collective rites and rituals in various cultures serve valuable functions in terms of those cultures' belief systems. Initiation rites, grief rituals, celebrations of the annual cycle of the seasons, and shared eating and drinking rituals—all tend to produce social cohesion, reduce ambivalence, increase conformity, and exert controls on socially unacceptable beliefs and behaviors. Equally important, they also tend to renew relationships among participants and between them and their deities.

But why do ritual celebrations and other corporate ritual occasions so frequently have strong religious orientations, even if they are not official functions of organized religious groups? The answer takes us to the heart of why crucial issues for fostering spiritually centered wellness in these turbulent times are illuminated by this book. In contemporary society—struggling with collective transition anxieties spawned by the twilight of the old millennium, reinforced by anticipatory anxieties concerning the dawning of the new millennium—shared sacred ceremonies have particular importance. Erik Erikson, in contrast to Freud, emphasized the health-sustaining functions of many religious rituals particularly in such a social context. He saw shared religious rituals as providing individuals and their faith communities with trust in a cosmic order that is just, loving, and continuing in time of kaleidoscopic change. For example, he understood the function of religious eating and drinking rituals such as holy communion as being to provide regular renewal of basic trust in parents, as they consume that which they regard as symbols of ultimate goodness. This trust renewal enables them to transmit vital trust to their children as they develop in troubled times.

I would add that, on a profound, often unconscious level, religious beliefs and belief-embodying rituals are ways of handling individual and collective existential anxiety. In contrast to neurotic anxiety, this anxiety flows from the human awareness of the mysteries and grief of time and continuing change, of aging and death. It flows from our species' haunting awareness that we are blends of animals and angels—rooted in nature with its sickness and death, and yet also transcending nature psychologically and spiritually, as creatures formed with a divine image at the heart of our deep Self. As animals who know we will die, we humans depend on group-generated religious rituals to help us cope with the existential mysteries in which all of our lives are immersed. There are no psychological or psychotherapeutic answers to existential anxiety. But, as Søren Kierkegaard, the grandfather of existentialism, once observed, a vital faith can transform it into a "school" in which spiritual growth occurs. Sacred rituals help sustain trustful faith so that it transforms our awareness of death and the living death of meaninglessness into a stimulus for creative living. Thus, these rituals liberate some of the creative energy tied up in existential anxiety, making it available to serve the longing to live what the Gospel of John called "life in all its fullness."

This book covers well a wide spectrum of rituals and liturgies focusing on individual and family life-passages and crises. It is my hope that there will be a sequel dealing with the pressing social and ecological crises of our times. Among these needed rituals of societal transformation are rituals of protest and "rites of rebellion." One example is the merrymaking Mardi Gras festival in New Orleans and in Latin American countries. Such festivals serve as relatively healthy release valves that drain off tensions from frustrations, sexual drives, and hostile impulses that accumulate in "polite" society. But many such rituals of protest are much more than social release valves. They are protests against oppression and the privileged groups that cause, and profit from, economic exploitation of the poor. Examples include the traditional farmers' masked dance in Korea, and the hilarious Doo-Daa parade spoofing the multimillion dollar "Rose Parade" preceding the Rose Bowl football extravaganza in Pasadena, California. The power of such rituals of protest are illustrated dramatically by the symbolic actions of the ancient Hebrew prophets, and by some contemporary prophetic spirits such as the following: Gandhi's fasting for freedom and leading a march of poor people to the sea to break the British monopoly by making salt illegally; the interfaith prayer protests accompanied by nonviolent resistance at the Nevada test site that symbolized our government's insane nuclear policies, past and present; and the interfaith "prayer meeting" of 5,000 people during the apartheid terror in South Africa. The latter was a passionate but vain attempt to prevent the bulldozing of "Crossroads," a huge squatters village of black workers and their families near Cape Town.

Another crucial area where rituals of social protest and transformation are desperately needed today relates to our species' catastrophic mistreatment of God's creation—the wonderful, living network of living things that is in us as we are in it. Our planet home is facing an awesome reality unprecedented in the four-billion-year story of continuing creation and evolving life. In biblical terms, ours is the first generation to hold in its hands the future health of God's creation. For the first time ever, one species (humankind) has the enormous power to damage irreparably the marvelous self-repairing systems of the biosphere. Upon this protective immune system all aspects of our healing and wholeness, including our spiritual health, ultimately depend. Decisions we make every day are helping to determine whether future generations inherit a healthy or a toxic earth.

The global eco-justice crisis is the human family's most serious health problem in its millennium-spanning existence on earth. Because the survival of a viable planet is at stake, this is the Mount Everest ethical issue towering over all the other global threats to human well-being. Because the root causes of the earth's rape are spiritual and ethical pathologies, clergy and congregations have strategic opportunities to help save a healthy earth, on which all future generations can live healthy lives. Utilizing empowering liturgies and symbolic rituals to raise consciousness and mobilize Christians for earth-saving action is an essential part of relevant ministry today![1]

Every aspect of a concerned congregation's life should highlight the eco-justice crisis regularly so that Christians will join hands with others in community efforts to enhance earth-literacy and earth-caring. The Earth Sabbath should become a major religious festival, supported by the worship, preaching, educational, and prophetic outreach programs of congregations. Christians should be challenged and guided in revising their earth-damaging lifestyles in the drastic ways that are needed if the planet is to be saved as a beautiful, bountiful place for people to be nurtured by the healing energies of nature. Individuals and families can celebrate the greening of their lifestyles with earth-energized rituals—in church and in their own backyards—committing themselves to continue helping to save God's precious creation. As Christians, we can learn much from the earth-grounded animal rituals of Native Americans and other indigenous people around the world, whose spirituality is centered on celebrating their love of the divine spirit's wondrous earth.

A striking illustration of prophetic earth-action rituals is that of the courageous women in North India who risk their lives by hugging the trees in their beloved forests to prevent the chain saws of the international lumber cartels from destroying their revered habitat. Another striking example of earth rituals of transformation is Wangari Mathai's prophetic planting of seven trees in her backyard on a day in June nearly two decades ago. She thus launched the Green Belt Movement in her native Kenya that has resulted in the planting of millions of trees, mainly by women and children. Reforestation has saved the precious topsoil from erosion and provided both much-needed firewood and food for the hungry. Wangari Mathai was mindful of the countless Kenyan women who, before the Green Belt transformation, were walking many miles to find twigs to cook their families' meals, and often carrying heavy earthen jars of water from the erosion-polluted streams. She said of the movement she had led, "We are lifting the heavy load that rural women have been carrying on their backs, one seed at a time."

A basic function of all dynamic religious rituals is to plant seeds of hope and help, of caring and change, and of commitment in the lives of worshipers. This book is a welcome gift to all those who would make new seeds available as they lead people who know and seek to live out Jesus' parable of the farmer who planted seeds in a field or the woman who seeded the bread dough she was about to bake with a tad of yeast. Clergy, who long for their faith communities to become more effective as places of healing and wholeness, will be challenged and guided by the authors of this book to implement the "fertile possibilities" that, as Hugh Sanborn has said, are evident throughout its pages.

---

[1]For a discussion of methods of eco-education, see chapter 10 of Clinebell's *Ecotherapy: Healing Ourselves, Healing the Earth* (Fortress Press & Haworth Press, 1996). "Healing Rituals in Ecotherapy and Ecoeducation" are discussed on pp. 216–20.

Introduction

Hugh W. Sanborn

Much has been made over the years of the importance of open, loving, committed and supportive church communities for faith development. Individuals and families that experience their ups and downs, joys and sorrows, successes and failures, spiritual breakthroughs and dark nights of the soul, within a sustaining community of faith, know how vital authentic Christian fellowship is for identity formation, growth and maturation in the faith, support and sustenance, and participation in ministry. Given this reality, it is surprising indeed that only two of life's passages or stage changes, pre-birth to birth (infant baptism or dedication) and childhood to adolescence (confirmation), and three major transitional events (believer's baptism, matrimony, and loss of a significant other), have been liturgically celebrated traditionally by most mainline Protestant churches. If the church is understood to be the faithful, growth-promoting, self-giving body of Christ, as the authors in this study believe it is, then it would be theologically consistent with this perspective for churches to develop a series of liturgies that contribute, from birth to death, to the nurture of this way of life within its members, families, and congregations. Underlying this study is the shared view of its authors that churches, if they are to provide effective spiritual nurture for their members throughout the life cycle, ought to be attentive to life's developmental passages and transitional events as potentially significant spiritual times for deepening and enriching faith.

Note that there are two distinct types of change being treated in this book, namely, developmental passages and major transitional events. Life's passages, as treated in this study, consist of the following stage changes: from (1) pre-birth to birth; (2) babyhood to childhood; (3) childhood to adolescence; (4) adolescence to young adulthood; (5) young adulthood to middle adulthood; (6) middle adulthood to later adulthood; and (7) later adulthood to life's completion or death. Major transitional events, on the other hand, refer to life experiences that may, and usually do, have significant impact on one's life and may or may not be related to one or more of life's passages. Major transitional events would include, but are not limited to, such diverse experiences as believer's baptism, marriage, divorce, the onset of or recovery from major illness, serious accidents, all kinds of losses, graduations, major vocational changes and moves, and retirement.

As stated above, some of life's developmental passages and transitional events, namely, infant baptism, confirmation, believer's baptism, matrimony, and loss of a loved one, have been liturgically celebrated by most mainline Protestant churches throughout their history. However, it has been and

1

continues to be theologically controversial whether baptism should be practiced soon after the initial passage of birth, or at a time of major faith transition, or in some way encompass both, or whether confirmation should take place during preteens, early teens, midteens or late teens. The reader will find a variety of theological options presented in the chapters that follow. It is to be hoped that the presentation of these theological perspectives will be helpful in clarifying and considering the issues as well as stimulating ideas about the liturgical approach that is most meaningful to individuals, families, pastors, and their congregations.

Since all the other passages and major transitional events have not been celebrated or affirmed through liturgy traditionally, it is the purpose of this book to break new ground in presenting the significance of doing so. All developmental passages and major transitional events are pregnant with potential for growth within individuals and congregations. The birth of a baby is not only a major breathtaking event in the life of the newborn; it holds deep and enduring implications for parental and family development as well as for the extended church family. Whether the church family into which the baby is born celebrates this passage into its care in the form of baptism, dedication, or some other form of celebration, the congregation as a whole has a nurturing role to play which embraces the baby, members of the baby's family, and the family as a whole. Celebrating the subsequent passages of this individual along the way to young adulthood and beyond with family and extended church family, as well as the major transitional events in his/her life, provide significant opportunities for development and maturation in Christian faith and identity for all who participate.

What is being implied above is that we Protestants in the mainline tradition have often given lip service rather than embodiment to our understanding that Christianity is a way of life. The human life cycle involves a number of difficult, often stressful, sometimes troublesome and painful, and sometimes joyous, rewarding, or liberating transitional periods and events. While most major transitional events seem to elicit some attention, care and support at least from pastors, too often our church communities, including pastors, are perceived by members to be of little help during, nonaffirming of, or even oblivious to, many of the major life-cycle passages. Are not understanding, support, affirmation, and celebration on the part of pastor and congregation as important during passage into childhood or middle age as during preparation for marriage? Drawing attention to all the life-cycle passages and helping individuals and families prepare for and move through them constructively, if accomplished with sensitivity, understanding, and empathy, can provide considerable guidance to individuals, families and congregations at critical periods of identity and faith development. Focusing on passages through liturgical affirmation and celebration is an important, if not essential, part of this process.

Since this study is about the use of liturgies in the church, a few things need to be clarified about the purpose and functions of liturgy as understood in the pages that follow. To state that the generally accepted purpose of liturgy is to worship and praise God is to focus on the raison d'être of liturgy, namely, fostering the God-person/God-community relationship. Relationship with the Source and Ground of our individual and collective Christian identity provides the primary framework for the receptive opening, giving , receiving, renewing, and growing that take place through effective liturgy. A complete worship experience, in brief, entails the movement into a deepening sense of relationship with the Source of all being and becoming—a spiritual movement that engenders confession, praise and thanksgiving and motivates and strengthens participants for Christian service.

Within this context, it should be noted that rite of passage, liturgy and ritual are closely linked. *Rite of passage,* Webster tells us, is "a ceremony in some cultures marking the passing to another, more advanced stage." *Liturgy* is defined by Webster as " the prescribed form for a public religious service," and *ritual* as "the observance of set forms or rites, as in public worship." A rite of passage, in other words, is one form of ritual or liturgy. In this book, we are using liturgy or ritual to include worship ceremonies which mark, affirm, and, when appropriate, celebrate both rites of passage and life's major transitional events.

Our emphasis in this study is on the enhancement of spiritual growth rather than the promotion of prescribed forms. Liturgy here refers to ceremonial space and time, potentially filled with expectation, excitement, possibility, and joy on the one hand, and anxiety, trepidation, reticence, and sadness or grief, on the other. It implies movement but may entail resistance to movement. It brings into focus a holy or spiritual time which may be potent with meaning for, and in some way significant or even critical to, the destiny of the individual and collective body. It attempts to express and contextualize the nature of one's spiritual experience and change through articulation, dramatization, and symbolic act—a process that, at its best, initiates the integration that must ensue if the passage or transition is to be successfully assimilated and completed. The liturgical form, then, is secondary, creatively shaped by participants to maximize spiritual growth.

In the pages that follow, the authors attempt to stimulate theological discussion and provide sample liturgies that elicit growth-promoting worship experiences for individuals, their families, and their congregations. Clergy and lay participants are encouraged to make use of the liturgies in whatever way concurs with their own needs, circumstances and theological conclusions, employing them in toto, in part, or in modified form, or reacting to them as disposable models useful only in provoking thoroughly new initiatives.

1
Birth and Infancy

Robert Tucker

A WINDOW OF LOVE

For an act that is so central to the church's self-understanding, so pervasive in its life, and so extensively practiced in its various communions, why does baptism have such divergent interpretations and forms?

Part of the answer must reside in water itself. Physically and symbolically, water cleanses, water refreshes, water accompanies birth, water is life-giving and life-sustaining. Water can also be terrifying and can bring death. Religiously, water played an important part in the rituals of ancient Judaism. People who had sexual intercourse or touched a dead body were unclean for religious worship until undergoing a washing for purification. Gentiles who wanted to become Jews entered a three-step process of circumcision, baptism, and sacrifice. Circumcision made one a child of the covenant between God and Abraham; baptism symbolically made a person part of a people who traversed the Red Sea in the Exodus; and sacrifice signified an acceptance of the Law given on Mount Sinai. These uses of water, in one form or another, are found in different understandings of baptism: cleansing from sin, new life, joining the church, and entering into the death, burial and resurrection of Jesus.

Adding to the diversity of understandings and practices of baptism found in the symbolism of water, there is the New Testament record itself. Jesus was baptized by John—a baptism of repentance—but there is no record that Jesus baptized or that the disciples were baptized. The apostle Paul was baptized but claimed that he, himself, had baptized few in Corinth, a church he founded (1 Corinthians 1:14–16). Adult converts were baptized, and that baptism was extended, at times, to their "household." Paul, in giving a theological basis for baptism, viewed baptism through the lens of his own dramatic change from persecutor to promoter of the church. It is clear, though, that baptism was an important part of the early church's self-understanding. The author of The Acts of the Apostles traces baptism back to the very first preaching of the apostles on the day of Pentecost.

It is only natural that a new movement will attract knowledgeable adults who are able to make a choice. For that reason, the baptism of adults in the New Testament is well documented. Baptism of individuals and also of entire households is recorded.[1] This certainly could mean that infants were baptized. But anything can be argued from silence, and the ambiguity in the New Testament record, combined with its silence on issues we now consider important, allows for differences in theology and practice among churches.

5

Although not a proof text for the baptism of infants and children, Jesus welcomed the children who had been turned away by the disciples, blessing them as "exemplary citizens" of the kingdom of God (Luke 18:15–17). The literature of the first century saw children as objects in need of discipline and training. Jesus took children seriously as persons. It is not to be lightly dismissed that the church fathers, as they increasingly favored the practice of infant baptism, cited this Gospel text in support of their claims.

Since the Greek word *bapto* means "to dip" or "to immerse," it is reasonable to assume that Jesus' baptism at the Jordan River meant immersion, and that this was also a practice in New Testament Christian communities. However, within a generation following Pentecost, the church allowed a variety of baptismal practices.[2] Although, visually, immersion is a vivid symbol of Paul's belief in baptism as dying and rising, immersion is symbolic, and the pouring and sprinkling of water is not automatically devoid of that same symbolism.

Much of the disagreement over baptism has centered in the "outward and visible act." Is it essential for there to be a personal conversion and confession of sins prior to baptism? At issue here is the efficacy of infant and child baptism. Does the Greek word for baptism determine the proper mode of baptism? At issue is the validity of sprinkling and pouring, alongside immersion. Is the act of baptism absolutely essential for a believing Christian? At issue is the relationship of baptism to membership in the Christian community. Does the water of baptism confer salvation on an individual? At issue is the question of the eternal life of those not baptized.

These issues are not to be casually dismissed, for they are a vital part of the dialogue we have with our biblical and theological heritage. However, just as when one focuses the eyes on a window pane, that which is outside the window goes out of focus, so to focus on the questions of baptism mentioned above—the outward and visible act—tends to blur the sacrament's core proclamation: the gospel of a loving God who reaches out to us humans, as infants when we are unaware of that love, and as adults when we least deserve it.

Baptism through the Centuries

In re-conceptualizing infant baptism, we find support in looking at the variations that have developed in the rite of baptism through the centuries, including more recent understandings that have developed in the twentieth century.

The origins of Christian sacraments[3] have been sought in the Greek and Roman religions, the official state religions, and the mystery religions. For our purpose here, however, rather than looking for specific historical antecedents, it is sufficient to note that Christian sacraments were part of a commonly accepted practice in all the sacred rituals of the era. They existed side by side and met a common human need.

The practices surrounding baptism changed over time and became more elaborate through the centuries. Early on, during the time of official persecution, a seeker needed a member of the Christian community as a sponsor. During this period, practitioners of certain professions—prostitutes or pimps, makers of idols, actors or entertainers, gladiators or soldiers—were required to find a new occupation prior to baptism. Also, a lengthy period of preparation, known as the catechumenate (from the Greek, meaning instruction), was instituted.[4] This was used for systematic doctrinal instruction and the exorcism of the evil spirits that ruled the candidate for baptism in her or his past. The time of baptism came to be limited to special feast days, mainly Easter or Pentecost, instead of immediately after conversion.

In the ecclesiastical records, we find the age at which baptism was administered varying in different places in both the East and West. In some places, immediate infant baptism was practiced due to the high rate of infant mortality. In other places, baptism took place after adolescence, so that the passions of youth would have subsided. Also of record are numerous examples of baptism being postponed until the individual's deathbed, so that the baptism would wash away more sins. The determining factor was the relationship of baptism to the forgiveness of sins.[5]

In the third century the question of why babies should be baptized was first given an answer by Cyprian of Carthage: the guilt of the human race in Adam was removed. This was articulated into a theological position of "original sin" by Augustine.[6] The role of the baptismal sponsors changed from being guarantors of the candidate's faith before baptism to making sure that the child received sound religious and moral teaching growing up after baptism. Also, with infants and children, pouring came to replace immersion.

During the Middle Ages, baptism underwent several significant changes. Instead of being salvation from a sinful life, baptism became salvation from original sin. Instead of being the beginning of a new daily life, baptism became necessary for life after death.

The Reformation rejected much of the medieval theology of baptism. Especially important was Martin Luther's citing of a passage from Augustine stating that what made baptism a matter of grace was the word joined to the water. The Anabaptists, in their reading of the Bible, rejected infant baptism as well as the method of pouring. John Calvin, in taking Paul's words on predestination to mean that God saved those who were "elected," stated that even if a person had not been baptized, he or she was already saved. Ulrich Zwingli went a step further and said that baptism was a sign of the faith that people brought to the sacrament but was not a cause of faith afterwards.

Just as the nineteenth century brought about a shift from a simplistic and nonhistorical view of the Bible to a developmental view, so, in the twentieth century, scholars began to see that liturgy also had its own development through the centuries. This discovery lent support to the idea that, since the sacraments have changed in the past, they are open to revision in the present and will probably continue to evolve in the future.

Liturgical scholars are discovering that in our pluralistic world it is difficult to confine the meaning that a sacrament has for people to its deliberately intended significance, that people in different places may interpret the same rituals differently, and that even people in the same location might, because of their differences in background and personality, experience a sacrament in a variety of ways. They are also learning that symbolic story and ritual are unavoidably polyvalent, that is, they inherently contain a rich ritual of meanings and values, some of which are deliberately intended and some of which are unconsciously communicated.[7]

Words describing current attempts to reshape the language and act of baptism are *acculturation*, used for the efforts to translate Christian understandings and forms into the equivalent cultural forms found in nations and cultures around the world, and *inculturation*, used for the efforts to create forms which might have been developed, had European Christianity not become the norm. The pluralism represented behind these words is a prominent feature of today's theological and ecclesiastical world.

During the four hundred years between the Reformation and Vatican Council II, the issues related to baptism in the Roman Catholic Church and Protestant churches underwent little change. Today, though, a number of theologians and movements have been re-conceptualizing the sacraments. Edward Schillebeeckx, Karl Rahner, Bernard Cooke, the theological thinking stemming from the process thinking of Alfred North Whitehead, the Pentecostal movement, and liberation theology all have placed their imprint on the way that we look at the sacraments.[8]

Into this heady and fermenting mix, the following understanding of the baptism of infants and children is offered.

A Theological Understanding of Baptism

Baptism proclaims the gospel: "In this is love, not that we loved God but that [God] loved us," and "while we still were sinners Christ died for us" (1 John 4:10; Romans 5:8). The baptism of infants, especially, allows us, with utter clarity, to see and proclaim the source of that divine love infusing our existence. Baptism is a window for love.

The general, and often trivial, way in which the word love is used should not stop us from being in awe at the truly radical nature of Jesus' understanding of the very center of this universe. In summarizing the law of Moses, Jesus said, "You shall love the Lord your God with all your heart and with all your soul, and with all your mind. And a second is like it: You shall love your neighbor as yourself'" (Matthew 22:37–39). The most common metaphor used by Jesus to describe God was "Father," not denoting a specific role, but the relational core of the universe. The parental love expressed in the well-known parable of the prodigal son is a prime example, for the parable is better understood as the parable of the prodigal father.[9]

Other New Testament writers were faithful to Jesus' message. In attempting to provide guidance to a very divided Christian community in Corinth, Paul wrote that love was the greatest gift of the Spirit (charisma) and that, among the lasting realities of faith, hope and love, "the greatest of these is love" (1 Corinthians 13:13). The writer John stated the centrality of love as boldly as he could: "God is love" (1 John 4:16).

The proclamation of this gospel is central to the baptismal service for infants and children that is proposed—that the graciousness of God which has touched and embraced adults in the Christian community is not limited to adult consciousness. The baptism of infants and children announces that love.[10]

This service affirms that baptism is an announcement of divine love and not the initiator of that love. Similar to a wedding service in which the promises of love and commitment are present before the ceremony itself, baptism states that the love of God is already present in the person's life before the words are spoken and actions are taken. Questions are asked of participants in both services, but the questions are a public affirmation of an already present reality. In the baptism of infants and children, the declaration of God's love shines forth with unqualified clarity.

All Life as Sacramental

Beyond the specific sacramental of baptism (and the sacrament of the Lord's supper), the conviction of this writer is that life—all life—is sacramental. Everything, potentially, has the ability to grab hold of one's being, to stand in awe before the graciousness of God, and to find illumination for the ongoing journey of life.

There is the sacramental quality of nature as seen in Brother Lawrence, the thirteenth-century lay monk awestruck in midwinter before the stark silhouette of a tree, realizing that life would sprout forth in the spring, and Martin Luther, who made a decision to take holy orders while sheltered from a violent thunderstorm. There is the sacramental presence of personal guilt or grief as seen in John Newton who, after four years of being engaged in the slave trade, could seek ordination and write such hymns as "Amazing Grace" and "Glorious Things of Thee Are Spoken." There is the sacramental presence of other committed Christians.

The title of this chapter is "A Window of Love." Windows break open the opaque walls of our dwellings to lighten interior space. All of life has the possibility of cracking open our preoccupation with the self and the world in the light of divine love. The sacraments are particular ways in which the church reminds itself of this love and announces it to others. It is in the baptism of infants and children that we have a window through which the Christian community sees, with utmost clarity, this good news.

A Service of Baptism for Infants and Children

As stated in the preceding section, infant baptism provides a special window on the centrality of God's love for Christian life and community. In this section, following a brief description of the preparation that takes place with the family, I will present a baptismal service that attempts to capture and communicate this perspective. For those who practice infant dedication rather than baptism, it should be noted that, with minor modifications, this liturgy may be easily converted into a dedication service.

Meeting with the Family

In order to explain the underlying meaning of the service and to relieve any anxiety over the unfamiliarity of the procedures, I meet with the family prior to the baptismal service. This provides an opportunity for parents to raise any questions they may have as we explore such issues as why baptism, except when there are extenuating circumstances, takes place in the midst of the worship community. Emphasis is placed on the fact that the congregation plays a significant role in the liturgy, promising to provide love, support and nurture for the newly baptized child and his/her parents. God's unconditional love is to be proclaimed and experienced as embracing the child and family as well as the total family of God.

Parents often find it helpful to recall their own wedding service when considering the meaning of their child's baptism. Just as the decision to marry and the commitment to the spouse preceded the wedding service itself, so, in the act of baptism, the service proclaims that their child has been, is, and will be loved.

In the baptismal service, then, we proclaim that which we Christians in faith know to be true. Nothing magical is understood to take place. Baptism, as a means of washing away original sin, is mentioned, not because people believe it, but because remnants of that understanding are found in the unexamined corners of people's minds. It is also a good counterpoint to the view of baptism expressed in the following service.

The final preparatory step is to go through the service itself, with each of the parents having a copy of the service in hand. I continue to emphasize and reiterate points which I consider important and to encourage the parents to ask questions. It is my hope that by the end of our preparatory session together, the parents will have a fairly good understanding of the intent and meaning of their child's baptismal service.

Baptismal Service[10]

(This baptismal service needs to be slightly altered if there is more than one child, if the child is adopted, or if there is only one parent.)

OPENING WORDS OF SCRIPTURE
Consider the incredible love that God has shown us
in allowing us to be called children of God—
and that is not just what we are called, but what we are.
Oh, dear friends of mine, have you realized it?
Here and now, we are God's children.
We don't know what we shall become in the future,
we only know that, if reality were to break through,
we should reflect God's likeness because we should see God fully!
We see real love, not in the fact that we love God,
but that God loved us
and, in Jesus, gave us the fullness of life.
Surely we, in our turn, should love one another!
(1 John 3:1–2; 4:9–11, Phillips, adapted)

A STATEMENT OF INTERPRETATION
Friends, here we celebrate life.
Here we celebrate the wonder of birth,
the joy of love,
and the graciousness of God.
We celebrate the birth of a child—
so natural and yet so miraculous—
rejoicing in the part we play in being co-creators of life,
standing in awe of the amazing complexity
of bone and tissue, mind and muscle, body and spirit,
marveling at the unknown future into which this person moves,
but always within the circle of God's love.
We celebrate the love of parents
that, out of longing, creates new life,
nurtures that life through years of growth,
and stands aside for that life's independence.
We celebrate the graciousness of God
who, in love, reaches out to us—
as infants, when we are unaware of that love,
as adults, when we least deserve it.
As that love has touched and embraced us,
so we affirm that this same love
has been with and continues to be with *name*.
We testify in this act of baptism
that God has given this child, and each one of us,
the opportunity and the courage to live in freedom
as we move, in faith, into the open future.

POURING WATER INTO THE FONT BY LAY PARTICIPANT

CALLING FORTH THE FAMILY

QUESTIONS OF PARENTS
> *Name* and *name*, do you, in bringing your child
>> before this community,
>> affirm your faith in the God who has created and loved us all?
> Will you endeavor to live out your lives
>> before your child in such a way that life itself
>> might become good news to *her/him*?
> Will you endeavor to keep *name*
>> under the ministry and guidance of the church
>> until she/he shall choose for *herself/himself*
>> whether or not to be a member of the Christian community?

RESPONSE OF THE CHURCH COMMUNITY
> We, representing this church,
>> along with Christians throughout the world,
>> are witnesses to this act of God's love.
> We promise, with our resources,
>> to assist the parents in their educational task.
> We promise, with our thoughtful concern,
>> to be an accepting and loving community.
> We promise, with our prayerful acts,
>> to make this child aware
>> of *her/his* deepest potential in Jesus the Christ.

ACT OF BAPTISM
> *Name*, I baptize you in the name of the Father,
> the Son, and the Holy Spirit. Amen.

QUESTION TO CHILDREN OF THE CHURCH
> The adults of this church have made a commitment to *name* today.
> You, too, will be important in *her/his* life.
> Will you, then, promise to welcome *name* as a part of your life?

CLOSING PRAYER AND BLESSING
> God of all creation and of this creation,
>> we praise you for the graciousness of your love showered upon us.
> We thank you for declaring your love for *name*
>> before *she/he* can fully know you.
> May the love that surrounded *her/him* from the beginning,
>> and is present now,
>> be evident throughout *her/his* life.
> We seek your blessing on [parents'] *name* and *name*.
> Support them in their struggle to be good parents.
> Help them to savor the days of joy
>> and sustain them in the days of difficulty.
> Whether we are young or old,
>> we ask that you would make our baptism real and complete,

by opening our eyes again and again
to the reality of your gracious love in our lives,
that we may live in the joy and power of your Holy Spirit. Amen.

CONCLUDING HYMN
Now thank we all our God with heart and hands and voices,
who wondrous things has done, in whom the world rejoices,
who, from our mothers' arms, has blessed us on our way
with countless gifts of love, and still is ours today.[11]

---

[1]In the New Testament, a person's conversion leads to that person's baptism "with all his house." We need to understand that concept in broader terms than our concept of the nuclear family. "Family is defined not only by (the) immediate family but also his slaves, former slaves who were now clients, hired laborers, and sometimes business associates or tenants." Wayne A. Meeks, *The First Urban Christians: The Social World of the Apostle Paul* (New Haven: Yale University Press, 1983), 30.

[2]From the Didache, c. A.D. 60–70: "Regarding baptism. Baptize as follows: after first explaining all these points, baptize in the name of the Father and of the Son and of the Holy Spirit, in running water. But if you have no running water, baptize in other water; and if you cannot in cold, then in warm. But if you have neither, pour water on the head three times in the Name of the Father and of the Son and of the Holy Spirit. Before the baptism, let the baptizer and the candidate for baptism fast, as well as any others that are able. Require the candidate to fast one or two days previously." Colman J. Barry, ed., *Readings in Church History*, vol. 1 (Westminster, Md.: Newman Press, 1965), 26–27.

[3]The Greek word used was *mysterion*. It was borrowed from Greek religions. Tertullian, writing around the year 210, first used the word *sacramentum* as a Latin equivalent, perhaps because it was the official word for Roman religious rites.

[4]A simple confession was no longer sufficient for baptism since non-Jews, who had no idea of the milieu in which Christianity arose, were seeking to join the church. A good description of this is found in Joseph Martos, *Doors to the Sacred: A Historical Introduction to Sacraments in the Catholic Church* (Tarrytown, N.Y.: Triumph Books, 1991), 147. Of all the material pursued on this topic, Martos' book has been the most helpful..

[5]Baptim had become an elaborate ritual, stretching over several days. Much of the ritual associated with baptism was an attempt, symbolically and ritually, to replicate in each person the death, burial, and resurrection of Jesus. Martos, 150.

[6]It needs to be recognized that the patristic view was anything but uniform. For example, "Irenaeus of Lyons, writing about the year 190, thought of baptism in terms of the renewal of all creation in Christ, receiving the Holy Spirit was the beginning of the divination of mankind." Martos, 150.

[7]Martos, 109.

[8]Ibid. A good, concise view of each of these movements is found in Martos, 109–27.

[9]The younger, or "prodigal," son occupies only the first half of the story, and the elder son occupies the second half. It is the father who holds the parts together and who is truly prodigal, i.e., wasteful, of his love.

[10]This service is amended from one developed first by W. Benjamin Pratt in *Ventures in Worship*, David James Randolph, ed. (Nashville: Abingdon Press, 1973),153–54.

[11]Martin Rinkart (1636), tr. Catherine Winkworth (1858), alt.

2

The Transition from Infancy to Childhood

Jerome W. Berryman

THEOLOGICAL AND PSYCHOLOGICAL CONSIDERATIONS

Theology and psychology will be asked to carry on a dialogue in this chapter to help us prepare to fashion some appropriate ways to mark the transition from infancy to childhood and then two further transitions within childhood during this remarkable period of human development.

The period called "childhood" roughly covers the time from about 2–12 years of age and incorporates enormous biological, psychological, and social changes. One of the most important changes is the developing use of symbols for communication with oneself and others and the ability to classify, order, and quantify one's understanding of the world. The spiritual changes are not as clear, apart from their relation to the development of one's thinking for expression, but the presence of spirituality dare not be overlooked or underestimated, as will be discussed later.

The influence of Jean Piaget's (1896–1980) research about children's thinking has sharpened our awareness of stages within childhood. We will use both Piaget's stage theory and common customs for schooling to divide childhood into easily remembered symmetrical periods of early childhood (3–6 years), middle childhood (6–9 years) and late childhood (9–12 years). Of course, children actually develop on their own timetables, despite the theories of scholars and times arranged for starting preschools and elementary schools.

The next section will be devoted to suggestions for liturgical actions to mark these three transitions during childhood which change the relationships among the children, families, and congregation. Another author will discuss the liturgical celebration for the transition from late childhood into adolescence, in chapter 3.

Theology will speak first in this dialogue. There seems to be an ambivalence in Christian theology about the importance, value, and definition of the child.

Second, we will take a look at what science can tell us about childhood. Instead of the usual emphasis on changes, we will examine five of the continuities between children and adults during this period. They are the means for participation in our lives together, for mutual respect, and through which we can all take part in the liturgies to be proposed.

14

Finally, we will propose some conclusions, drawn from the conversation between theology and science, about what to keep in mind as we create the liturgies to mark these special moments in human experience. By this use of action, symbol, and space, children can know deeply that they are as real and important as grown-ups and that their journey, full of changes as it may be, is both whole and holy.

It is important to keep in mind that this author is an Episcopal priest, so many of my references assume the great tradition of the *Via Media*, steering a course between Geneva and Rome. What is said, however, may be of interest and have practical importance for people of all denominations and other religions by implication.

The Church's Confusing View of Children

The raw material for a theological appreciation of childhood is to be found in the Synoptic Gospels. Some information may be found by comparing Jesus' view of children with the views found in the Jewish, Greek, and Roman worlds of the first century, but the picture is far from clear. We can at least acknowledge this complexity and attempt to learn from it. We will also examine the testimony of the church during later centuries as it struggled to better understand our origins in childhood. The theology and sacramental practice, however, were as confusing as Jesus' parables in the first century.

Jesus and the Children

Hans-Rudi Weber's *Jesus and the Children*[1] discussed how children were perceived of by people in Athens, Sparta, and Jerusalem, and how that view contrasted with the view of Jesus. Jesus is not recorded as having said anything directly about the nature of children, but there are some inferences that can be made.

First, Jesus was, perhaps, realistic about children. The tendency to idealize children was studied by George Boas in *The Cult of Childhood*.[2] In tracing this idea from the time of Plato to the twentieth century, Boas' search is related to the tendency to think of all origins as ideal. Sometimes earlier times, or more primitive cultures found in one's own time, have been idealized. Today this tendency is more likely to take the form of idealizing such concepts as Real Men, Woman, Folk (rural), the Irrational, or the Collective Unconscious as well as the Child. The romantic view of a Golden Age or a Noble Savage can be invested in the Child, but Jesus was apparently immune to any of these varieties of idealization.

A hint of Jesus' realism about children may be found in his comment about children sitting in the marketplace. (Matthew 11:16–19; Luke 7:31–35) They call to their playmates without listening to adults. We can pipe, wail, or even offer them something to eat and drink, but they will not listen. Getting children to listen is a matter of knowing how to be open to their true nature and our own rather than using loud voices or bribes. Wisdom is justified by her children (deeds), and we adults are "children" who need such wisdom no less than they do.

Second, if we want to know the Kingdom, we need to *become* like a child. Jesus' parabolic challenge to the disciples' dispute about greatness is found in all three synoptics. (Matthew 18:1–5; Mark 9:33–37; Luke 9:45–48)

The disciples were disputing about who was to have the greatest power of position in the Kingdom. In response to their complete misunderstanding of his words, Jesus set a silent child in their midst. "Whoever welcomes one such child in my name welcomes me; and whoever welcomes me, welcomes not me but the one who sent me" (Mark 9:37).

Children may not listen, as in the marketplace, but there are times when they do not speak, as in the parable. What they have the potential to do at any time is receive. Children absorb life as they absorb food to grow, but the disciples' will to power would not let them absorb anything but themselves. Despite this, however, Jesus was also showing them that he received the disciples as one might receive a child, or the Kingdom. They did not understand this until later.

The parable, of course, does not tell us what the nature of the child is. We must discover what is hidden by the child's silence, but much of this nature has to do with receiving as a paradoxical way of entering. Children enter by being welcomed, while the disciples were trying to force their way in by right.

Third, children *are* Kingdom-bearers. The Kingdom belongs to them, so they are blessed as creatures of worth in themselves and not as bearers of Torah, as the Jews thought. Their value was not in their future contributions to the state as citizens, as the Greeks of Athens thought, or as well-trained soldiers, as the Spartans thought. Neither was their worth defined as personal property, as the Romans thought. "Let the little children come to me; do not stop them; it is to such as these that the kingdom of God belongs." (Mark 10:14) This is not something the children will discover when they grow up. They are *already there*.

This story of Jesus' blessing the children is also found in all three synoptics. (Matthew 19:13–15; Mark 10:13–16; Luke 18:15–17) Again, the child is used as a parable. What children need are blessings. They do not need more misunderstood words or frustrating actions like those of the disciples who tried to push them away. This parable of action also suggests that we adults are such "children" as well. We too need blessings so we can bless, as when God revealed to Abraham his true nature, a nature that has overtones of the Kingdom ringing in it.

The Church and Children

There is an ambivalence about children in the history of the Christian church. This ambivalence comes in part from the parabolic nature of Jesus' view of children, but there is also another source. Children are closely associated with women.

Margaret Miles wrote: "In the Middle Ages Aristotle's doctrine of woman as a misbegotten and deformed male crossed easily into Christian speculation about Eve and her secondary and derivative creation."[3] Not only was Eve secondary; she was also the one who "led Adam" into disobedience and therefore was the one who brought sin into the world.

Tertullian (c. 160–c. 230) is an example of how emphatic a church father might be. He wrote: "Do you know that each of you women is an Eve?…You are the gate of Hell, you are the temptress of the forbidden tree, you are the first deserter of the divine law."[4]

It was primarily Augustine (354–430) in his *Confessions* who gave anti-sexual views their classic formulation. He proposed that the transmission of sin was through sexual intercourse. The only way out of this natural infection is by baptism which cleanses us of the stain left by our parents' erotic impulses when we were conceived.

When Miles traced the medieval development of the concept of the grotesque, she found it in the expression of attitudes toward women. Women came from the perversely bent rib, so they were included among the grotesque. What is most important is that their monstrosity would not go away; it could only be hidden by careful adherence to socially approved appearance and behavior.

Rosemary Radford Ruether has elaborated on this theme: "Historical Christianity defined women as inferior, subordinate, and prone to the demonic. These images justified almost limitless violence against them whenever they crossed the male will at home or in society. Woman as victim is the underside of patriarchal history."[5] For example, the period from 1484 to 1692 in the Catholic and Protestant Christian West saw hundreds of thousands of women burned at the stake or drowned as witches.

The contempt for women and their bodies, as well as the violence directed toward them, has provided the social context for an uncertainty about infants who have just arrived through such a sinful doorway. It was not even clear in the Middle Ages whether women and children were considered human beings. At least in 585 during the Second Synod of Macon, a general council for all of France, the sixty-three males, bishops and their representatives, debated the question: "Are women human and fully 'person' (homo)?" It was decided that women were human, but the question of children was left unresolved in theology. Aries wrote in his *Centuries of Childhood*:

> In medieval society the idea of childhood did not exist; this is not to suggest that children were neglected, forsaken, or despised. The idea of childhood is not to be confused with affection for children: it corresponds to an awareness of the particular nature of childhood, that particular nature which distinguishes the child from the adult, even the young adult. In medieval society this awareness was lacking. That is why, as soon as the child could live without the constant solicitude of his mother, his nanny, or his cradle-rocker, he belonged to adult society.[6]

In practice, there is at least the suggestion that children were not given much consideration at all. When we raise the question of whether children are born sinful, our modern temperament may put too much urgency into the question.

During the New Testament period, a profession of belief was an integral part of baptism (Acts 2:38; 8:16; 10:48; 19:5; Romans 10:9; 1 Corinthians 6:11), but there is little else known about additional details. The candidates were probably adults at first, but it is possible that children might have been baptized when whole households were converted.

The regular baptism of children was noted by Origen, Tertullian, *The Apostolic Tradition*, and Cyprian in the third century and by Asterius about 340.[7] Toward the middle of the fourth century, however, the baptism of children apart from emergency seems to have become the exception.[8]

A tendency to wait for baptism until later in life developed because, as Tertullian argued, little children are sinless and do not require the forgiveness of sins, which baptism confers.[9] Saints who were children of Christian parents and who were not baptized until they were older were Ambrose, Augustine, John Chrysostom, Gregory of Nazianzus (the son of a bishop), Jerome, and Paulinus of Nola.

By the end of the fourth century the custom changed again. There was a return to the practice of child baptism. Gregory of Nazianzus was one of those who argued for it, although he did not yet make a case for infant baptism.

By the sixth century in Rome the candidates for baptism were assumed to be infants.[10] During the second half of Lent, the babies were assembled at first on Sundays and later on weekdays for three scrutinies (later seven). It was impossible to have the traditional examination of the candidates, since now they were infants, so the scrutinies were to ensure that the evil spirit departed from them.

The rite was complicated but included mainly prayers and exorcism. Salt was placed on the tongue for wisdom. When the creed and Lord's Prayer were said, it was only in theory that the little ones could be inferred to have learned them.

In the sixteenth century the Council of Trent led a movement toward uniformity that required infant baptism. It had become so common by this time that liturgical books ceased to include any specific rite for adults, and in many places regulations required not more than a week to pass between birth and baptism.

One result of the infant-baptism custom was that the rite began to be thought of as a child's naming ceremony. Another result was that communion and confirmation split off from baptism. The gift of the Holy Spirit, now linked with confirmation, was conferred by the bishop when the child was at least seven years old. One needed to be confirmed to be admitted to communion.

The Byzantine Rite, found in the oldest surviving liturgical document, the Barberini *Euchologion*, required that infants be included in the eucharistic liturgy. Today this practice is no longer required, but it is certainly not prohibited.

Sometimes a historical accident played a part in the development of theology. English practice insisted that a child should not be admitted to communion before confirmation. This came about when Archbishop Peckham, at the Council of Lambeth in 1281, complained of the damnable negligence of confirmation. He ordered that no one would be admitted to holy communion, except in danger of death, unless he or she had been confirmed.[11]

In 1542 Calvin drew up an order of baptism for his church in Geneva. Children were to be brought either on Sunday afternoon at the time of the catechism or on weekdays after the morning sermon. The minister was to deliver a long discourse to expound the meaning of baptism. There followed a simple ceremony that trimmed away almost all the nonscriptural elements that had encrusted the rite during the previous centuries.

Does baptism signify the initiation of the child into the church family or not? If the child is a member of the family, then he or she should be able to come to the table and be nourished with family food and by the family's presence. If baptized children cannot receive holy communion, either they are not part of the family and baptism is meaningless, or holy communion is meaningless for all baptized Christians.

The status of a child became theologically contradictory by sacramental practice, sometimes by historical accident. Another criterion for defining a child had developed, which seemed to give this cogency.

The Fourth Lateran Council (1215) took notice of children by rejecting the earlier custom of openness and excluding infants from holy communion until they reached the "age of discretion." Spiritual maturity was linked to a single trait, the use of reason. At the Council of Trent (1545–1563) this position was affirmed. Trent went on to add that only children who had reached the age of reason could be admitted to confirmation.

Other sacraments, such as anointing, were delayed as well. Bernard Poschmann wrote: After the Council of Trent, it was often stated that those who were admitted to communion were also capable of receiving extreme unction. In practice this also came at fourteen years of age. The present practice of administering communion at an age when a child is able to go to confession began in the seventeenth century.[12]

The use of the trait of reason also was inconsistent with the age at which one's religious education ought to begin. Children were considered able to be educated years before they were allowed to receive the nourishment of holy communion or the other sacraments, except for baptism.

St. Clement of Rome, an early bishop writing about A.D. 96, wrote to the Corinthians: "Let our children receive a share of education in Christ: let them learn how strong is humility before God, how powerful pure love before God, how beautiful and great the fear of God, and how it saves all who live in it in holiness, with a pure heart" (1 Clement 21:8; compare 62:3). The normal setting for this instruction was probably at home, as it was in the Jewish household.

The importance of the home for religious education was confirmed by John Chrysostom. He was ordained as a priest in 386 after being a hermit, and appointed to the archbishopric of Constantinople in 398. He was banished in 403, recalled in 404, and died in 407. He wrote in "On Vain Glory and How Parents Should Bring Up Their Children" (45:1–2) that Bible stories should be taught in a way to arouse children's interest:

> When the child really knows the story, wait a few days and one evening say, "Tell me the story of the two brothers." If they start to tell you about Cain and Abel, stop them and say, "No, I don't mean that one, I mean the story about the other two brothers, the one whose father gave a blessing." Then remind them of a few important little details without mentioning the brothers' names. When they have told you the whole story properly, go on to the next part.[13]

We have now looked at inferences about the personhood of children indicated by the sacramental practice of the church, theological pronouncements, and views about their religious education. When we move to North America to discuss the connection between theology and child-rearing among Protestants during the early centuries of our settlement the picture of the "Christian" view of children continues to become more complex.

Philip Greven studied the relationship of child-rearing and theology at the beginning of our country's history.[14] The three views of children used by Protestants at that time focused on their will.

The evangelicals thought the child was born in sin and that a willful child was a child of pride. Pride blocked the ability to know one's dependence on God. The task of parents and schools was to break the child's will for the child's own good. Jonathan Edwards was an enlightened example of this viewpoint.

The moderates were caught between duty and desire. While the evangelicals were self-suppressed, the moderates were self-controlled. They learned how to compromise between duty and desire with children, but they still believed in the need for self-denial. These parents tried to bend the will of their children. An important example of this view is the Adams family of Braintree, Massachusetts, who gave the United States many remarkable public servants.

Genteel families valued fond affection over conscientious discipline. A sense of duty was expected, but it was based on a reverence and love for parents rather than a fear of them. These parents did not try to break or bend the will of their children. They encouraged it. The families of Governor Thomas Hutchinson of Massachusetts, the Allens of Pennsylvania, and the William Byrds in Virginia are examples of this belief.

Today the child-rearing practices of Americans still follow the same three attitudes toward the child's will, although in most cases the theological connection has evaporated. What is more dangerous for children is the still lingering assumption that children are born evil. If children are bad by nature

(nature has replaced theology), then there is no reason not to beat some sense into them, to civilize them, to make them more human.

It is no wonder that Christian people in congregations are confused and often unconscious of how they act toward children as a result of this confusion. It is hard for the church to help mitigate this violence toward children until its most potent language, the symbols and gestures of liturgy, become powerfully clear about whether or not children are real people. The ambivalence about women needs to be addressed by this means as well.

How to communicate liturgically about the personhood of children, which is our subject here, will be taken up in a later section. First, however, we need to know how children are seen by science in order to help us create appropriate liturgies to mark their transitions during childhood.

The View of Children from the World of Science

Charles Darwin was one of the first to keep a detailed diary of a child's development. His *Biographical Sketch of an Infant* (1877) followed the activities of his son, Doddy, from birth. Darwin reflected on the causes of his child's behavior, noting when emotions such as fear or anger were first shown, and discussing when this behavior first showed signs of reason. On this side of the Atlantic, Stanley Hall published his "Notes on the Study of Infants" in 1891. He is often considered the father of child psychology in North America.

The development of reasoning has a special interest for us here. This is the aspect of being human that defines us with respect to other species and suggests the appropriate time for admittance to holy communion, becoming a full person sacramentally.

Jean Piaget (1896–1980) made the study of cognitive development his life work. For the English-speaking world this developmental view was applied to religious education by Ronald Goldman in England, whose doctoral thesis at the University of Birmingham in 1962 was developed into such books as *Readiness for Religion: A Basis for Developmental Religious Education* in 1965.[15]

In North America, James W. Fowler expanded the use of the cognitive point of view to include not only religious education, but the growth of human meaning as "faith stages."[16] In Europe, Fritz Oser used stage theory to better understand what he called "religious judgment."[17] Oser and his associates focused on the relationship between the person and Ultimate Being (God) when considering what he or she should do in various situations.

The developmental perspective is about discontinuity, or at least differences, between children and adults. Our focus here, however, will be on continuities. The reason for this shift of attention is to find ways that all members of the congregation can connect with the transitions the children are making. The continuities we will use as our means of connecting are: feelings, existential awareness, play, spirituality, and creativity. We will begin with discussion of feelings.

Feelings

David Elkind played a prominent role in bringing the work of Piaget to the attention of North America. His first published studies about the cognitive development in religious understanding were in the early 1960s.[18] These identified the stages of children's thinking about their Jewish, Catholic, and Protestant institutions and beliefs. Most children before the age of eleven or twelve were not able to understand religious concepts as they were understood by most adults. Instead, the children gave meanings to these concepts which reflected their own views of the world.

Despite Elkind's interest in the changing ways children think, he also has stressed the emotional continuity between adults and children. He has argued that while most adults believe children and adolescents are like them in their thoughts and unlike them in their feelings, the reverse is true.

It may be that thinking, feeling, and acting can be separated artificially for research, but it is not true that these distinctions are separate processes. They are instead specialized forms of action.

Maturana has suggested that living systems are structurally organized to engage in the process of producing more of themselves.[19] They are *"autopoietic,"* a word he invented to emphasize that at every level of life, from cells to missionaries, there is a tendency to form additional like-structured entities. In a living system there is a unity between product and process.

Emotions as bodily predispositions underlie, support, and create readiness for action. These predispositions make classes of behavior more probable or less probable. Directionality is always involved.

At any given time we are moving this way or that way in space, and emotion is with us all the time as our system continually changes state in connection with shifting circumstances. Emotion does not precede or follow action. It is the bodily support that a class of actions requires.

Language is one of many classes of action that emotions support. If you are in bed mulling over something, such as buying a house or taking a vacation, you are already involved in the process of acting. You may find many points along the way to reverse the process until you sign a contract and put your money down, but even then the action is still not complete, although it will be more costly to get out of it.

Our conceptual premises are related to how our bodies are constructed and function, so our conceptual schemes are not really rational. The problem that appears, however, is that since we are self-reflecting creatures, when we have language, we tend to reify the tripartite division of thinking, feeling, and acting. This introduces apparent conflicts within ourselves, because language traps us into thinking that there is a little person inside who thinks, another one who feels, and another one who acts. In actuality we are a single living system acting.

Daniel Goleman's *Emotional Intelligence*[20] has argued in another way for the unity of thinking, feeling, and acting as an expanded view of intelligence. He calls for emotions to be thought of at the center of "aptitudes for living."

His work has summarized the current state of research concerning our emotions.

Goleman calls emotions "impulses to action." The body clearly changes as each emotion prepares the body for a different kind of response. For example, with anger blood flows to the hands, making it easier to grasp a weapon or strike an enemy as the body prepares for vigorous action. Love prepares the body for the opposite of the "fight-or-flight" mobilization shared by fear and anger. There is a bodywide calm and contentment that aids cooperation.

The primary emotions we share with children are like the primary colors of blue, red, and yellow, which can be blended into a whole rainbow of colors. Goleman says the main "candidates" for these primary emotions are: anger, sadness, fear, enjoyment, love, surprise, disgust, and shame.

Each emotion has a basic nucleus. The first ring of influence beyond the defining core emotion involves moods which are more muted and longer lasting than emotions. The second ring of influence is temperaments, which constitute a readiness to evoke a given emotion or mood that makes people the way they are. The third and outer ring, perhaps about to spin out of control, holds within its bank of influence the emotional disorders such as clinical depression or unremitting anxiety. One enters this zone of feeling when he or she feels perpetually trapped "in a toxic state."

The issue of anxiety brings us to the next continuity that children have with adults. It is an awareness, marked by anxiety, of our own existential limits.

Existential Awareness

The awareness of the limits to human existence pervades the experience of individuals all their lives, and it is what we have in common with other human beings regardless of where or at what age we find ourselves. F. H. Heinemann wrote in *Existentialism and the Modern Predicament*[21] that the way (Heinemann refers to this as "key-symbol") to solve the problem of philosophies that rely too much on being either too objective and reasonable or too subjective and emotional is to start with an awareness of humankind's being in the world, responding.

Meaning comes from being in interrelation with other elements of existence. Despite the difference in language domains (existential philosophy and biology) used and the time of writing (1953 vs. 1987), this is compatible with Maturana's view of existence as a coordination of actions which human beings have the ability to describe with language. Putting aside Descartes' *cogito, ergo sum* and taking up the starting point, *respondeo, ergo sum*, enables us to align the analysis of biology, psychology, sociology, and religion, despite their different perspectives and ways of speaking.

The ultimate limits that we share take many forms and may be subdivided and mixed, but there are four primary boundaries we cannot cross. We cannot cross them, because they both attract and repel us. If we move toward them they repel us. If we try to ignore their presence and move away, attempting to build up a defense against knowing our limits, they attract us. We may use all the energy we might otherwise put into growth, development, and an expansion of awareness to try to ignore their compelling presence.

An existential philosopher's treatment for the problem of existence is to become aware and honest about our limitations as human beings. This awareness and acceptance can release most of the energy, set aside to maintain our defense against such knowledge, for creating and realistic living. Enlarging one's frame of reference to the ultimate one allows many of what seem like problems to disappear, because they no longer matter or have meaning when seen from our ultimate boundaries.

Many existentialist philosophers used literature to express their understanding of life, because analysis, taking the problem apart, only challenges the intellect. The whole person needs to be challenged to integrate one's boundaries into his or her living. This is best done indirectly through symbols, such as liturgy or art, in order not to raise our defenses too high or fix them too deeply and rigidly. The knowledge of our limits can easily overwhelm us, so we must construct a destructive defense if no constructive one can be found such as authentic, constructive creativity.

Four of the existential issues that stimulate anxiety for children and adults are: death, freedom, existential isolation, and meaninglessness. An approach to dealing with these boundaries from a psychological point of view has been argued by Irvin D. Yalom.[22]

Yalom noticed that some issues in therapy arise because of an individual's confrontation with the "givens" of existence. The conditions will not go away. The goal of therapy is not to make them disappear; such thinking would be deluded in itself, for these issues color everything we do. Therapy can help, however, and so can the religious traditions of liturgy and care.

The virtue of Yalom's position is that it combines the insights of philosophers, the existential analysts of Europe, and the humanistic psychologists of North America with a deep appreciation for traditional empirical research. When one adds the insights of religion for healing to this approach, one has a powerful tool, indeed. Let us now take a closer look at these four limits to our being and knowing.

The reason death causes anxiety is that, in Maturana's terms, living systems are self-creating and remain so until they disintegrate. We cannot say if cells, insects, fish, reptiles, birds, or mammals are aware of this, but we are. The core existential conflict or paradox for us is that we desire to live forever and know we will not.

The paradox of freedom involves the absence of external structure. We are in a structural drift without meaning, as Maturana argues, until we create meaning with language. We are free, but our wish for ground and structure clashes with our awareness of groundlessness. Furthermore, we must take responsibility for the meaning we create with language. People move toward freedom until they discover it is real and possible, implying radical responsibility. They then move away from it. When they move away from it, the threat softens, so it becomes attractive again. The paradox is an unrelenting and powerful one.

The third limit case is existential isolation. It is neither interpersonal isolation accompanied by the feeling of loneliness nor intrapersonal isolation from the parts of oneself, felt as estrangement. It is fundamental isolation. We must enter and leave for ourselves. There is always a gap between us and both everything and everyone else.

As Maturana has reminded us, we are a closed neuronal network. If we take our biology seriously at our most fundamental level of awareness, we may wish for contact, for protection, and to be part of a larger whole. At the same time, and just as powerfully, we do not want to be swallowed up by a larger system and disappear.

Fourth, we are creatures who need meaning, and yet we know that the meaning we have is meaning we have created or inherited from someone else who created it. How can we have confidence in a meaning if we or some other human being is the source?

There is another reason the paradox cannot be resolved. Chaos makes us anxious, and certainty makes us bored. We long for certainty, but when there is certainty we cease to be a living system and become fixed like a crystal. This terrifies us, so we flee toward chaos again, then back toward rigidity, and back and forth again and again.

None of these boundary paradoxes can be resolved at a personal level of experience and thought. We need to step outside the language domain of everyday life or science and move into the transformational language of religion. Only then can we understand and live with such a contradiction by transcending it.

There are people today working in multidisciplinary settings that focus on the emerging science in the area between order and chaos. M. Mitchell Waldrop, describing the work of Chris Langton at the Santa Fe Institute, noted science's shift from asking how systems are made to asking how they behave. This shift has illuminated the concept of "the edge of chaos." Others call this area complexity.

Whatever the name of this class of behaviors might be, it involves the components of a system which never quite locks into place, yet never quite dissolves into turbulence either. This is exciting, because, as Waldrop wrote: "These are the systems that are both stable enough to store information, and yet evanescent enough to transmit. These are the systems that can be organized to perform complex computations, to react to the world, to be spontaneous, adaptive and alive."[23]

This "edge of chaos" is what I propose Jesus was stimulating with his parables about children, and it is what I intend to arouse within and among the children who gather to mark important transitions in their lives by the symbols and actions of liturgy. When the coordination of actions we live in is at the "edge of chaos," the coupled systems not only stimulate but help generate life for each other. We are, to change language domains, creating in the image of the Creator. This is why we are sensitive to such a presence in the universe.

Play

It is true that both children and adults can play, and sometimes they play together, but it is sometimes difficult for adults to play with children. This blocks communication and understanding that might otherwise take place in this medium across the stages and ages in the congregation and in families.

John Hull has suggested in *What Prevents Christian Adults from Learning?*[24] that we are reluctant "players" because of our schooling. We often have less tolerance for cognitive dissonance than children, because we have been trained to be right. Being right is sane, good, and deserving of a reward. To play is reduced to being a waste of time. There is no practical product arising from this activity.

There is an aspect of play in liturgy, but some, such as Romano Guardini and Hugo Rahner, S. J., would go even further. Rahner called for a theology of play, a *theologia ludens*, and a morality of *eutrapelia*, the "well-turning" ones who live with the balance of laughter without being reduced to flippancy or sarcasm. Guardini wrote that worship is "a kind of holy play in which the soul, with utter abandonment, learns how to waste time for the sake of God."[25]

Jane M. Healy wrote *How to Have Intelligent and Creative Conversations with Your Kids*,[26] because she realized that in most adult-child communication the children are supposed to only listen. If they are asked questions, the response expected is usually limited to a "Yes" or "No."

"Well, how was school today?"
"OK."
"Did you learn anything interesting?"
"Not really."

Schooling compounds this problem by modeling more of the same kind of one-way communication. The teacher asks questions and the children are to give the right answer. Next question.

Healy proposed that adults ask a completely different kind of question to engage in two-way conversations with children. Play is fundamental to this process. One of Healy's proposals for a question was, "How might the world be different if people were born with wheels instead of feet?" Let the play begin!

Her book was written in response to a father who said, "I don't want to be difficult, and I'm sure we should talk more with our children. But the last thing my wife and I need is another guilt trip! We're both working, and our time is so limited. Don't just tell us to have 'intelligent' conversations with our children. Tell us how."

Healy realized that she knew how to do this at the level of intuition, but she did not know how to tell anyone how to do what she did naturally. How to have a playful conversation with children is possible to learn (or should we say relearn). Although play may be sleeping, perhaps it can be awakened. This too is something we need to keep in mind as we think about how to liturgically mark the transitions in childhood.

Spirituality

The fourth continuity between adults and children we will examine briefly is spirituality. We have already discussed how both children and adults are aware of feelings, existential issues, and a need for play. There are five reasons why I also assume that children already know God.

The first reason is empirical, and is based on a study that links adult religious experience with childhood. Edward Robinson discussed the religious experiences of about 600 children in *The Original Vision.*[27] This study did not begin as one about children. Childhood experiences were mentioned spontaneously in 15 percent of the first 4,000 responses to an adult study.

Some of the childhood experiences reported in the Oxford study had been remembered and valued for more than fifty years. In addition, even when adults misinterpreted or rejected what the children told them about their experiences of a power greater than themselves, the children continued to value their experiences, because, as one adult remembered, "I knew what I knew."

The second ground for this assumption is strategic. If we teach children about life and assume that God is not present, we tend to withhold language about God and permission for expressing such an experience during childhood, the most important period for language acquisition. I would rather err on the side of God's presence than absence, and give children the language to identify, name, and value such experiences.

Related to this strategy is a double bind for empirical research. We cannot learn from children about their religious experiences unless they have the language, permission, and support to express these experiences. Since language helps shape the world one lives in, the language, permission, and support we give to children to speak of God "tips" their interpretations of reality toward God. If we do not do this, the research will tip toward a world without God. A neutral study is impossible.

Samuel Terrien's *The Elusive Presence*[28] is a biblical theology that uses the experience of the mystery of God to integrate the meaning of scripture. I would add only that this journey begins in childhood and that children, from an early period, need both nourishment for the journey and the tools to make the journey. The only way to learn a language in a way that will be useful is to use it while you are learning it. If it is true that children have the same feelings and existential issues we do, they also need a *theologia ludens* to make sense of it.

Third, children need religious language to deal with their existential limits, as we have said, but this is more than an educational issue. It is an ethical issue. Human beings are born into a situation limited by death, fundamental aloneness, the threat of freedom, a need for meaning, and other existential boundaries. These existential edges to life limit but also define us. They cannot authentically define us if we cannot allow ourselves to be aware of them, and that is difficult unless we can find a safe place to be while that transforming process takes place. The liturgy, artfully offered, is such a place.

Fourth, the collapse of the old arguments for discrediting theistic experience has left room for considering this assumption to be reasonable. It used to be that the lack of agreement about descriptions of such an event (conflicting claims argument) and the correlation between prior beliefs and such descriptions (reductionist argument) seemed persuasive. The broader view of how scientific knowledge is construed, and the development of the cumulative case for empirical evidence about the experience of God, brilliantly summarized and contributed to by Caroline Franks Davis,[29] have expanded the concept of what counts as "evidence" to include religious experience.

The fifth reason for making this assumption comes from my own experience as a child. I, too, encountered the presence of a Power I could not understand or speak of, but it was very real. Later I learned that this Power might be related to the "church God" whom I experienced primarily in social terms. Keeping the door open between the Power children cry out to in terror or delight and the church God is possible. Play, it seems to me, is the key, i.e., godly play.

There are two kinds of play and both are needed to play the ultimate game worth playing. One is the play of "as-if" which keeps us connected with tradition and our culture. There is also the play of "what-if" which carries us beyond tradition and culture (without becoming disconnected because of "as-if" play). This "going beyond" play leads us to creativity.

Creativity

Whatever we do to mark the transition from infancy to childhood and the transitions within that period of life, it needs to involve the children, the parents, and the congregation in a liturgical act that stimulates feelings, existential issues, play, the child's experience of the mystery of the presence of God, and creativity. We turn now to examine this last continuity.

The language of our liturgical action should be the language of symbol and gesture. The language of one's tradition links the play of liturgy with what we have received from the tradition with the play of what will become, the transformation in the liturgy. This is a combination of "playing-as" to give us a safe place and "playing-as-if" to experience transformation. To discuss the process of how to begin to think in a new way we need to return to the work of Piaget and bring the story up-to-date.

The cognition relied on for transformational communication is much broader than the mathematical-logical kind of intelligence that Piaget studied, Goleman introduced to religious education, and which Fowler and Oser have developed in such detail. The work of Howard Gardner may provide the key to unlock a new and broader view of how to be with children and how transformation might take place despite our developmental differences in thinking.

Gardner began his career in the tradition of Piaget, but he proposed a view of human development in his first book that focused not on cognitive development alone. He followed the rich integration of what he called the making function, perception, and feelings. He returned to the theme of creativity (making) in *Creating Minds: An Anatomy of Creativity Seen Through the Lives of Freud, Einstein, Picasso, Stravinsky, Eliot, Graham, and Gandhi* in 1993.[30]

Our liturgical communication needs to be at least as broad as the seven ways of knowing that Howard Gardner has proposed: logical/mathematical (Einstein), interpersonal (Gandhi), intrapersonal (Freud), musical/rhythmic (Stravinsky), verbal/linguistic (T. S. Eliot), visual/spatial (Picasso), and body/kinesthetic (Martha Graham).[31]

The making function (creativity) that he stressed in his developmental theory for the arts is also fundamental to our marking of the transitions in childhood by liturgical action. It is a creativity that needs to be open to the seven ways of knowing and creating, so each person present can be renewed in his/her own unique way.

This liturgy also needs to invite children, parents, and the congregation into the mystery of the presence of God rather than conclusions stated in propositional language about that presence. This will call forth the urge to create in each participant and give each an opportunity in a safe place to transcend one's ordinary, personal existence to be part of something larger. This engaging of our creativity brings us into the area of complexity where living creatures need to be in order to be truly in the image of the Creator of the universe.

Conclusion

We have discussed the confusing view the church has taken across the centuries. We have learned that this confusion can be dangerous as well as inconsistent. In such confusion people might act out for unconscious reasons and endanger children in addition to not understanding them. This liturgy needs to state clearly yet broadly that children are creatures in need of blessing, as are we, in order to bless.

We have also mentioned the cognitive differences between children and adults, but we have chosen to focus on the commonalities among us all: feelings, existential limits, play, spirituality, and creativity. These doorways need to be kept open so we can visit each other in these profound ways during the liturgy.

We also need to incorporate into our liturgy the seven ways of knowing that Gardner has proposed: logical-mathematical, interpersonal, intrapersonal, musical/rhythmic, verbal/linguistic, visual/spatial, and body/kinesthetic. These avenues of knowing need to be present to celebrate each one's uniqueness as well as our corporate unity in this act of supporting and nourishing transformation.

We need to be reminded in closing what Tom Driver wrote in the concluding pages of his book, *The Magic of Ritual: Our Need for Liberating Rites That Transform Our Lives and Our Communities,* about transformation and liturgy.

> The liminality of ritual is the power of transcendence, of no-saying, of expressing what society and culture deny, of unmasking pretension,

of elevating persons and things of "low degree," of "putting down the mighty from their seats" (Luke 1:52–53). It is the power Shakespeare called imaginative, to "give to aery nothing a local habitation and a name."[32]

We need not only all of the above but a touch of Shakespeare's poetry as well. In the next section we shall try to propose ways to "give to aery nothing a local habitation and a name" to mark transitions of children that also involve our adult ways of being in the world as parents and members of congregations.

CELEBRATING CHILDHOOD TRANSITIONS

In the previous discussion we demonstrated the ambivalence of the church toward children. We also noted how adults and children can find common experiences in their feelings, existential awareness, play, spirituality, and creativity. The liturgies proposed in this section will attempt to make clear the positive regard of the church for children and their growth as people and as Christians. The commonalities between adults and children will be used to draw all into the communication, and a broad view of the way children know will inform our design.

A Few General Considerations

There are several practical matters that need to be addressed in addition to the theoretical foundation formulated in the last chapter. A primary concern is that any liturgy designed needs to be do-able. It cannot be so complicated and take so much time for preparation that it will never get done, at least after the first time.

A second practical matter to keep in mind is that all the participants need to be prepared and to take part. This includes the celebrant, the congregation, the child, and the parents, however they may be arranged. To be playful, for example, does not mean anything goes or that one can talk and act in the liturgy without attention to the depth and poetry in what one says and does.

Third, it should be kept in mind that what is done speaks louder than the words one uses. How this is done is as important as what is said and done. The words need to be kept at a minimum, and they need to be open to all people present from the youngest to the oldest. This means that the communication needs to be available to all ages.

Finally, what is done must be real. If children are given jobs to do or things to prepare, they need to be supported, and their work needs to be treated with the same respect and care that would be given to anyone in the congregation.

The Early Childhood Transition

For a time the baby is content to remain in the arms of the mother or father and to participate through their actions. The child absorbs what they are doing and the pattern of the action becomes familiar. One day, however, the little one will reach out to take part personally.

When little children begin to reach out for the elements of holy communion, it is time to begin to think about preparing the family for a first communion. Once children begin reaching out, it means that they can now feel rejected when they are refused.

No one knows in advance when a child will reach out. If it is quite early, then the family can help the little one take part. When the child is about two or three years of age and walking, it is time to mark the child's participation with a special act of acknowledgment. The transition from being a baby to becoming a child is at hand.

There are many ways of making one's first communion. Long and important traditions are established in many denominations. What I will suggest here puts all these traditions to one side. It is an effort to say what would be most appropriate for the children.

The first communion preparation begins with a visit to the priest[33] by as many in the family as possible. The formality of the visit is difficult for everyone involved, but it is important to connect the child with the church through the place and the priest.

What is done during this visit counts more than the words spoken. The child will remember the people and the place rather than what is said, but this does not mean that one can be careless with words. It is important to begin to use the language of the Christian tradition with understanding and love, for the child is learning that language and the feelings that go with it, whether or not anyone is paying attention to the language lesson going on.

After a few minutes in the priest's office, everyone can go into the church. Now the priest can show everyone the most important gestures and symbols in the context of the place where they are used in worship. Talking about this in some other setting is only words about words. Here the words can be associated with the symbols and action.

Special attention is given to the gesture of the Holy Spirit's coming down at the epiclesis (invocation). The hands are held over the elements. The gesture of the offering is also shown. The hands now lift up the bread and wine to God.

The child is then asked where the bread and wine come from. "On this coming Sunday, your special day, the bread and wine will be brought by you and your family. Carry the bread with two hands and someone else in your family will carry the wine. I will be here waiting for you. You don't need to worry. This is fun, and I will be happy to see you and your family."

The priest then shows the child and his or her family how he will kneel down to receive the bread from the child at eye level. The priest will then receive the wine at the eye level of the adult or other child and receive the other offerings as well.

Careful preparation is important so all will feel comfortable, but God will enjoy what happens regardless of any awkwardness. The congregation also can enjoy this, especially if the celebrant takes delight in such Godly play and keeps everyone at ease. The balance of formality, order, and play is a lovely art that can keep the liturgical life of a parish deeply engaged with the Holy Spirit and dancing lightly at the same time.

After the first communion, the child and his or her family need to mark the day's celebration with a formal yet playful meal together at home or in some other special place.

Baking the bread in the form that is customary for use in your parish is also possible, but this may be too time-consuming and make the liturgy too complicated to be enjoyed. The visit with the priest is already a lot of significant time to invest.

The Transition from Early to Middle Childhood

The transition to middle childhood has to do with reading. When the child enters the first grade, he or she is beginning "real school." Preschool, as its name implies, prepares the child for this important moment. In real school one learns how to read.

The behavioral sign for this transition, then, is readiness to attend first grade and to learn to read. At this time the child is not reading with great comfort, so let us call these children "word-readers." We will talk about "paragraph-readers" when we discuss the transition to late childhood.

It may seem like an old-fashioned approach to tie the transitions within childhood to reading. After all, this is the age of television. On the other hand, despite television and computers being used in many school programs, the schools are still primarily engaged in ushering children into the print culture.

Why not use television, which is more widespread than literacy? The reason is that children do not need to develop any skills to watch television, except pushing the button to turn it on, and television develops no skills. One does not get better at watching television by watching more television.

Since there is no challenge to mastering television watching, there is no sense of accomplishment. Furthermore, the onset of watching marks no developmental period, since we may begin watching television as infants.

The conceptual content of television is leveled by its dependence on visual images to carry its message along whether one is watching *Sesame Street*, the news, or a car commercial. The images are designed to evoke an emotional response rather than one to encourage the use of the imagination or critical reasoning.

In addition, the kind of social setting in which the television invites the child to engage is destructive to human communication. The video speaker will not respond. We must respond to its changing images and sound. It is a monologue that you must listen to on its terms.

It seems to me that children are learning this form of communication well from the example of the speaker with whom they spend so much time. The result for human interaction is that they are either restless until entertained by images or until they speak. In the case of the former, they cannot listen to another human being, so they cannot engage in a conversation. This breaks down human communion and makes it unholy.

The ability to watch television, therefore, seems a poor choice to use as a symbol for critical transitions in the lives of human beings. You might ask: What about computers? Computers still require literacy to use them, although they are moving toward an oral and image culture as well.

Childhood is intertwined with literacy. In the Middle Ages one was an adult by seven years of age, because by the age of seven one had command over speech, even though there was no writing for most people.

Neil Postman wrote in *The Disappearance of Childhood* that childhood is not "a biological category." It is "a social artifact."

> The idea of childhood is one of the great inventions of the Renaissance. Perhaps its most humane one. Along with science, the nation-state, and religious freedom, childhood as both a social structure and a psychological condition emerged around the sixteenth century and has been refined and nourished into our own times. But like all social artifacts, its continued existence is not inevitable. Indeed…the idea of childhood is disappearing, and at a dazzling speed.[34]

Childhood is not only "a biological category." It is a "social artifact," and needs to be not only acknowledged but supported for human development. The liturgy marking the transition into middle childhood, however, is not only about reading. It is also about participating more fully in worship, serving others, and having a real place in the life of the church in addition to worship and Sunday school.

The liturgical marking of this transition has three parts. First, there is the liturgy in the church when the children's names are called, their transition is spoken about, and they are given a *Book of Common Prayer*. Second, there is some kind of service project that they and their classmates do with the help of their Sunday school teacher. Third, there is a real job in the church that they and their family can sign up for, such as being greeters or helping take care of the building and the yard.

This time the preparation is done by the child's Sunday school teachers. When the children come into the first grade, the lead teacher invites the families to come with their children to the Sunday liturgy about the middle of October for a special presentation. By this time a sense of the group has formed in their Sunday school class, and the teachers have prepared the children for receiving the gift of a *Book of Common Prayer*.

The preparation for receiving the prayer book involves using a simplified version with pictures that the children can use to find their place in the worship service. Each picture has a word from the headings in the prayer book to identify it. This is to help with the transition from the pictures to the book itself. In the meantime the book can be brought to church as a symbol of participation.

The children are called forward with their families. The priest says something like this to the whole group: "You are really growing up. It is amazing that you are in the first grade now. It is time for you to have your own prayer book, so you can bring it to church with you. Your mom and dad will help you find your place. The ribbons already mark the place for what we are doing in worship today. We love to have you here. It makes us happy to give you your own prayer book to keep and use, because it shows you belong here. God bless you all." Again the celebrant gets down to each child's eye level for the presentation.

The transition to early childhood involves bringing the gifts forward for holy communion. The gift that the child gives at this level is also a gift to others, but these others are not in church. A carefully guided introduction to a group service project is the second part of this transition.

An example of a service project is visiting older people from the congregation at home or in a nursing home. The children will go with their Sunday school teacher, with some parents helping to drive. Another example is bringing food and toys to children who are homeless. The experience needs to be one that is not overwhelming, so the children can feel enough in control that they can look back on the experience as something really fun and worth repeating.

Finally, it is important to begin to have a real job in the life of the parish. The children and their parents may sign up to be greeters at the door. Another real job would be for the children to help mothers or fathers with altar guild duties. A third example of a real job is to help take care of the church or the yard and garden.

The Transition to Late Childhood

The transition to late childhood also will be marked by a liturgy in the church, a service project, and a real job. Let us begin with the liturgy in the church.

When the children enter the third grade, they are more comfortable reading. They can read whole paragraphs with understanding rather than just a word at a time. In addition, at church they have been supported by their families and Sunday school teachers to use or at least to bring their prayer books to church and Sunday school, and they are learning their way around in its pages.

Since the children are reading well by this time and their ability to discuss what they read is more fluent, it is time for them to be given a Bible. There are a number of respectful editions, as opposed to cute, cartoon and trivialized editions. The illustrations need to be strong and realistic.

The purpose of giving the children a Bible at this stage is to show them that their growing abilities are appreciated and to challenge them to continue their growth in understanding as their journey progresses. As you will see, it is also a means for them to begin to take a new kind of leadership in the parish.

This time, the child is brought to the priest's study to visit with him or her alone. They talk about what is going to happen in the liturgy and why the child is being given a Bible. This is a time to talk about what the Bible is and how important it is. Perhaps the priest even has a Bible to show the child that he or she was given at an early age.

During the liturgy in the church, the child will be named again before the congregation and be celebrated again at another coming of age. The celebrant may say something like this: "Now that you are in the third grade, it is important for us to congratulate you and to honor your new place in life by giving you this Bible. It is a symbol of our respect for you and your growing up. It gives us all a way to share with you something that is very, very important to all of us. May God bless you in your journey throughout life, and may you keep this with you always to show you the way."

This time, the priest does not get down at the child's eye level. This is more formal and grown-up. Now there is a handshake and there is not as much informal kidding around. It is still fun, but that is noticed by the twinkle in the priest's eye and genuine respect and love in his or her voice.

When the celebration is over, a reception is held at the church with as many of the congregation present as is possible. They need to come and visit with the third graders and get to know them better. Perhaps someone dressed up like a biblical character can come to entertain and to talk with humor about his or her experiences. This "biblical" person can also congratulate the children.

The service project that accompanies this rite of transition takes the child beyond home and the congregation. These children are often ready to visit a soup kitchen, if it will not overwhelm them. Visiting the elderly and doing projects at the church continue to be important. It is also time now to be more conscious about bringing gifts of money. Perhaps the children will have an allowance that they can share with the church.

The real job for these children is to usher and greet without their parents but in small groups. Parents and younger children will be present to help, but these children need to do this by themselves.

Another real job is to help with leading worship. Now it is time for the children to read the scriptures publicly. This will involve a visit to the parish priest or the Sunday school teacher to prepare to read with understanding. A long passage can be divided up into smaller parts, so a few children can work on a passage together.

In addition to reading the scriptures in church, the children also need to have a few times each year for them to respond to the scriptures with their own kind of "sermon." This is a chance for singers, dancers, and poets to join in the creativity with their special talents.

Conclusion

As you can see, these liturgies take time for the priest, Sunday school teachers, the parents and the congregation. The way we spend our time is how we show what (and whom) we value. These liturgies are intentionally shaped to value children, not as the future of the church, but as part of the present church.

[1]Hans-Rudi Weber, *Jesus and the Children* (Geneva: World Council of Churches, 1979).

[2]George Boas, *The Cult of Childhood* (London: The Warburg Institute, 1966; reprint, Dallas, Texas: Spring Publications, 1990).

[3]Margaret R. Miles, *Carnal Knowing: Female Nakedness and Religious Meaning in the Christian West* (Boston: Beacon Press, 1989), 162.

[4]Tertullian, "On the Apparel of Women," quoted in "Feminist Theology and Religious Education," Elizabeth Dodson Gray in *Theologies of Religious Education*, ed. Randolph Crump Miller.

[5]Rosemary Radford Ruether, "The Western Tradition and Violence Against Women," in *Christianity, Patriarchy and Abuse*, ed. Joanne Carlson Brown and Carole R. Bohn (New York: Pilgrim Press, 1989), 37.

[6]Phillipe Aries, *Centuries of Childhood*, (New York: Knopf, 1962), 128.

[7]"The Fourth and Fifth Centuries," E. J. Yarnold, S.J.; *The Study of Liturgy*, ed. Cheslyn Jones, Geoffrey Wainwright, Edward Yarnold, S.J.(New York: Oxford University Press, 1978), 95.

[8]J. Jeremias, *Infant Baptism in the First Four Centuries* (SCM 1960), 11–18; *The Origins of Infant Baptism* (SCM 1963), K. Aland, *Did the Early Church Baptize Infants?* (SCM 1963) noted at 85 of *The Study of Liturgy*.

[9]"The Fourth and Fifth Centuries," 96.

[10]"The West from about A.D. 500 to the Reformation," J. D .C. Fisher, E. J. Yarnold in *The Study of Liturgy*, eds. Cheslyn Jones, Geoffrey Wainwright, Edward Yarnold, S.J. (New York: Oxford University Press, 1978), 111.

[11]Ibid., 115.

[12]Bernhard Poschman, *Penance and the Anointing of the Sick* (London: Herder and Herder, 1951), 255.

[13]Henri I. Marrou, *A History of Education in Antiquity* (London: Sheed and Ward, 1956), 315.

[14]Philip Greven, *The Protestant Temperament* (New York: Knopf, 1977).

[15]Ronald Goldman, *Readiness for Religion: A Basis for Developmental Religious Education* (London: Routledge & Kegan Paul, 1965; reprint, New York: Seabury Press, 1970).

[16]James W. Fowler, *Stages of Faith: The Psychology of Human Development and the Quest for Meaning* (San Francisco: Harper and Row, 1981).

[17]Fritz Oser and Paul Gmunder, *Religious Judgement: A Developmental Approach* (Birmingham, Alabama: Religious Education Press, 1991).

[18]David Elkind, "The Child's Conception of his Religious Denomination: I, The Jewish Child," *Journal of Genetic Psychology* 99 (1961): 209–25; "The Child's Conception of His Religious Denomination: II, The Catholic Child," *Journal of Genetic Psychology*, 101 (1962):185–93; "The Child's Conception of His Religious Denomination: III, The Protestant Child," *Journal of Genetic Psychology*, 103 (1963):291–304.

[19]Humberto Maturana and Francisco Varela, *The Tree of Knowledge: The Biological Roots of Human Understanding* (Boston: Shambala, 1987). For the application to psychology, please see Jay S. Efran, Michael D. Lukens, and Robert J. Lukens, *Language Structure and Change: Frameworks of Meaning in Psychotherapy* (New York: W. W. Norton and Company, 1990).

[20]Daniel Goleman, *Emotional Intelligence: Why It Can Matter More Than IQ* (New York: Bantam Books, 1995).

[21]F. H. Heinemann, *Existentialism and the Modern Predicament* (New York: Harper and Brothers, 1953; Harper Torchbooks, 1958).

[22]Ovrom D. Yalom, *Existential Psychotherapy* (New York: Basic Books, 1980).

[23]M. Mitchell Waldrop, *Complexity: The Emerging Science at the Edge of Order and Chaos* (New York: Simon and Schuster, A Touchstone Book, 1992), 293.

[24]John M. Hull, *What Prevents Christian Adults from Learning?* (London: SCM Press, 1985).

[25]David L. Miller, *Gods and Games Toward a Theology of Play* (New York: Harper Colophon Books, 1973), "Chapter Six." This is a good introduction to religion as play. Both Guardini and Rahner's work are introduced in the context of a theology of play. A discussion of play in relation to religious education may be found in Jerome W. Berryman, *Godly Play: An Imaginative Aproach*

to Religious Education (San Francisco: Harper SanFrancisco, 1991; reprint Minneapolis: Augsburg Fortress, 1995).

[26]Jane M. Healy, *How to Have Intelligent and Creative Conversations with Your Kids* (New York: Doubleday, 1992).

[27]Edward Robinson, *The Original Vision: A Study of the Religious Experience of Childhood* (Oxford: Religious Experience Research Unit, Manchester College, 1977).

[28]Samuel Terrien, *The Elusive Presence: The Heart of Biblical Theology* (San Francisco: Harper and Row, 1978).

[29]Caroline Franks Davis, *The Evidential Force of Religious Experience* (Oxford: Clarendon Press, 1989).

[30]Howard Gardner, *Creating Minds: An Anatomy of Creativity Seen through the Lives of Freud, Einstein, Picasso, Stravinsky, Eliot, Graham, and Gandhi* (New York: Basic Books, 1993). The book referred to as his "first book" is *The Arts and Human Development* (New York: John Wiley and Sons, Inc., 1973; reprint with new introduction New York: HarperCollins, Basic Books, 1994).

[31]Howard Gardner, *Frames of Mind: The Theory of Multiple Intelligences* (New York: Basic Books, 1983).

[32]Tom F. Driver, *The Magic of Ritual: Our Need for Liberating Rites That Transform Our Lives and Our Communities* (San Francisco: HarperSanFrancisco, 1991), 190.

[33]Following my Episcopal tradition, I will use "priest" through this chapter, but you may read "minister" or "pastor" or whatever term is common to your own tradition.

[34]Neil Postman, *The Disappearance of Childhood* (New York: Vintage Books, Random House, 1994), xii.

3
Growing toward Committed Discipleship

Laurence Hull Stookey

A Proposed Process

An Alternative to the Problems of Confirmation

In almost all denominations, recent "confirmation training" has been a matter of "too little, too soon." Add to that the difficulty that the very concept of confirmation is in trouble in many quarters. No longer accepted as a kind of second-stage rocket that sacramentally "completes" infant baptism, what is confirmation: A ritual termination of several sessions of straight catechesis ("the pastor's class for youth")? An assertion of Episcopal prerogative (in denominations in which only bishops can confirm)? A religious accommodation to culture in recognition of puberty?

So tangled are the issues, and so diverse the suggestions as to how to settle them, that this chapter seeks to do an end-run around the problems. However the churches may officially settle the issue of confirmation (and they will likely settle it in different ways), there is growing recognition that a renaissance of mature Christian discipleship is urgently needed, that this depends upon disciplined preparation now largely missing in the church, and that therefore a new concept of and concrete plan for moving into adult faith is needed. What is envisioned here is an extended process of preparation which goes beyond the cognitive and didactic models of the past and is not unlike scouting movements in scope and seriousness.[1]

Five Characteristics of a Program toward Adult Discipleship

What are the characteristics of such a process? Five are crucial: (1) It is extended over a significant duration of time, not over six or eight weeks. (2) It springs from the weekly liturgy of the congregation. (3) It wrestles with opportunities for concrete local expression growing out of the liturgy. (4) While resources may be provided "from above" (by national denominational and ecumenical agencies, for example), each participating congregation fully owns its own program. (5) It is ecumenical to every possible extent. Let us look at each in turn.

(1) Ideally, the process should extend from puberty to the threshold of adulthood, encompassing the years of senior high school. Activities perhaps would not be of equal intensity throughout the entire period, but would accelerate toward a peak at the age of sixteen or seventeen.

The rite set forth in the next chapter is designed for the entry point. Some denominations may want to interpret this entry point as "confirmation," and thus adapt the rite accordingly to accommodate existing denominational rites of confirmation. More likely, if a traditional "confirmation rite" is desired, that would be used at the far end of the process. But the process itself is free-standing and can function as readily in churches which have no tradition of confirmation and desire none.

The Sunday morning component of the program has to do largely with attendance by youth at congregational worship (see number 2). The rest of the program probably best occurs at some other time, thus avoiding the some-times pejorative (at least to this age group) connotations of "Sunday school." Nor are weekly sessions (however defined) mandatory. While small groups that meet regularly to encourage interaction and provide mutual support are assumed to be at the core of the program, some aspects of the process may be worked through by individuals who report regularly to a mentor, rather than in group sessions. In order to be sustained for three or four years, the program will require variety and flexibility, though always with deliberate, careful supervision and consistent accountability.

(2) The program is liturgy-based. Its goal is to teach growing Christians to pray in the fullest sense: not just as individuals but in corporate bodies in communion with the church catholic; not merely in words of intercession but in actions that embody the hope of the petitions. What happens from Sunday afternoon through Saturday evening is a self-conscious working-out of the faith expressed and shared on Sunday morning.

Thus, for example, on Sunday the congregation typically prays for (a) the sick and shut-ins; (b) the dying and those who mourn; (c) the leaders of our nation and the world; (d) the cause of peace and justice; and (e) the mission of the church. At various age-appropriate points during the multi-year process, this can lead to activities such as the following:

Prayers for the sick and shut-in may provide an entrée into learning the skills of Christian visitation in hospitals and homes. These may also lead into discussion and study of the issues of health care in our society and the tangled matter of the responsibility of adult children toward aged and infirm parents (an issue often very apparent to youth because of the needs of their own grand-parents).

Prayers for the dying and those who mourn may provide consideration of the Christian understanding of death generally and the funeral practices in particular; subsequent discussions of heroic medical procedures, living wills, decisions to terminate life support systems, organ donation, and euthanasia can then hardly be avoided.

The church's intercession on behalf of national and international leaders will grow into far-ranging discussions of the entire political process. These can dovetail with local school curricula in government and citizenship, yet must go beyond these by confronting the explicitly Christian dimensions of living in this world while critically examining the standard assumptions of secular values. The ever-present reality of political corruption and deception can lead into engagement in the Christian tension between the reality of intractable sin and the drive toward sanctification. As those engaged in the process approach the age of eighteen, such discussions will increasingly focus on their responsibility as Christian voters, jurors, and potential holders of public office.

Sunday prayers for peace and justice should occasion weekday study of the history that underlies gender, racial, ethnic and political tensions, issues of power and the control of land and resources, of defense and disarmament, and of values represented by the fiscal priorities undergirding these.

And the prayers for the mission of the church can lead in a dozen directions ranging from church polity as a means of expediting (or impeding) action to questions about global evangelization and the interaction of the various religions of the world as these respect or compete with each other.

All of this, simply based on five selected kinds of Sunday intercessions! But more than that happens on Sunday. The use of scripture and sermon in Sunday service will compel consideration of methods of biblical study and the theology of preaching: Is the Bible to be read differently from other books? Is the sermon to be heard differently from other kinds of persuasive discourse? Why or why not? Are the biblical writers and today's preachers simply expressing individual opinions; or does the fact that we are part of a community of faith enter into the picture in important ways?

The use of water in baptism and bread and wine in communion should open into avenues of exploration as diverse as ecology and ecclesiology. And Sunday's hymns and creeds will provide a rich curriculum for prayer, study, and reflection.

It should be amply evident that a serious liturgy-based process can readily fill up three or four years as a preparation for life as Christian adults. The process itself, not simply its content, is the point. For the process is intended to develop habits such that attendance at worship throughout life will continually occasion related thought and action. Too often "confirmation training" at puberty or shortly thereafter has been viewed as the end of the process for formal religious education ("graduation from Sunday school," in many cases) rather than as the formation of habits and methods to be used throughout a lifetime of committed Christian faith and action. As a consequence, adult participation in Sunday worship has been viewed as optional (for those who "need it" or "like that sort of thing") and essentially irrelevant to life the rest of the week.

It is to be hoped that as a by-product of liturgy-based training for youth, adults will also be reeducated. The worshiping congregation, observing the process, may come to find new meaning for itself in the integral relationship of liturgy to life.

(3) The examples already given indicate what is meant by local expression, and more abound: working with problems of homelessness; looking into local health care options, particularly for the poor; dealing

with irrational fears of AIDS and the neglect of those in the community who suffer from it; sponsoring open forums or debates by political candidates; assessing manifestations of and reasons for local (as well as national) history of racial fears; working on problems springing from the closing of a nearby military base; assessing the cleanliness of local water and air are and how they can be improved.

(4) All of this should make it clear why a program has to be tailor-made. Denominational, national, and regional agencies may provide helpful resources. But if the program does not have concrete manifestations locally, the incarnational thrust of the Christian faith is lessened, or even denied.

However, "local" does not necessarily mean every congregation separately, or even town by town. The geo-political makeup of each region can provide guidance for work that is fully cooperative yet concrete. The process suggested here is so visionary as to overwhelm most congregations singly; but it is less daunting if congregations work together based on geographic proximity and mutual interest.

(5) That cooperation should be fully ecumenical—indeed catholic. The unity the church already has is often concealed by our propensity for independent action; nor is more unity likely to be attained by separate and separated work. The sharing of ideas and resources across denominational lines is mandatory; and ideally the study and support groups should consist of youth from the different cooperating faith traditions.

True ecumenical involvement in the program will mean honest confrontation with conflict—as when Protestant youth are exposed at the same time to the beliefs of a Roman Catholic pro-life advocate and a Unitarian pro-choice leader. But learning how to deal with just differences among Christians is a crucial part of mature faith and witness.

Ecumenism should be carefully considered even at points where it may seem less than efficient. For example, while Baptist, Presbyterian, Lutheran, and Methodist youth may see the advantages of meeting together to discuss core beliefs or cooperative action projects, they may be inclined to meet separately to discuss their several forms of polity because this is efficient: Why should Baptists "waste their time" learning about Methodist annual conferences or Lutheran synodical structures? Well, perhaps for the same reason that American students in a civics class study the British Parliament and the Russian Politburo: Often we understand—and critique—our own practices best by comparison and contrast.

Scope and Stance of the Program

The program as outlined above may seem prohibitive in scope. Certainly it will be if we suppose that everything must be the responsibility of a volunteer from the congregation—the prototypical youth leader. At least one reason for conceiving the program cooperatively is that it then can draw widely upon community resources. It is a foundational assumption that the program does not call for leaders who themselves must become thoroughly knowledgeable about education, medicine, politics, and so on, in order to "teach" all of these things to youth. The program calls for coordinators who identify in the congregations, as well as in the broader community, educators, health-care professionals, political leaders, and the like, who can make presentations, suggest topics for discussion, and recommend materials for reading or viewing on videotape. (It goes without saying that these coordinators will themselves become significant learners, so that the process will have an important "ripple effect" that extends beyond the age range of fourteen to seventeen.) And as participating youth move closer to adulthood they should be encouraged themselves to seek out and suggest resource persons and data.

What is needed directly from the church itself throughout the program is expert guidance in the catholic Christian tradition and contemporary theological outlook. For example, such a program may or may not include discreet units of historical study ("the early church," "problems and possibilities of the faith of the Middle Ages," "the Reformers of the church"), or theological issues ("doctrine of creation," "christology"). But it will necessarily be infiltrated with historical perspective and theological undergirding.

To cite one example only. A Christian consideration of war and peace needs to be informed by the following at least: (a) the biblical tension between Jesus' teaching of turning the other cheek, on the one hand, and, on the other, the Old Testament practice of war and Pauline statements about obedience to civil authorities; (b) the pre-Constantinian pacifism of the church which precluded consideration of soldiers as members; (c) the Augustinian theory of "the just war" and its later development; (d) the resurgent pacificism in the left-wing of the Reformation; (e) recent church documents, from John XXIII's *Pacem in Terris* to various denominational papers on peace and related issues.

Any discussion of war and peace that ignores these is not yet deliberately Christian and could readily be held in a public high school classroom. The point of the church's program is not merely to produce involved citizens but to nurture Christians who intentionally bring faith to bear on their citizenship.

Considerations in Face of the Challenge

By now, most readers will be muttering that all of the above is obviously the construct of an ivory-tower academician who doesn't know the difference between a youth program in a local congregation and a seminary curriculum. The theological professor-author offers the following considerations in response.

First, not all young people may be attracted to everything suggested here. But youth who are capable of mastering the intricacies of the game "Dungeons and Dragons" (to say nothing of computer technology) are under-challenged by the youth programs of most local churches. What they do encounter in church (usually at the age of twelve or thirteen) often leads the very best among them too readily to conclude that Christianity is a "Mickey Mouse operation" not worthy of their serious adult involvement. Too often we have failed to grab young people at the point of their nascent idealism and capacity to respond to challenge and have settled for meeting their personal social needs (clubs, group excursions to amusement parks, and sessions on sexuality and drug abuse—all quite necessary but hardly definitive for understanding the scope and seriousness of Christian discipleship).

Second, seminary-trained church professionals ought to function in the congregation primarily as "theologians-in-residence." They are to share with the congregation what they have experienced in the church's academy (which surely is one of the primary reasons for having church owned-and-operated schools of theology). If they see themselves more as personal therapists, bureaucratic administrators, or interest-group organizers than as teachers of the faith, something is amiss, and congregations have a right to call for the reordering of priorities. Too many pastors (it is less true of religious education staff persons) are "out of the loop" in terms of parish education and think their obligation is fulfilled through an annual four or six weeks' "confirmation class," usually for those in their junior high years. Certainly the clergy and other theologically trained persons should be at the center of planning and oversight of the discipleship process.

Third, the program envisioned here is no more ambitious than the catechumenate of the ancient church, in which three years of regular study were normally expected in preparation for admission to the sacramental fellowship. Further, various renewal movements of the church have established requirements of extended disciplined study. (Note, for example, the ambitious catechetical demands of the Protestant reformers or the class meetings of the early Methodists, both of which provided regular study and extended oversight.)

Most likely a full-blown program will need to be phased in over a period of years, with careful preparation and evaluation at each stage. Good record-keeping concerning programming will be invaluable to those repeating the process in future years; and it is to be expected that those youth who complete the program will themselves be excellent candidates for the leadership of it thereafter.

PRELIMINARY BLUEPRINT FOR A RITE

Purpose and Design

Many rites of the church are ways of demarcating time, establishing identity, and providing encouragement and support. Such is the rite suggested here. It marks passage from the time of childhood, when Christian responsibilities are limited and largely outside the realm of deliberation, into the time of adolescence, when serious thought must be given to the nature of the faith and when the foundations must be built under mature thinking and doing.

Those who engage in the rite are thereby identified as having serious intent to be expressed in disciplined ways. Here a delicate balance must be achieved. It is not likely all youth in a congregation will engage in the program of growth toward committed discipleship. Nor is it necessarily desirable that all should—for this could evidence parental or peer pressure rather than the personal interest and commitment demanded by such a program. Hence there is a danger of elitism. On the other hand, there is the danger of debilitating reductionism, which challenges no one, and ignores vast human potential if such a program is not available to those who can engage in it.

Care must be taken, therefore, to commend and encourage those who enter this venture, without implying that these are "the true believers"—the only ones really serious about the faith—or that this is the one and only route by which youth can become committed disciples of Jesus Christ.

Because attrition is avoidable in any program of such duration and intensity, care also must be taken lest we imply that this rite inaugurates a covenant that cannot be broken without severe onus to those who leave the program. Still, the church is seeking to offer support so that reaching the goal will not only be attainable but joyful.

Such support must be congregational in the broadest possible sense. The congregation must enthusiastically embrace the program from its inception, and participation in the rite is a crucial way to signal and intensify that ownership. For this reason (as well as the fact that this is a liturgy-based program), the rite is to be an act of congregational worship. Normally this will be a Sunday morning service, though possible exceptions come to mind.

If the program is being done cooperatively, whether by several congregations of the same denomination or by parishes of different denominations, it may be helpful to hold the service at some time other than Sunday morning in order that members of all participating groups can attend. Those planning the service will need, however, to engage in "sanctified scheming" to ensure such attendance; for too often joint services attract disappointingly few persons and thus seem to indicate a lack of enthusiastic support.

"Sanctified scheming" means that if the service is to be held in the building of Congregation A (which will therefore be the most likely to attend due both to convenience and a sense of being proper hosts), the choir of Congregation B will be asked to sing, and the handbell group of Congregation C to participate also. Members of Congregation D will be responsible for refreshments. Greeters, ushers, and other personnel will be selected from families not represented in any of the aforementioned categories and will not be relatives of the youth participating in the rite, and so on.

It is also possible that a congregation planning such a rite for its own youth alone may wish to have a "special" service (on Sunday evening, for example) as a way of highlighting the importance of the occasion. There are pros and cons to such a decision; but if the option is chosen, a similar "consecrated conspiracy" should be employed to ensure a worshiping assembly at least as large as that which gathers on a good Sunday morning.

What is supplied here is not a recommended liturgical text (which in itself would be far less that the liturgy enacted) but only a "preliminary blueprint." In the field of architecture, such drawings provide tentative basic specifications in two dimensions, not three-dimensional realities or firm decisions about detail. As the discipleship program itself must be tailor-made, so also the introductory liturgy must be specifically designed in order to reflect accurately the process being entered into.

Local planners should consider well what needs to be signaled through the rite and how this best can be achieved. Choice of persons to participate is crucial. If, for example, this is the program of one denomination only, can its ecumenical character be declared by having members of other denominations participate in the rite? Surely the congregation should itself be broadly represented by the selection of persons of various ages, both sexes, various ethnic and social groups as leaders in the rite. While the pastor may act as presider, to have a clergy-dominated rite is to send a signal that is in conflict with the basic intention of the program.

Also crucial is the choice of symbolic tokens to be presented to the youth who enter the program. Each young person probably will be presented with a Bible and a hymnal (or a hymnal plus a book of congregational rites, if the denomination binds these in different volumes). But additional presentations may vary from person to person—first to reflect differing interests, but also to suggest that specific responsibilities may be delegated to particular individuals with a view to later sharing within the group.

By way of example: A youth who wants, but does not have access to, good national and international news coverage may be presented with a subscription to a weekly news magazine, while another young person with a keen interest in biblical study may be given a one-volume Bible study guide or videotape program designed for laity. Still another may receive a subscription to an appropriate periodical for youth. Each in turn can then share with the group from the content of his or her respective resources. Some presentations may be denominationally specific: a lectionary guide may be appropriate to Lutherans but not to Baptists, for example. Presentations during the rite will not only indicate the scope of the program but may also suggest to adult members of the congregation how their own faith can be enhanced and expressed through the use of similar resources.

The Service in Outline

The rite of commitment to the program most likely will be located in the order of worship following the reading of scripture and its exposition in a sermon. This placement indicates that Christian commitment grows out of, and is guided by, biblical study and the heritage of the Christian community (for scripture is the first layer of tradition). The prayers of intercession at the end of the rite logically flow into the general intercessions of the congregation, however these are usually organized and conducted. If all the youth participating in the growth in discipleship program are already admitted to the table of the Lord, the service may culminate in the eucharist as both a sign of strength for the journey and a form of family fellowship.

If this is not a regular Sunday morning service, the choice of hymns, scriptures, prayers, preaching theme, and the like can all be specific to the occasion. If the rite is inserted into the regular Sunday service, the choice of day will be crucial, particularly in lectionary churches, since some Sundays lend themselves better thematically than others.

Suggested elements in the rite and a logical ordering of them follows.

PRESENTATION OF THE YOUTH

At the appointed place in the order of service, youth will come to stand before the congregation, accompanied, perhaps, by their parents or other adults acting as sponsors or primary supporters. Their names may be read aloud by a person whose role in the congregation makes this logical: chair of youth work or church membership secretary, for example.

STATEMENT OF PURPOSE

Then a succinct introductory statement can be read, embodying the basic theology and intention of the program. This may be done by the program coordinator, or the chair of the committee that has planned or oversees the program.

ASSENT OF THE YOUTH

Next, those enrolling in the program express their assent and intention. The degree to which this is done informally or through actual vows should be considered carefully; the determination may well depend upon whether this rite is seen to be part of a more official denominational action such as confirmation, admission to church membership, or admission to the table of the Lord. Upon this determination also may depend the matter as to whether the statements of assent should be conducted by the pastor or someone else.

In all cases, however, indication should be given that assent has been duly considered prior to this occasion, with full knowledge of the demands of the program. The seriousness of the endeavor does not lend itself to "walk-in" participation; under no circumstances should leaders of the rite visually survey the congregation and then ask, "Are there any others present who may wish to take part in this program even though they have not previously decided to do so: if so, let them also now come." As magnanimous as such a gesture may seem, it degrades the importance of this rite and the program generally among those who have thought it through carefully.

PRAYER OF COMMITMENT

This may be a unison prayer on the part of the youth—perhaps even one they have jointly written under careful guidance; or it may be a prayer spoken on their behalf by a representative of the congregation or by the pastor.

PRESENTATIONS

Items useful to those entering the program and symbolic of its nature and scope may then be presented to each young person. For example:

- Study Bible in contemporary translation with helpful annotations.
- Table of lectionary readings.
- Hymnal, or hymnal and separate liturgy book used in Sunday worship.
- Devotional guide for use in private prayer.
- Outline of the scope and design of the program of growth toward committed discipleship.
- Subscription to appropriate periodicals, whether religious or "secular" publications, that concentrate on issues of pressing concern to Christians.
- Notebook to be used for "journaling."
- Items related to the specific work of the parish or denomination: congregational or denominational history, annual parish report, manuals of policy and polity.
- Directory of community services, governmental offices and officials, social agencies, ecumenical agencies.
- Certificate of entry into the program.
- Identifying insignia (such as a pin or pendant) of suitable design.

It may be determined that as a kind of annual recognition and reaffirmation, when new persons are brought into the program, those already in it will be recognized also. In that case, certain presentations may be made the first year and others deferred to various stages along the way. A Bible and hymnal would certainly be needed from the beginning; but it is unlikely, for example, that denominational polity would be studied until much later, or that fourteen-year-olds would be much interested in reading *Time* or *Newsweek*.

WORDS OF SUPPORT AND COMMENDATION

These may be prepared and presented by designated persons; or they may be solicited informally from the congregation; or both may be done in combination. Some thought should be given as to how to close off *ex tempore* remarks. As a part of the commendation, handshakes may be exchanged between youth and designated persons, and the peace may be exchanged in a

manner familiar to the congregation, after which the youth and other participants may return to their seats. (It may be well to seat them before the words
of support and commendation if some extended period is envisioned for this
act.) Some brief word of commending grace may be offered before they are
seated.

INTERCESSIONS

Here there may be intercessions for all who participate in the program—
not only the youth but their leaders and the sponsoring congregation as a
whole.

These specific intercessions may lead into broader intercessions for the
church and the world according to the usual patterns of congregational prayer.
Thus the specific rite for the youth flows back into the broader pattern of
congregational worship; and the service concludes with offering, prayer of
thanksgiving, eucharist, hymn, dismissal and blessing, etc., according to local
and denominational patterns for a congregational liturgy.

Some Models for the Spoken Acts

The words spoken in the rite will need to be carefully prepared locally;
but since nothing is more intimidating than a totally blank piece of paper to
most people who are asked to write such words, the following are offered as
starting points.

PRESENTATION OF THE YOUTH

We now call forward the following persons and offer our support as they
begin the program of growth toward committed adult discipleship. *[Name of
each person is read.]* We are grateful for your faith and welcome your commitment to this program.

STATEMENT OF PURPOSE

Jesus instructed his followers this way: "Any who would come after me
must take up the cross daily and follow me." We understand this to mean that
mature Christian discipleship is not assumed casually or continued haphaz-
ardly. God welcomes us into the church from the moment of birth, but expects
increasingly more of us as we grow in years.

Therefore our congregation encourages the participation of its youth in a
process of growth toward committed discipleship. The program extends
throughout high school, and seeks to move persons through the teenage years
into the time of mature, adult Christian responsibility. The program springs
from the regular worship of the congregation and explores the many ways in
which Christian prayer manifests itself in practical living.

Into this process we have invested great talent, energy, and resources; and
to this process we now welcome these persons.

ASSENT OF THE YOUTH

You have already thoughtfully explored the purpose and design of our
program and have expressed your desire to be a part of it. We ask you now to

declare this publicly before the congregation, that we may know of your faith and may support and encourage you along the way. Is it your sincere intention to participate in this program as a way of responding to God's love, so that you may be effective disciples of Jesus Christ throughout your life?

RESPONSE
It is; and I seek the help of God and of this congregation.

PRAYER OF COMMITMENT
Gracious God, by your goodness made known in Jesus Christ you call forth from us lives of thankful prayer and service. Accept the intentions of *these* your *sons and daughters*. Guide them step by step on their journey toward adulthood, that they may grow in wisdom, kindness, strength, and goodness. Keep them faithful as they pursue the work to which they now pledge themselves; give them strength equal to the challenge and joy in all they learn. Make them conscientious ministers on behalf of your creation and servant-inheritors of your righteousness; through Jesus Christ, our Savior. Amen.

SELECTED STATEMENTS OF PRESENTATION
[Bible] The Scriptures record the faithful struggle of God through the ages to make divine love known in our midst. In this Bible, seek God's call to you and the ability to respond with all of your heart and mind and strength. In the congregation on Sunday, the scriptures are opened and interpreted to you. Throughout each week read and ponder again what you receive on Sunday, that active faith may spring alive within you.

[Lectionary guide] This is the organized way we use to read scripture in the congregation. When you cannot be present with us on Sunday morning, you can nevertheless ponder these same passages and be united with us is study and growth.

[Hymnal/prayerbook] Here are the praises and prayers of many generations of Christian people across the earth. These we borrow and pass on as we worship together. Use these also in weekday devotion for inspiration, guidance, and an increase of understanding.

[Subscription] In response to your own consideration of what may be helpful in your life, we give you a subscription to (*name of publication*). By the reading of it we hope that you will become more aware of the world around you and better equipped to use the talents God has given you.

[Community directory] Within this directory of community services and agencies, you can discover ways to be of assistance to others and to seek assistance for yourself in times of need. By this, be reminded that God has bound all of us—church members and nonchurch people alike—in a common society. We live not for ourselves, but for one another under the gracious purpose of God.

[Insignia] Accept this pin as a visible sign of your commitment. We encourage you to wear it at all the activities of our congregation so that we may be reminded of your faithfulness, and so that we may not fail to support you with our prayers, our love, and any other help that we can offer.

WORDS OF SUPPORT AND COMMENDATION

Individuals within our congregation now offer to you assurances of support, and express the joy we feel together as you take this step toward Christian adulthood…

INTERCESSIONS [*a litany*]

O God, our Maker and Guide:

We hold before you these young women and men of our congregation. Strengthen their determination to follow your way faithfully throughout life. Stretch their minds and fill their hearts with understanding and generosity. Help them to develop the gifts you have put within them, and to discover abilities still hidden from their view. Lord, in your goodness:

Receive our prayer.

We praise you for the dedication of all who plan, direct, and oversee the work of this program. Help them discern the workings of the Holy Spirit in our midst; and give them steadfastness in purpose and action. Lord, in your goodness:

Receive our prayer.

Continually work within all of us, blessed Lord, lest we lose sight of our own responsibility and opportunity in this work of growth. Show each of us how we also may more fully take up the cross and serve you according to our abilities and opportunities. Make this and all communities of your people true fellowships of mutual care and sacrifice. Lord, in your goodness:

Receive our prayer.

These specific intercessions may then lead into the more general intercessions of the congregation.

---

[1]There is no implication here that churches involved in various scouting programs should jettison them to make room for explicitly Christian programs of disciplined training. There is, however, on the horizon a certain threat to church scouting programs. Increasing legal challenges to explicit affirmations of God in Boy Scouting, for example, could lead to a church-state issue if the courts decree that atheists must be admitted to scout troops as a matter of civil right. Should that happen, and should congregational sponsoring of scouting be disrupted, the church might well consider developing its own [coeducational] program of training to fill the void. Such a program need not (likely, should not) be closely patterned on existing scouting models, but could well copy the seriousness and duration assumed in the lives of those who take part in scouting programs. Programs of Christian education during the teenage years often have been embarrassingly undisciplined and undemanding by comparison.

4
Coming of Age

Hugh W. Sanborn

THE FINAL STAGE OF THE CHRISTIAN RITE OF INITIATION

Introduction

After attending a bar mitzvah service a number of years ago, I pondered the possibility of developing a "coming of age celebration" for my daughter and son, a worship service and festive dinner party that would celebrate their passage to young adulthood. That bar mitzvah service, which included communication between family members, passing on of tradition, affirmation of the maturing young person, the reading and interpretation of scripture by the initiate, and the giving of gifts, was quite impressive. Something seemed amiss, however. Was the initiate actually developmentally ready to be proclaimed a young adult?

The bar mitzvah service is centuries old, practiced by Jews since at least the thirteenth century.[1] During earlier centuries of bar mitzvah practice, the initiate was indeed expected, if not always prepared, at age thirteen or soon thereafter, to assume the responsibilities of a young adult, including apprenticeship and marriage. The same was true, of course, for the initiate's Christian counterpart.

In the twentieth century, the age for assuming the responsibilities of young adulthood has changed considerably due to prolonged years of pre-college education, dependence on parents and single status. Given these realities, I have become convinced that to be efficacious as a liturgical celebration of passage, the Christian rite of initiation to adulthood must be timed to correspond to the appropriate developmental period marked by concomitant events and decisions. In our present era, that time arrives at the average age of eighteen or at the time of high school graduation.

The purpose of this chapter is to present the case for a three-stage process approach to Christian initiation, consisting of baptism, confirmation and coming of age, with emphasis on development of the latter as the completion stage of the rite of Christian initiation.

Roberts' Contribution

In his insightful book, *Initiation to Adulthood: An Ancient Rite of Passage in Contemporary Form*,[2] William O. Roberts, Jr. presents a cogent and convincing

51

case for restoring the lost rite of Christian initiation to adulthood. Referring to the findings of anthropologists and historians of religion, Roberts presents the significant features of initiation rites, emphasizing the importance of the basic separation-transition-incorporation pattern followed by all rites of initiation. He then identifies scriptural models of initiation and explores the form of the initiation rite in the early Christian community. Baptism, faith education, confirmation and first communion are identified as the primary components of the early Christian initiation rite. Roberts deplores the fact that the unity and significance of the Christian rite of initiation were lost through subsequent centuries as the components were separated, reinterpreted and/or assigned different functions. His book concludes with a description of the exceptional confirmation program he and his congregation have developed in an effort to reinstate the lost rite of initiation.

While Roberts' study is not without problems, Roberts has, in my view, made a major contribution to the Christian community in recognizing the importance of, and forcefully arguing the case for, restoration of the Christian rite of initiation. I view the position presented here as a modification and extension of Roberts' main thesis.

The Problem

To expect adolescents or youth, at the conclusion of confirmation (whether or not the preparatory program for confirmation conforms to a rite of initiation passage), to view themselves and function as young adults, disturbs my developmental sensitivities. The fact is that the confirmands are, as adolescents, in the transitional stage of development between childhood and young adulthood. Parents, church families, schools, and, until recently, courts and most of the laws of our country have viewed adolescents as youth most of whom are not yet ready, as psychologists attest, to assume the responsibilities of young adulthood. Thus, to identify this important rite of passage so completely with confirmation, as Roberts does explicitly and most traditional forms of confirmation do implicitly, appears to me to be unrealistic and abortive and to establish false expectations. Following confirmation, adolescents continue to function as youth and to wrestle with their ambivalent feelings (i.e., feeling at times like children and at times like adults), parents continue to relate to their offspring as youth, churches continue to encourage the newly confirmed to participate in youth groups rather than singles groups, and our society (if not all our laws) continues to view adolescents as minors.

It is a curious fact that Roberts conveys considerable understanding of the transitional developmental processes and ambivalent dynamics of the adolescent stage, on the one hand, and yet assigns the rite of passage to young adulthood to age fifteen and sixteen, on the other hand. As he states quite clearly: "Only if one remains true to the task of one's age will one eventually pass out of it."[3] In agreement with Roberts on this point, I take the position that fifteen- and sixteen-year-olds in our culture are adolescents or youth who are in the transitional stage between childhood and young adulthood, developmentally ready to make some initial commitment to church membership, but not yet ready to assume the responsibilities of young adulthood.

Several factors led Roberts to identify the rite of passage to young adulthood with confirmation and place it at age fifteen and sixteen: his desire to counter the dissolution of the rite over the centuries through separation of its various components, his church's tradition, the demanding schedules of older teenagers, and the needs of youth and their parents.[4] The latter three factors indicate the practical reasons for inviting eighth and ninth graders to participate in confirmation. Solid and sound as these reasons are for supporting confirmation for this age bracket, they do not support completing the rite of initiation at this stage. Since it is the first factor that provides such support in Roberts' view, attention must be given to this significant point.

While it is true, as Roberts points out, that components of the rite of initiation were separated by the church over the centuries, it would appear that the present problem is less their separation than their loss of identity as components of a cohesive process. (Though Roberts contends that incorporating that component known as baptism into the initiation rite at age fifteen and sixteen should be the norm, he himself stops short of suggesting that the church cease practicing infant baptism in order to be consistent with this norm.)[5] Their separation, so bemoaned by Roberts, may in fact be a positive development in light of modern understanding of the developmental process. It is my position that infant baptism, confirmation and coming of age are most adequately viewed as liturgically marking three separate developmental passages in the process correctly described as the Christian rite of initiation. Once this is recognized as a cohesive process, I am convinced, the problems Roberts has with the age issue and infant baptism may be satisfactorily resolved. After all, faith development, the maturation process in the faith which is integrally related to the total maturation process, is the primary concern. If Roberts is correct in arguing that confirmation is an important component of the rite of initiation, and I believe he is, it is far more realistic to shape confirmation to accomplish a specific faith development task appropriate to that age group and to see it as one passage in a larger process, than to convert it into a comprehensive initiation rite.

I am arguing that the problem with both traditional forms of confirmation and Roberts' innovative program of confirmation[6] is the unrealistic, premature completion of the rite of initiation. Instead of being confirmed as members[7] of the church who are moving toward the rite of initiation to young adulthood and the responsibilities that entails, the newly confirmed are abortively proclaimed to be young adults already. But as any adolescent will confirm—no pun intended—neither do their elders (parents, high school teachers, church youth leaders, etc.) treat them as young adults, nor do they consistently view themselves as, or feel comfortable when cast in the role of, young adults. Realistically, adolescents understand themselves to be and are viewed as youth on the way to becoming young adults. They should not be robbed of the opportunity to complete their rites of passage in the fullness of time.

The Solution

In our culture, as noted above, the appropriate time to celebrate the end of the transition stage of adolescence and the beginning of young adulthood is the time of graduation from high school at about age eighteen. High school graduation clearly marks the end of the chapter of adolescence or youthhood. For most graduates, the questions common to young adulthood loom large before them. It is not surprising that many graduates take a trip with or without parents—when it is with parents, it is often viewed as the final family vacation—as a brief interlude between the end of the old stage and the beginning of the new stage, with all the problems and responsibilities the new stage entails. For the new stage is as threatening as it is exciting, requiring leaps into unexplored territory and promising new freedoms that can be claimed and enjoyed only as difficult decisions are enacted. Moving away from home to enter full-time employment or attend college, becoming acclimated to a new community, choosing the academic and/or social groups to associate with, deciding whether to attend and become involved in a new church, are but a few of the challenges facing young adults as they move away from the security of the familiar.

The fullness of time, then, is marked by high school graduation, the secular event that signals the coming of age or that the passage to young adulthood has begun in earnest. It is at this exciting, joyous and yet stressful time in the life of individuals and their families that the final event in the rite of initiation should be celebrated by the church. The service should focus on the individual initiate: (1) his/her separation from family and, when appropriate, from the local church family; (2) his/her growth, struggles, developing identity, and readiness to assume the responsibilities of young adulthood; and (3) his/her incorporation into service of the larger society and Christian church, emphasizing the contributions the individual has to make as a young adult in communicating his/her developing faith through worship and the promotion of Christian values and community-building. The service as a whole should communicate confidence in and joyous affirmation of this particularized coming of age process.

Three Stages of the Christian Rite of Initiation

The coming of age passage is to be understood as the third and final stage in the three-stage process of the Christian rite of initiation: baptism, confirmation and coming of age—see the chart on the following page. Note that each passage follows the separation-transition-incorporation pattern of all initiation rites. The passage of baptism, at the average age of one year, denotes separation from the mother, the transition to life and nurture in the world, and the resulting incorporation into family and potentially into the extended family of the church. At the average age of fourteen, the passage of confirmation represents separation from childhood, the transition to adolescence or youth, and incorporation into the church family and potentially into the wider church and society. The coming of age passage, at the average age of eighteen, marks separation from adolescence and family and possibly from the local church family, transition to young adulthood, and incorporation into the larger church community and society.

Three Stages of the Christian Rite of Initiation

LITURGICAL CELEBRATION	SEPARATION	TRANSITION	INCORPORATION	SYMBOLIC
STAGE I **Baptism** (Age: between 0–2 yrs.; aver. age 1 yr.)	mother	life and nurture in the created order	family, and potentially into church family	primary separations
STAGE II **Confirmation** (Age 13–15 yrs; aver. age 14 yrs.)	childhood	adolescence	church family, and potentially into wider church and society	essential transitions
STAGE III **Coming of Age** (Age 17–19 yrs.; aver. age 18 yrs.)	adolescence, family, and often local church family	young adulthood	larger church community and society	major incorporations

Note also that each of the three passages, due to the primary characteristics of each, may be viewed as symbolic of one component of the separation-transition-incorporation pattern: baptism, celebrating the potentiality of the separated newborn, symbolizes life's primary separations; confirmation, celebrating the potentiality within the changes taking place during adolescence, symbolizes life's essential transitions; the coming of age, celebrating the potentiality for full adulthood, symbolizes life's major incorporations. Coming of age completes the initiation rite precisely because, at the age when most individuals are prepared to make this passage, it deals intentionally and decisively with the developmental task of moving toward the widest forms of incorporation required of Christian adults. That task requires that one become not only independent, but also interdependent or incorporated successfully into the larger communities of church and the world. Thus, in the liturgical celebration of the coming of age passage, the individual is affirmed and blessed as one who, having entered the coming of age process, is preparing to assume the responsibilities of young adulthood in society as well as the church.

The coming of age passage also marks the fulfillment of the promise of infant baptism. It is in this sense that I concur with Roberts in viewing baptism as an important part of the completion of the Christian initiation rite. The suggestion resulting from the United Church of Christ and Disciples of Christ union dialogue pertaining to baptism provides a helpful approach which is consistent with the process understanding of the Christian rite of initiation presented here. That dialogue proposed viewing baptism as a process beginning with what has been traditionally known as infant baptism and concluding with what has been traditionally labeled adult or believer's baptism.[8] Such an approach is not to be construed as two baptisms or baptizing and rebaptizing. Rather, it recognizes that Christian initiation is a process that takes place over years and is completed only when the initiate proclaims his/her faith and becomes a member of the body of Christ. It thus follows that, in fulfillment of the initial phase of baptism, the second and final phase of one's baptism in Christ takes place at the coming of age service.[9]

Finally, the coming of age passage demarcating the final stage of the Christian rite of initiation raises a significant issue, namely, at what stage does one become a member of the church, at confirmation or the coming of age celebration? While it is my view that joining the church would be more appropriate at the coming of age passage, given the well-established tradition of membership decision making following confirmation, any attempt to change this basic process would no doubt meet with considerable resistance. There are other options, however, which would remain consistent with traditional practice as well as with our best understanding of the stages of human development.

One option would be to distinguish between some form of preliminary membership and full membership, the former to be granted at confirmation, and the latter to be granted at the coming of age celebration.[10] Realistically, as I have argued, youth are not prepared to assume the responsibilities of full membership at the close of the confirmation stage. However, adolescents are prepared to make an initial commitment to church membership at that time and to assume responsibilities commensurate with youth. Making such a membership differentiation both affirms the confirmation process and contributions adolescents as youth can and do make to the life of a congregation, and emphasizes the importance of moving toward assuming the responsibilities of full membership. Even, and perhaps especially, when young adults leave their home churches soon after full membership is granted, the timing and significance of this event could make a major difference in the way the church community is perceived by these initiates.

Perhaps a less radical and more generally acceptable option would be a modification of what is meant by formal membership in the church. Though Christian churches have always considered all baptized persons of whatever age to be informal members of the body of Christ prior to declaration of formal membership, the latter has been understood as *adult* membership. If formal membership were to be modified to include youth who have completed confirmation as well as adults, no change in practice would be required. The only change entailed would be broadening our understanding of what is the present predominant practice.

Summary

The primary purpose of this section has been to present the rationale for the church's inclusion of a liturgical celebration marking the important passage to young adulthood. I have proposed viewing baptism, confirmation, and coming of age as three stages of the Christian rite of initiation, baptism as a process consisting of two phases, and church membership as being modified in some way to make it consistent with modern developmental understanding. However, I feel that one's view of baptism and church membership is of far less consequence to the main thesis of this chapter than one's understanding of confirmation and coming of age passages. Only when coming of age is recognized as a passage, separate in time and function from confirmation, will the Christian rite of initiation be adequately completed and thus fully restored.

A SERVICE OF CELEBRATION

Introduction

In the preceding section, I attempted to clarify the rationale for approaching coming of age as the third stage in the process of the Christian rite of initiation, the first two stages of which are baptism and confirmation. Coming of age, which takes place in our culture at the time a youth graduates from high school or at the average age of eighteen, is marked by significant movement away from parent-youth and toward adult-adult modes of relating, acceptance of new responsibilities, and involvement in new social, vocational and/or academic communities. It is a time of joy and of stress, a time of leaping forward and of pulling back, and a time of new freedom and independence and of anxious testing of one's competency and adequacy as a young adult. It is clearly a major passage which the church needs to recognize, provide assistance with, and celebrate as an important point in the fulfillment of the promise of baptism and confirmation.

The purpose of the present section is more practical than theoretical. I attempt to: (1) present one approach to preparation of the individual and her/his family for this celebration of passage; and (2) offer a sample coming of age service that embodies liturgical communication and enactment of the Christian rite of initiation to adulthood.

Approaching Coming of Age

As noted above, the coming of age period in one's life, centered in the secular event of high school graduation, is a time of considerable excitement, expectation and stress. Emotions of family members are often frayed and tempers short as graduation approaches. Since the individual and her/his family may experience a range of moods from joy and elation to anxiety and grief, it is an opportune time for the individual and her/his family to participate in a series of sessions with the pastor in preparation for celebrating the coming of age passage.

Depending on the number of persons preparing for the final stage of Christian initiation, the pastor might meet with either a group of individuals or with each initiate separately. If the former approach is employed, it is still important that the initiates have the opportunity to share their anxieties, struggles, and concerns individually with their pastor as well as in the group situation. In either case, the sessions should provide opportunities for self-evaluation, examining the growth that has taken place in one's life since confirmation. This process should include: (1) evaluation of relationships, accomplishments, growth needs, goals, and plans; (2) clarification of values and faith development; (3) assessment of how one is experiencing the passage to Christian adulthood and movement toward independence; and (4) appraisal of one's commitment to the local church and to the wider church and society.

A number of resources and exercises can be used for these sessions, from books and films to creative art and physical and mental exercises. One could not begin to list all the useful materials available today to stimulate learning and growth experiences. Every Christian educator has her/his favorites. Suffice it to say that I would make use of books such as the helpful comprehensive study by Gerald Egan and Michael Cowan entitled *Moving into Adulthood: Themes and Variation in Self-Directed Development for Effective Living* (Belmont, Ca.: Wadsworth, 1980) along with the Bible and written materials on church membership and denominational and World Council of Churches' instrumentalities. I also recommend films such as *Parable, Everybody Rides the Carousel, Roots* or the television series *Peter and Paul;* creative expressions through art, such as finger painting one's independent self or conveying one's faith stance in a drawing or poem; and exercises such as the trust fall, conveyance of one's feelings for another through touch,[11] or a group fantasy about being adults. The important thing is to be selective of available materials in order to provide enough significant opportunities for the sharing of vital issues and self-learning to take place within a set number of sessions. The initiates themselves should participate in the shaping of these preparatory sessions.

During the period of time that the initiates are meeting with the pastor, it is also important that parents meet in their own group or separately with the pastor to share the anxieties, struggles and concerns they are experiencing. A group experience can be very reassuring to parents as they discover that stressful relationships are common to most families during this period.

The final phase of the preparatory period should consist of family sessions in which the initiate, siblings and parents meet together with the pastor to share their thoughts and feelings about the coming of age passage. This can usually be accomplished in one or two sessions, after which the initiate and her/his parents meet alone with the pastor to prepare the coming of age service.[12] Due to the nature of the content of the service, these final preparatory sessions are likely to elicit the expression of any feelings held back during earlier sessions. When this occurs, processing these feelings is essential to the completion of the preparatory process.

Coming of Age Celebration

The service given below is intended to be a sample liturgical embodiment of the coming of age passage. It has been shaped to include a statement of purpose, direct communication-enactment of passage by initiate and parents, moments of sharing by important others, selected scriptural passages, young adult's faith journey, litany of the faith tradition, commitment (or recommitment) to church membership, laying on of hands, and symbolic act of discipleship. Some initiates, families and their pastors will want to omit or add parts; others will want to start over, or at minimum modify much of the form and content. Some, for instance, will want to add communion, the Lord's Prayer, or a favorite poem or piece of music, while others will want to omit the footwashing ceremony, litany or gift giving. I encourage this process, hoping that each initiate, family and pastor will creatively shape the service to convey the meaning of the coming of age passage for that initiate, family and congregation.

Furthermore, the length of the coming of age service may vary considerably, depending on time, place and the desires of the initiate and her/his family. The service given below is intended to be a thirty- to forty-five minute celebration held, similar to a wedding, as a private afternoon or evening service in the sanctuary. If the celebration were to be incorporated into the Sunday morning service, it would probably be preferable to shorten the liturgy to ten or fifteen minutes. In any event, the initiate, family and pastor will want to consider these matters carefully in order to plan a celebration responsive to the needs of all involved, as well as appropriate to the setting.

The suggested order of service is as follows:

CALL TO WORSHIP (pastor)
Initiate walks with parents to front of sanctuary.

INVOCATION AND STATEMENT OF PURPOSE (pastor)

PREPARATION FOR PASSAGE (initiate, parents, and pastor):

Parents: Share memories of childhood and adolescence, recalling serious and humorous events, communications, moments, etc., and express feelings and concerns, concluding with expressions of love, affirmation and support. Statement might begin with words similar to the following: "We accompany you to this special place in the spirit of celebration, but also with a sense of sadness, to say goodbye to our teenage daughter/son."

Daughter/son: Responds, sharing her/his thoughts, feelings and concerns, concluding with a statement similar to the following: "The time has come for me to say goodbye to you as the parents I have needed throughout my childhood and adolescence. I know you will always be there for me, but no longer will I need what I once needed from you as parents." Embracing each: "Goodbye, Mom; goodbye, Dad."

Pastor: Addressing parents with words similar to the following: *(mother's name)* and *(father's name)*, you cannot travel the path that *(initiate's name)* must now travel. You have given your *daughter/son* of your very life and being, nurturing *her/him* in Christian values, relationships and faith to the best of your ability as you promised to do at the time of *her/his* baptism. *She/he* has become a young woman/man ready to follow a new path that will lead to full independence and responsibility for self as well as to contributions that will be unique to *her/his* developing identity and vocation. She/he must walk this path alone with *her/his* God, but as *she/he* has chosen to fulfill *her/his* baptism through full membership of (or with renewed commitment to) *(name of church)* and dedication to service of the wider church and human community, *she/he* will always have an extended family encouraging, affirming and supporting *her/him* throughout *her/his* life's journey. Say farewell to your *daughter's/son's* youth and continue to trust God to be with *(initiate's name)*, and *(initiate's name)* to be growing in her/his relationship with God."

Parents: Addressing *daughter/son* with words to the effect of: "Go, go with our love and with our blessing into the difficult yet exciting stage of young adulthood. When next we embrace, we embrace as adults."

Parents are seated: initiate takes seat next to or across from pastor.

SOLO   "You're Becoming"[13]
Written by singer Wendy Aldwyn especially for a coming of age celebration.

MOMENTS OF SHARING
Selected persons from extended family, congregation and community

SCRIPTURE READINGS (initiate)
At least one passage selected and read by initiate, perhaps with an interpretation

PASSING THE FAITH TRADITION THROUGH LITANY (initiate, parent and/or grandparent, and congregation)
Written by initiate, family, and pastor during joint preparatory sessions

STATEMENT OF FAITH JOURNEY (initiate)
Written by initiate during preparatory sessions

AFFIRMATION OF COMING OF AGE PASSAGE (pastor, parents, siblings and other relatives and/or selected persons)
Through membership or renewed commitment ceremony, laying on of hands, and pastoral blessing

HYMN AND SYMBOLIC ACT OF CHRISTIAN SERVICE (initiate and parents or other selected persons)
The hymn, one selected by the young adult, is sung by the congregation as the young adult washes the feet of parents or selected persons or performs some other act of discipleship.

PRESENTATION OF GIFT(S) (by parents or perhaps church and/or others)

NEW RELATIONSHIP EMBRACE (young adult and parents)
A symbolic enactment of the new adult-adult relating

CLOSING PRAYER (pastor)

BENEDICTION

Much like a wedding, the coming of age celebration, as I envision it, is followed by one final form of celebration. A reception, dinner, dance party, or similar festive event might be scheduled to take place after the coming of age service.

A passage has taken place completing the Christian rite of initiation process. All Christian churches—Protestant, Roman Catholic or Eastern Orthodox—could profit significantly from this or some other form of recognizing and celebrating coming of age.

[1]Cf. "Bar Mitzvah," *The Standard Jewish Encyclopedia*, ed. Cecil Roth (Garden City, N.Y.: Doubleday, 1959), 234, and "Bar Mitzvah," *The Universal Jewish Encyclopedia*, ed. Isaac Landman, 2(New York: *Universal Jewish Encyclopedia*, 1940), 73.

[2]New York: Pilgrim, 1982. See also William O. Roberts, Jr., "Christianity's Lost Rite: Initiation to Adulthood," *The Christian Ministry*, 14 (May 1983), 24–28.

[3]William O. Roberts, Jr., *Initiation to Adulthood: An Ancient Rite of Passage in Contemporary Form* (New York: Pilgrim, 1982), 104.

[4]Ibid., 78–82 and 112.

[5]Cf. ibid., 89–90 and 169.

[6]See ibid., 124–74. Much of the content of the confirmation program developed by Roberts and his congregation is of excellent quality and could be easily modified, with a few significant alterations, to meet the requirements of the three-stage approach discussed herein.

[7]The underlying assumption, whether verbalized or not, is that membership means *adult* membership. This issue will be raised again at the close of this chapter.

[8]See "Baptism and the Lord's Supper," *Study Series on the Covenant*, prepared by the United Church of Christ–Christian Church (Disciples of Christ) Steering Committee, 1981, 2.

[9]How this final phase of the process of baptism is to be practiced is not the concern of this chapter. Suffice it to suggest that one might expect a wide variety of styles of practice developing, from verbal affirmation of baptism's fulfillment to full immersion.

[10]Again, the way these forms of membership are differentiated in practice is not the concern of this chapter. Some churches might assign some specific service to preliminary or youth members, while others might withhold voting rights or restrict eligibility for nomination or appointment to church leadership positions.

[11]In the touch exercise, a volunteer stands in front of the group with eyes closed. Other members of the group, individually or together, may then go up to the person and convey their feelings through some form of touching. The leader decides when the time is up, and then another volunteer stands before the group.

[12]Siblings who are assigned a special role in the service would, of course, be included in these sessions.

[13]Due to space, "You're Becoming" has not been included in this chapter. If you desire to see a copy of this song, please write and request it.

5
Believer's Baptism

O. I. Cricket Harrison

INITIATION INTO NEW AWARENESS

In the document *Baptism, Eucharist and Ministry*, baptism has been affirmed as one of the common treasures of the churches, regardless of the form through which it is administered. Each of the differing forms of baptism offers its own richness of symbolism and meaning. Infant baptism beautifully depicts the saving grace of God, freely offered to human beings. Believer's baptism is also a gift to the church from and through God's saving grace, but perhaps more graphically indicates a point of new beginning, of regeneration, of cleansing. In believer's baptism, the motif of cleansing can be seen perhaps more clearly, for the candidate coming for baptism receives from Christ through the church "a bath of purification from the guilt of sin, witnessing to repentance and looking forward to the coming reign of God and administered now in the name of Jesus."[1] Believer's baptism may, because of the age of the candidate, more fully embody the separation of one being baptized from the old life and one's movement into the new life of community. In this baptism becomes, both to the candidate and the community, "a sign of repentance and the purification from sin."[2]

In the second chapter of Acts, Peter is reported to have preached to all the crowd gathered on the day of Pentecost, ending with these words: "Therefore let the entire house of Israel know with certainty that God has made him both Lord and Messiah, this Jesus whom you crucified" (Acts 2:36). Hearing this, the crowd was "cut to the heart and said… 'what should we do?'" (Acts 2:37). Peter's response was straightforward and immediate: "Repent, and be baptized every one of you in the name of Jesus Christ so that your sins may be forgiven; and you will receive the gift of the Holy Spirit. For the promise is for you, for your children, and for all who are far away, everyone whom the Lord our God calls" (Acts 2:38–39). Peter realized that God's call is to all people. A believer is to respond first by confessing Jesus as Christ—and then by being baptized. Hence the baptism of older children, adolescents and adults illustrates an important baptismal theme—that of "the individual's response to the call of God."[3] More clearly stated, baptism is God's action through the church in response to the person's confession, or the confession made by those answering on behalf of an infant. Although candidates truly decide to present themselves for baptism, the church must remember always to embody in its teaching and liturgical practices that it is God who, in and through the saving works of Christ, is the active agent in baptism:

Repentance must now mean a turning to *Christ*, and the forgiveness of sins reveals that *Christ* has now the authority to do this; for God *through Christ* has given [humankind] the promised salvation, has created the new eschatological community of salvation and bestowed on it [the] Holy Spirit...From the human viewpoint baptism is the individual, spiritual and corporeal visible expression of repentance and trust, of self-giving and confession of faith; the individual visibly demonstrates and testifies to his [or her] faith in the presence of the community before entering the community. From the divine standpoint baptism is the visible sign of grace, directed towards this one individual person, and the guarantee and presentation of God's justifying grace proclaimed and given to the believer.[4]

In this sense, baptism of adolescents and adults signifies for the entire worshiping community the ongoing dialectic of faith, the continuing conversation between God and humankind. In the act of believer's baptism, God reaches out *through the church* and offers the gift of new life in Jesus Christ to those individuals who have come to faith.

More than a sign of a new beginning for an individual, then, believer's baptism is (although it is not always adequately interpreted as such) a rite of initiation into a community of the new creation. Baptism is never solely a decision or action of the individual alone. We do not choose to be baptized as much as we submit to baptism as a sign of God's grace in having chosen us. Believer's baptism, or the confirmation of one's baptism, is one of the most visibly powerful ways we live out God's claim upon us. Baptism reaches beyond us, not only setting us in the midst of a faith community, but also causing us to become an enacted witness to Christ before our children and others with whom we come in contact. The individual believer is not alone in her or his decision of faith for

...the essential part of the Christian message is the idea of salvation for the whole community of people, of which the individual is a member. Closely linked to the idea of the Christian's message is the outward sign, which is at once a sign of grace and vocation for the individual and...of reception into the community of the people of God: baptism (cf. Ephesians 4:1–5).[5]

By bringing a person into full relationship with the community of faith, believer's baptism can be an identifying moment as one becomes newly aware of one's new identity before God. Indeed, believer's baptism can be seen as an initiation into the "eschatological community of salvation."[6]

To better understand the nature of this eschatological community, one needs to consider the concept of *covenant*. Ronald E. Osborn describes God's covenantal work with the church as fourfold:

This company to which we belong is a covenant-community. God brings it into being as, together with God and with one another, we voluntarily assume a sacred bond.

First, God binds the divine Reality to us, as members and as church, to God—to God's love, God's will, God's mission, God's power. Second, God binds us to one another in sacred community, and in fidelity we seal the bond. Being a disciple is not a private vocation. It is a calling within community. Most of us find that community in a congregation.

Then God binds us to the whole body of Christians, and we make ourselves one with all of them. This relationship comes to expression in community and country-wide gatherings, both denominational and ecumenical. Various regional, national and international bodies enable Christians to demonstrate the unity in the common covenant.

Finally, in making covenant with us, God binds us to all humanity, indeed to the entire world. Jesus lived and died for every human being and for the entire cosmos. The risen Christ is Lord of all. In making covenant we commit ourselves to living out the meaning of his lordship everywhere. When we speak of church, we speak of covenant-community.[7]

If baptism is, as Osborn asserts, an act of covenant-making or covenant-sealing, then the process *of preparation for baptism* becomes at once more urgent and more complex. The community of faith must be prepared to teach each candidate the meaning of covenant, what we understand and believe to be the nature of God, the community's self understanding of being a people called together by God in the name of Jesus, the nature and mission of the church as the body of Christ, and the Christian's calling to stewardship on behalf of humanity, the world, and the entire cosmos.

These meanings cannot be taught in a discrete period of time. One cannot take in all there is to know about the meaning of baptism in a four- or six-week class with the pastor. Indeed, just as infant baptism is completed through confirmation, believer's baptism is also a learning process that is centered in the daily life of the faith community as much as in special preparatory classes. One comes to know the meanings of baptism as one begins to live out one's new awareness of being a child of God within a transformational community of faith. In other words, we come into a new faith identity even as we identify ourselves with a covenant-community. One of the many dialectics of faith is that we come to know ourselves best as individuals before God as we recognize ourselves as members of faith community.

Marjorie Suchocki sees baptism as an entrance point not only into the faith community but into a realm of sacred time, a realm in which God's saving act in Jesus Christ is not only past but yet to come, and offered not only to individuals but to communities: "Baptism, as the sacrament of entrance, is not only apostolic proclamation in continuity with the past, nor is it only the openness to Christ and reception of Christ mediated to us through the future. Baptism is also the acceptance by the many of the baptized one in the community of the present."[8] It is in the present that one responds to the claim and call of God; it is in the present that the baptized person is *incorporated* into the faith community.

Charles Foster sees the faith community as a complex, living reality, even as he recognizes the symbolic nature of the name "faith community." For Foster, faith community is a "symbolic description of *the gathered responses of people to the initiative of God, in which both our corporate identity as the body of Christ and our personal identities as his followers are revealed.*"[9] Foster cautions those who nurture Christians in their growth in faith not to assume that others' faith journey is dependent on the teacher/guides. Foster is clear that God is the initiator of community. God calls persons into community; individuals do not somehow band together to look for God. This view of God as the one who calls us into relationship is especially important in the context of believer's baptism, where it is easy and tempting to claim the primary action as the human's decision to enter into communion with God, rather than seeing baptism as the embodiment of the human's response to a claim and call and care that has always been present but never fully acknowledged.

Just as important for Foster is the understanding that community is not only "vertical" (God relating to persons) but also "horizontal" in dimension as Christians are "caught up in their common allegiance to Christ as the head of the church, in the awareness that, where two or three are gathered, the binding presence of God in Christ is also present."[10] This person-to-person connection within one's new faith identity is admittedly complex in nature, for it consists not only of all the relationships one has to a group in the present, but also all the formative experiences the person has received up to the moment of baptism. Furthermore, the faith community brings all the formative experiences, the faith history if you will, of the community. For the Christian faith community, we draw much of our faith history from the stories of significant God-relationships recounted in the scriptures. But we also draw our individual and corporate identities from sources even more universal than the ancient stories of our faith. Foster borrows Carl Jung's notion of "archetypal participation" to describe the way in which a song or symbol or action can project "a common experience in our lives that actually transcends the immediacy of our own experience…participation is much more than mere involvement in an activity…It is a process that arises from the springs of the collective well of human history."[11]

Foster notes that our collective past emerges in surprising ways, as we struggle to make meaningful our daily existence. Images and feelings we have not personally experienced can "break through" our own patterns of thought and behavior, and cause us to reinterpret our present situation in new ways. Or these largely unconscious processes can "intrude" on present reality making it possible for us to see the familiar in new and ever-changing ways.[12] In other words, just as an individual continually reinvests the stories of her or his life with fresh meanings, so the church defines and redefines its rituals through the eyes of its growing faith memories. Baptism in the name of Jesus not only brings to mind Jesus' own baptism by John the Baptist; it also helps the gathered faithful recall Jesus himself. Just as Jesus' life has to be reinterpreted through his death and resurrection, so baptism becomes richer in meaning when seen through the eyes of Easter faith.[13]

Easter was a redefining moment for the faithful who first encountered the risen Christ. Their feeble hopes were vindicated and strengthened, their trust in the promises of God was sealed, but more than that, the qualities of their relationships were irrevocably altered and transformed. They were no longer people of doubt but of conviction; they were no longer hopeless, but found new hope in the life-giving power of love. They were called out of themselves into a new reality that they were now *witnesses* on Christ's behalf. This sense of sharing in a common experience and being called to a common action is described by Foster as an experience of Christian fellowship.[14]

Foster deepens this notion of fellowship by exploring Victor Turner's concept of *communitas*. Foster understands Turner to use this term in describing moments in human life when an event occurs in which the organizing structures of society break down and allow new relationships, new community, new trust to emerge, such as the rescue and cleanup efforts that began in Oklahoma City almost as soon as the explosives were detonated at the federal building in April 1995. *Communitas* pulls us ever out of our individual isolation into relationship with God and God's people: "It is a remembered event transmitted by story, ritual, and creed to subsequent generations. It is a social and cultural event, transforming lives and relationships, and often ecclesiastical structures and political processes…It is the creative Spirit of God present."[15]

John Westerhoff shares much of Foster's passion for the community of faith being a primary communicator of the faith. Specifically he sees baptism as a mark of faith. It is not a momentary occurrence, nor is it a repeatable event. Rather, baptism is best seen as an "entrance upon a lifelong journey…to actualize the implications of a new inheritance. Baptism not only starts us on the way of faith, but it signifies to the whole world that we are among the company of those who are signed, sealed, owned, claimed, and commissioned to do Christ's work in the world."[16]

The dialectic between one in unity with, and yet distinct from, the many emerges yet again. Believer's baptism is an entrance to a community of faith, but it cannot be collapsed into a mere rite of belonging. Baptism is not an initiation piece such as the wearing of a silly hat or pledge board in order to join a sorority or fraternity. Alexander Campbell, one of the founders of the Christian Church (Disciples of Christ), was adamant that baptism was not to be reduced to a ceremony required to join the church. If that had been the case, according to Campbell, the command to be baptized would read "repent and be baptized, every one of you, for admission into the church."[17] Baptism marks a person's inclusion in the church. Perhaps it is better to say that baptism of adults marks the person's *awareness* of inclusion in the body of Christ, for God has already included the person in the community of salvation, and it is that act of grace to which the person responds by submitting to baptism.

Baptism is an act of incorporation into the faith community, but it is also, in John Macquarrie's words, a "rite of vocation."[18] Macquarrie specifically refers to baptism as a rite of vocation into the "general ministry of the church."[19] But it is clear, viewing Macquarrie's discussion of baptism in full, that he sees it as an "unfolding."[20] That is to say, baptism is a rite that becomes understandable as we begin to live the implications of God's claim upon our lives. If baptism can be considered a process of discovery, as Macquarrie appears to believe, then it might not be too far a stretch to venture that baptism is a rite of vocation into self-discovery as well as ministry. That is, as a person is incorporated into the community of faith, he or she begins a conversation, already begun by God, as to what one is to do and to become as a person of faith. Hence, another facet of Christian vocation is that of searching out one's identity before God and expressing that identity in service and witness.

Baptism at any age, and in any form, marks the beginning of the search for Christian identity by naming us before God and the community. James E. Griffiss notes that naming someone or something is an act of power:

> To give a name to a person is to locate her within the history of a people, to express one's hopes and dreams for her, and to call upon God for her protection and care. To know another person's name can also mean to have power over him and to know something about his inner reality, spirit or soul. And for Christians, of course, the name which we are given in baptism is the name by which we are known to God.[21]

Griffiss notes that having a name before God allows us to enter conversation with God. Through baptism we become God's own children and can enter into an intimate relationship with God such as Jesus modeled in calling God "Abba."[22] Because we have entered into this process of intimacy, our confessions of faith become filled with meaning: "All that we have to say about God finds its meaning and justification in the relationship we have with the God whom, we believe, we can call by name and who, we believe, hears us."[23]

This dialectic of relationship and meaning extends to the symbols of our faith as well. As the community affirms and renews its common symbols, new meaning is invested in them. So the familiar practice of baptism can be filled with new, perhaps even startling insights for a community of faith as much as for the baptismal candidate. These multiple layers of meanings, while they may be distressing to those charged with preparing candidates for baptism because of their complex and ever-changing nature, actually invests the rite of baptism with power. Griffiss clearly sees this abundance of meanings as providing present depth and future richness to an ancient ritual of the church:

To speak of the water of baptism, for example, calls forth the whole history of our relationship to God as we know it in Jesus Christ. Perhaps because the Jewish people and early Christians lived in a sparse and arid land, the image of water figures largely in Scripture. But water is also fundamental to human life. We all need water in order to survive. As most scientists would now say, we human beings, and all other animals, came from the water. And indeed most people seek out the oceans or lakes for their annual holidays. There is something about water which both strengthens and comforts us.

But there is more to the water of baptism than merely a return to the primal elements. In the Old Testament there is the story of the flood with which God cleansed the earth. Early Christians, such as the writer of 1 and 2 Peter, used the image of the flood and the ark in order to signify the church as the ark of salvation. When the people of Israel were wandering in the desert, Moses struck a rock and water gushed forth. Jesus himself calmed a storm at sea and even, we are told, walked on the water to demonstrate his power over it. All those images, and there are many more, come together when we speak of the water of baptism. In baptism, we are not only washed of our sins but made new, brought into a new relationship with God, and incorporated into the church.[24]

Griffiss' understanding of past history becoming present reality is similar to Suchocki's insight that the believer receives the hope of a future in Christ through the receiving of the ancient gift of baptism. But even as we are named and known and brought into relationship with the family of faith through baptism, we discover that this God who has loved humanity from the world's beginnings and has revealed that love in the life, death, and resurrection of Jesus, is still the God who is hidden, unrevealed, and at least in part, unknowable: The sacramental elements "also carry with them the hiddenness of Christ, a real presence, that cannot be fully grasped or conveyed in words."[25]

It is the hidden God who through Christ is revealed. It is the hidden God who through the church is revealed in the gift of baptism. It is this same hidden God who calls the believers to witness to the world the love that has called them together and makes of them one people. It is this same hidden God who calls us to become living expressions of what it means to be people of faith. Everything we do, everything we say, is now to be seen and interpreted in light of our baptism. To respond in faith is a lifelong proposition. The faithful person is one who remembers the vows of her baptism and lives them out in celebration, confession and commitment. Geoffrey Wainwright understands the struggle toward Christian identity as being "achieved only dialectically, through self-surrender which becomes a reception of the self from the Other."[26]

Thus baptism takes us full circle—out of ourselves and our accustomed ways of looking at the world, into a world of mystery and wonder where God embraces us and names us and sets us in the midst of a community of transformation. Within that transformative community, we are cared for, comforted and challenged. Through our participation in the sacraments we receive the living mysteries of God; through our sharing both of Sacred Story and sacred stories we are woven into the very fabric of God's new creation. Indeed, the new awareness we receive as we are initiated into the life of faith through baptism, is the awareness of God alive in Christ, actively bringing all creation to wholeness and calling us ever to be *initiators*, story starters if you will. God witnesses our baptism, and in turn we become witnesses to the love of God calling people to new life as expressed in baptism.

"SHALL WE GATHER AT THE RIVER?": A CELEBRATION OF BELIEVER'S BAPTISM

Shall we gather at the river, where bright angel feet have trod, with its crystal tide forever flowing by the throne of God?[27]

Because baptism is filled with such a large variety of possible meanings, the process of preparation must include multiple introductions to the various meanings of this ancient rite of inclusion and incorporation. Baptismal preparation must address issues of personal faith identity (Who am I before God?), corporate faith identity (Who are *we* before God?) and sacred vocation (To what particular opportunities for witness and service is God calling me/us?). Within each of these questions is embedded a number of meanings and nuances for baptism. These disparate meanings cannot be taught in a discrete period of time. One cannot take in all there is to know about the meaning of baptism in a four or six week class with the pastor. Growing toward believer's baptism is an on-going learning process that is centered in the daily life of the members of the faith community as much as in special preparatory classes.

Because this preparatory process or catechesis is grounded in the community of faith, the community of faith should not only participate as helpers, supporters and teachers of the baptismal candidates, but as true disciples, learners, seekers of the faith. Since catechesis is "the [lifelong] process by which we make Christians,"[28] the members of the community of faith need to hear again and again Christ's command to "make disciples," for "the burden of baptismal work is upon the *Church*, the baptizers, not the one who is being baptized."[29] John Westerhoff and William Willimon are quick to assert that God is the primary actor in baptism: "The promises of salvation, conversion, growth, and life are *God's* promises administered through the *church*—not through the good intentions of the candidate."[30] Since the faith community is the body who administers baptism on God's behalf, it is the same body that gathers to witness the baptism of the believer. Part of the preparation for baptism, then, must involve the teaching of the meaning of baptism to the faith community. The community needs to be learning the stories of faith that both enrich and enhance the multi-faceted rite of baptism. Just as the early church required a lengthy preparation time before a convert was deemed prepared for baptism, so the living history of God's saving acts revealed in scripture must be presented and re-presented in light of the present situation in which the community of faith finds itself.

Ronald Osborn suggests that each foundational statement of faith has a corresponding symbolic value present in the rite of baptism:

> Our baptism recalls and imitates the baptism of Jesus in the Jordan River (Matthew 3:13–17). Following him in this manner, we covenant to be his disciples and join him in his desire "to fulfill all righteousness."
>
> Our baptism dramatizes our personal confession of the faith the church proclaims. It enacts the basic elements of the primitive Christian tradition "that Christ died for our sins...that he was buried, that he was raised on the third day" (1 Corinthians 15:3).
>
> Our baptism performs outwardly what happens inwardly in the new believer. The disciple voluntarily dies to an old life, to everything unChristlike and unloving within us apart from Christ, and rises to walk in Christ in "newness of life" (Romans 6:3–4; Colossians 3:5–17).
>
> Our baptism, by its action, suggests that in taking off our old garments to enter this bath we lay aside an old life. In the water we are cleansed of sin and guilt. As we put on a clean white robe, we put on Christ. (See 1 Corinthians 6:9–11; Galatians 3:27; Colossians 3:1–14).
>
> Our baptism is an act of initiation which incorporates us into the church, the body of Christ. The Holy Spirit comes to us within the community of the faithful, which the Spirit has created and sustains. Plunged into the life of the church, we make covenant with the great company of Christians in the whole world, and they with us. (See 1 Corinthians 12:12–13).
>
> Our baptism identifies us with all humanity. As Jesus was made one with all humankind and died on the cross to redeem them all, we also by being made one with him in baptism are made one with all those for whom he died. In baptism we commit ourselves to a life of love and self-giving like that of Jesus. (See 2 Corinthians 5:14–15).[31]

From scriptures such as these we can tease out the elements for a biblical theology of baptism. But William Willimon insists the early church held dear a number of stories including "Jesus walking upon the water, calling to the disciples who watched him from a boat; Moses striking the rock in the wilderness to bring forth water; Noah and his family in the ark and others."[32] These stories and the images they carry attach themselves to one's physical experience of baptism. In this manner, one's baptism takes on meaning that had not yet been discovered.

While thorough Bible study can indeed enhance one's appreciation and understanding of the rite of baptism, William Willimon and John Westerhoff propose a number of other areas of concern that are also elements of the catechetical process:

The normative nature of adult baptism, to which exceptions can be permitted only for the children of the faithful; the theological significance of baptism as the means by which persons are made Christians; the communal, public nature of baptism as a rite to be celebrated within a person's or family's worshiping community; the fact that baptism grants full and complete membership in the church along with the right to full participation including Holy Communion; the essential nature of lengthy and serious participation; the importance of sponsors...who are chosen by the congregation and prepared to provide pre- and post-baptismal catechesis and companionship in the journey of faith; the non-repeatable nature of baptism; and the need for the continual renewal of our baptismal covenant and lifelong catechesis will each need to be addressed.[33]

Baptismal catechesis, then, used as its primary content the nature of God, the nature of the church as the people of God and the body of Christ, the nature of baptism itself—both as enacted sacred story and as historical practice of the church—and finally the nature of human beings as responsible (response-able) creatures created, cared for, chosen, called, claimed, and named by God in Christ.

Such a preparatory curriculum for baptism is understandably lengthy and admittedly complex. This is to be expected considering that baptism is an ancient rite—most likely pre-dating both Judaism and Christianity—that is multivalent in its symbolism. To use a familiar phrase from Paul Ricoeur, baptism carries with it a "surplus of meaning." There is always more meaning yet to unfold for the candidate and the faith community.

Westerhoff and Willimon suggest that preparing candidates for baptism is a ministry properly entrusted to a group of spiritual leaders within the congregation:

> A group of faithful adults must be chosen and educated as catechists [to] prepare persons for baptism. These adults need a sound historical and theological understanding of baptism and an understanding of the rite of baptism; a strong foundation in Bible, church history, theology and ethics; a maturity of faith and life; a personal spiritual discipline; and the ability to offer spiritual direction and counsel. A parish program to equip persons for this significant lay ministry is the first step in any relevant program.[34]

These communities of spiritual leaders become teachers and mentors to those presenting themselves for baptism. Westerhoff and Willimon see a person's movement toward baptism in three stages.

The first stage is *inquiry*, a questioning time that helps to clarify the depth of a person's desire for baptism.[35] The catechist here acts much like a gatekeeper at the gates to a feudal town, making sure that each person entering truly has business being there. In Westerhoff's and Willimon's model of catechetical process, the second state is specifically named *preparation*.[36] Each inquirer is assigned a sponsor and admitted into the faith community as a *catechumen*:

> ...expected to attend worship regularly, to acquire a knowledge of salvation history as revealed in the holy scriptures of the Old and New Testaments, to grow in the spiritual life of prayer and devotion, and to practice a life of Christian service and social action in accordance with the Gospel.[37]

The third stage is *candidacy*, a final period of intense discipline and examination in which candidate and sponsor alike undertake the disciplines of prayer, fasting and personal reflection in order to assure the candidate's spiritual and emotional readiness for baptism.[38] Once the candidate is ready to make a commitment of faith, his or her sponsor becomes a companion throughout the entire ritual process itself.

A Service of Christian Baptism

Persons become disciples of Christ as they are moved by God's spirit
>to turn away from sin and evil,
>to make a profession of faith,
>to receive God's renewing grace through baptism,
>and thereby to become one with the whole people of God.

Although these steps may be separated in time, they are one action. This unity is most fully expressed when they follow one another in the same service of worship. However, in keeping with many local traditions, the first two actions may take place at one service and the latter two in another.

Normatively, baptism takes place within a congregation's regular Sunday worship service following a sermon relating to the baptismal theme. Baptism is followed by sharing in the Lord's supper with the new members. Baptisms may also be conducted as a part of an Easter vigil or in a separate service. The material which follows may be adapted to these various circumstances.

Since baptism receives persons into the universal church, the service is designed to be sensitive to the larger church's understanding of how baptism is properly administered. The ecumenical convergence statement on baptism found in *Baptism, Eucharist and Ministry* states: "Within any comprehensive order of baptism at least the following elements should find a place:

> the proclamation of the scriptures referring to baptism;
> an invocation of the Holy Spirit;
> a renunciation of evil;
> a profession of faith in Christ and the Holy Trinity;
> the use of water;
> a declaration that the persons baptized have acquired a new identity as sons and daughters of God;
> and, as members of the church, called to be witnesses of the Gospel."
> [Baptism 4.1]

The church has always baptized persons in the name of the Father and the Son and the Holy Spirit. Thus, it is appropriate to ask the candidates to affirm these words of baptism. Although God transcends all names and forms, the use of the word Father for God is normative in all churches to this date. Alternative wording is provided for making this affirmation.[39]

BAPTISMAL COLLECT
Restless Spirit,
you brooded over the waters of chaos
    and with a word caused light and life to be.
In a flutter of dove's wings,
    you claimed Jesus as your own
    as he rose from his baptism at the hands of John.
Through wind and flame,
    you sealed the gathered community as a Pentecost people
    entrusted with the ministries of witness and service in the name of Christ.
Come to us now, we pray.
Help us to be sensitive to even your lightest whispers
    and make us strong through the power of your lifegiving word. Amen.

RENUNCIATION OF EVIL AND CONFESSION OF FAITH
  The Renunciation of Evil and Confession of Faith may take place either as persons come forward at the Invitation, or in the baptistery prior to the act of baptism.

Name(s) come/comes before God and this congregation today to confess Jesus Christ as Lord and Savior.
Name, I now ask you:
Do you renounce evil, repent of your sins, and turn to Christ?
I do.
Do you confess that Jesus is the Christ, the son of the living God,
and do you accept and proclaim him to be Lord and Savior of the world?
I do.
Looking to your baptism
in the name of the Father, Son and Holy Spirit,
do you, in the company of all Christians,
believe and trust in God the Father, who made the world;
and in his Son, Jesus Christ, who redeemed humankind;
and in the Holy Spirit, who gives life to the people of God?
I do so believe and trust.

Or:

Recalling that Jesus told us, "Go, therefore and make disciples of all nations, baptizing them in the name of the Father and of the Son and of the Holy Spirit," I ask you: Do you believe in God the Source, the fountain of life; and in Christ, the offspring of God, embodied in Jesus of Nazareth and in the church; and in the liberating Spirit of God, the wellspring of new life?[40]
I believe.

Look with joy to your baptism.

SCRIPTURE SENTENCES

Hear these words from holy scripture:

Each sponsor may read one of these or other appropriate scripture passages, espe-cially a scripture that has particular importance for the candidate.

In those days John the Baptist appeared in the wilderness of Judea, pro-claiming, "Repent, for the kingdom of heaven has come near." Then Jesus came from Galilee to John at the Jordan, to be baptized by him. John would have prevented him, saying, "I need to be baptized by you, and do you come to me?" But Jesus answered him, "Let it be so now; for it is proper for us in this way to fulfill all righteousness." Then he consented. And when Jesus had been baptized, just as he came up from the water, suddenly the heavens were opened to him and he saw the Spirit of God descending like a dove and alighting on him. And a voice from heaven said, "This is my Son, the Beloved, with whom I am well pleased." (Matthew 3:1–2; 13–17)

Now the eleven disciples went to Galilee, to the mountain to which Jesus had directed them. When they saw him, they worshiped him; but some doubted. And Jesus came and said to them, "All authority in heaven and on earth has been given to me. Go therefore and make disciples of all nations, baptizing them in the name of the Father and of the Son and of the Holy Spirit, and teaching them to obey everything that I have commanded you. And re-member, I am with you always, to the end of the age." (Matthew 28:16–20)

Peter said to them, "Repent, and be baptized every one of you in the name of Jesus Christ so that your sins may be forgiven; and you will receive the gift of the Holy Spirit. For the promise is for you, for your children, and for all who are far away, everyone whom the lord our God calls to him." And he testified with many other arguments and exhorted them saying, "Save yourselves from this corrupt generation." So those who welcomed his message were baptized, and that day about three thousand persons were added. They devoted them-selves to the apostles' teaching and fellowship, to the breaking of bread and the prayers. (Acts 2:38–42)

Do you not know that all of us who have been baptized into Christ Jesus were baptized into his death? Therefore we have been buried with him by baptism into death, so that, just as Christ was raised from the dead by the glory of the Father, so we too might walk in newness of life. For if we have been united with him in a death like his, we will certainly be united with him in the resurrection like his. (Romans 6:3–5)

If you confess with your lips that Jesus is Lord and believe in your heart that God raised him from the dead, you will be saved. For one believes with the heart and so is justified, and one confesses with the mouth and so is saved. The scripture says, "No one who believes in him will be put to shame." (Romans 10:9–11)

In Christ Jesus you are all children of God through faith. As many of you as were baptized into Christ have clothed yourselves with Christ. There is no longer Jew or Greek, there is no longer slave or free, there is no longer male and female; for all of you are one in Christ Jesus. (Galatians 3:26–28)

STATEMENT OF PURPOSE

The statement may be read solely by the celebrant, or responsively by the celebrant and congregation.

From apostolic times persons have become disciples of Christ by confessing that Jesus is God's Messiah—the Lord and Savior of the world. In obedience to Christ's command and in likeness to Christ's example, they have been baptized. Today we joyously receive new disciples into Christ's one, holy, apostolic and universal church. Through baptism we are brought into union with Christ, with each other, and with the church of every time and place.

Through baptism we are buried with Christ, that we like him, may be raised from the dead to walk in newness of life.

Through baptism into Christ, God graces us with the gift of the Holy Spirit to forgive our sins, to cleanse us from all wrongs, to clothe us with God's own righteousness, and to strengthen us all our days.

Through baptism into Christ we gain a new identity as sons and daughters of God, and receive a new life-purpose of Christlike ministry by word and deed.

Let us each remember and rejoice in our own baptism as we join in receiving these new disciples into Christ and Christ's church.

PRAYER

Gracious God, we thank you that in every age
you have made water a sign of your presence.
In the beginning your Spirit brooded over the waters
and they became the source of all creation.
You led your people Israel
through the waters of the Red Sea
to their new land of freedom and hope.
In the waters of the Jordan,
your Son was baptized by John
and anointed with your Spirit
for his ministry of reconciliation.
May this same Spirit
bless the water we use today,
that it may be a fountain
of deliverance and new creation.
Wash away the sins of those who enter it.
Embrace them in the arms of your church.

Pour out your Spirit on them
that they may be agents of reconciling love.
Make them one with Christ,
buried and raised in the power of his resurrection,
in whose name we pray. Amen.[41]

If the candidate has not already made a confession of faith, it may appropriately be done at this point, followed directly by the act of baptism. As each candidate enters the baptistery, her or his sponsor makes a brief statement, essentially pronouncing a blessing on the candidate. This statement may take the form of a reflection on the meaning of baptism or it may be a recounting of a significant moment, event or insight shared by sponsor and candidate during the catechetical process.

BAPTISM

The celebrant leads each candidate into the baptistery and lowers her or him into the water. This descent into the waters may be made either backward, forward or by use of a chair upon which to sit as water is poured over the head...

By the authority of Jesus Christ, I baptize you, *name,*
in the name of the Father and of the Son and of the Holy Spirit. Amen.

Or:

Name, by the authority of Jesus Christ, you are baptized
in the name of the Father and of the Son and of the Holy Spirit. Amen.

Immediately after the administration of the water, as hands are placed on the head of each person, the celebrant says to each:

The Holy Spirit be at work in you
to do far more than you dare ask or imagine,
keeping you in the knowledge of Christ's love,
too wonderful to be measured.

POST-BAPTISMAL PRAYER

We give you thanks, O Holy One,
mother and father of all the faithful,
for *this your child/these your children*
and for the grace acknowledged here today
in water and the Holy Spirit.

Embrace us all as daughters and sons
in the one household of your love.
Grant us grace to receive, nurture, and befriend
this new member/these new members
of the Body of Christ. Amen.

Give to the newly baptized:
strength for life's journey,
courage in time of suffering,
the joy of faith,

the freedom of love,
and the hope of new life;
through Jesus Christ who makes us one. Amen.

As the newly baptized dress, the congregation may celebrate the occasion in a number of ways:

1. A member of the congregation may read scripture passages designed to assist the worshipers to meditate upon and recall the significance of their own baptism. Readings may include: Jeremiah 31:31–34; Mark 1:14–20; Matthew 16:24–27; John 14:15–18; John 15:1–11; 1 Peter 2:4–10; Romans 8:11–17.

2. The congregation may sing hymns expressing its commitment to Christ.

3. The choir may sing an anthem of praise and devotion to Christ.

WELCOME

When all are dressed, the celebrant enters the chancel, moves behind the Lord's table, followed by the newly baptized and their sponsor/companions who gather facing the table in front. All carry small unlighted white candles. Taking a lighted candle, (either from the table, or using a paschal candle), the celebrant says such words as these:

Jesus said: "I am the light of the world. Whoever follows me will never walk in darkness but will have the light of life" (John 8:12). Receive this light. Shine as a light in the world to the glory of God.

The celebrant lights a first candle. The light is then shared with all those gathered. After all candles are lighted, each person places the lighted candle on the Lord's table in an act of consecration. Having the new members turn toward the congregation, the celebrant may lead the congregation in welcoming the new members, using these or similar words:

Name(s), God has blessed you with the Spirit
and received you by baptism into the one,
holy, catholic, and apostolic church.

With joy and thanksgiving,
we welcome you into Christ's church,
joined together with all those who in every place
call on the name of our Lord Jesus Christ.
Together let us encourage one another,
building up each other within Christ's body.
Together let us esteem one another in love,
praying without ceasing for every good grace
to grow into the full likeness of Christ.

Each person may be seated in a specially reserved section for receiving holy communion, or anywhere within the congregation. The service may proceed by sharing in the Lord's supper.

At the end of worship, the minister and the sponsors give a member(s) a sign of welcome (e.g. the kiss of peace or the right hand of fellowship). A Bible may be presented.

CONGREGATION:
In the name of Christ we welcome you.
May we grow together in unity,
and be built up onto the body of Christ in love,
to the glory of God, now and forever. Amen.

Post-Baptism Catechesis: The End of the Beginning

Westerhoff and Willimon assert that there is actually a fourth stage in baptismal catechesis. Once the process of inquiry, preparation and candidacy has been completed and a person is baptized, the lifelong process of living the faith begins. Hence the faith community must stand ready to support and nurture the newly baptized as they seek "to understand the meaning of the sacraments and to experience the fullness of corporate life in the church."[42] In short, the newly baptized need ample opportunity to "try on" their new faith identities in order to make sense of their vocation as followers of Jesus Christ.

A. Roger Gobbel echoes this concern that the learning/teaching process, indeed, the critical faith task of meaning-making, not end with the completion of the ritual of baptism. For Gobbel, it is essential to understand that God's work is full and complete in baptism, but as human creatures we must struggle all our lives to renew our sense of our baptisms and to re-integrate those new meanings into our faith identities:

> The claims and promises are God's claims and promises. They are declared to infants as well to adults. Whether we consider the Baptism of an infant or an adult, completeness and wholeness are marks of those claims and promises. Some things are settled with finality, completeness, and wholeness. To whom we belong and who we are are matters that have been determined. We belong to God, are claimed by God, and are children of God, inheritors of eternal life. Nothing need be or can be added to our Baptism. Nothing is yet to be done to complete our Baptism. God's work is complete.

> Between our Baptism and death, we are to live the baptismal life in faith. In the world, we are to be, to live, and to do who we already are—children of God. While Baptism is complete and whole, life in Baptism is always marked by surprises, the unexpected, and an amazing and exciting newness. Time and time again, we ask the question, What does it mean for me to be a baptized person? Responses to this question will result from active participation in the process of interpretation and the work of constructing understandings of ourselves as baptized persons.

> The responses we give to the question, while proper, right, and faithful for today, may not be proper, right, and faithful for tomorrow. We may be committed to our responses and regard them in some sense as absolute, but we dare not regard them as final, complete, or

unchangeable. In new seasons and situations we encounter new events and new demands, calling us anew to remember who we are, requiring us to ask the question again, and challenging us to achieve new understandings and responses never imagined or anticipated. We have the task of making new sense and constructing new understanding of ourselves as the people of God.[43]

Far from being unchanging and unchangeable, God is profoundly touched by the happenings of our lives. As we live out our faith vocations, God continually offers us the best choices that our previous choices will allow. Within the community of faith, we receive permission and encouragement to ask hard questions of God and of ourselves. In and through the rhythms of our shared faith life, members of the community come to know themselves more profoundly as God's own people, called, claimed and newly named through God's loving actions in Jesus Christ.

A Closing Meditation
Shall we gather at the river, where bright angel feet have trod,
    with its crystal tide forever flowing by the throne of God?

Yes, we'll gather at the river, the beautiful, the beautiful river;
    gather with the saints at the river that flows by the throne of God.

On the margin of the river, washing up its silvery spray,
    we will walk and worship ever, all the happy golden day.

Ere we reach the shining river, lay we every burden down;
    grace our spirits will deliver, and provide a robe and crown.

Soon we'll reach the shining river, soon our pilgrimage will cease;
    soon our happy hearts will quiver with the melody of peace.

Yes, we'll gather at the river, the beautiful, the beautiful river;
    gather with the saints at the river that flows by the throne of God.

Drawing imagery clearly from Revelation 22:1, Robert Lowry, the composer of this beloved camp meeting hymn, made a number of important statements that can be applied to baptism. First, the question is addressed to a community; the text clearly questions a relational "we," not an isolated "I." Baptism is a faith action which takes place within the context of a gathered people. Second, the consummation of the life of faith will be the people gathered in God's presence in continual praise and worship. Baptism sets us on a trajectory that leads always to that Constant Presence, that Holy Mystery we know through faith in Christ as God. Third, human burdens are set aside, God's free gift of grace is offered, and the crown and the robe of salvation are given to the faithful. Through baptism we receive the freedom, the lightness, the joy of new life in Christ. Furthermore, God delivers us from all that would bind us and clothes us anew in the garments of salvation. Finally, the life of faith is a pilgrimage that has, as both its origin and destination, the loving heart of God. Baptism sets us on a path, gives us a direction in which to travel, and confirms our hope that in Christ we have a home, we have a name, we have God's own peace to sustain us through all the vagaries of life. Baptism soaks us in the restless waters of new creation, and that restlessness stirs us ever to search for God until at last, in God's holy embrace, we find our rest, our hope, our joy.

> In water we dive, and cannot draw breath
> then surface alive, rebounding from death.
> Our old self goes under, in Christ dead and drowned.
> We rise, washed in wonder, by love clad and crowned.[44]

> Yes, we'll gather at the river, the beautiful, the beautiful river;
>   gather with the saints at the river that flows by the throne of God.

---

[1]Hans Küng, *The Church* (Garden City, N.Y.: Doubleday Image Books, 1976), 116.

[2]Ibid., 149.

[3]J. Cy Rowell, "Baptism," in Iris V. Cully and Kendig Brubaker Cully, ed., *Harper's Encyclopedia of Religious Education* (San Francisco: Harper & Row, 1990), 52.

[4]Küng, 270 and 272.

[5]Ibid., 172.

[6]Ibid., 116.

[7]Ronald E. Osborn, *The Faith We Affirm; Basic Beliefs of Disciples of Christ* (St. Louis, Mo.: Bethany Press, 1979), 56–57.

[8]Marjorie Hewitt Suchocki, *God, Christ, Church; A Practical Guide to Process Theology* (New York: Crossroad, 1984), 148.

[9]Charles R. Foster, *Teaching in the Community of Faith* (Nashville: Abingdon Press, 1982), 20–21.

[10]Ibid., 29.

[11]Ibid., 31.

[12]Ibid., 32–33.

[13]A fuller discussion of this important process of redefinition can be found in Hans Küng, *The Church*, 266–86.

[14]Foster, 34–37.

[15]Ibid., 44.

[16]John H. Westerhoff III, *Bringing Up Children in the Christian Faith* (Minneapolis: Winston Press, 1980), 5.

[17]Alexander Campbell, *Christian Baptism: With Its Antecedents and Consequents* (Bethany, Va.: printed and published by Alexander Campbell, 1853), 256, as quoted in Mark Toulouse, *Joined in Discipleship; the Maturing of an American Religious Movement* (St. Louis, Missouri: Chalice Press, 1994), 113.

[18]John Macquarrie, *Principles of Christian Theology*, 2d ed. (New York: Charles Scribner's Sons, 1977), 461.

[19]Ibid.

[20]Ibid.

[21]James E. Griffiss, *Naming the Mystery; How Our Words Shape Prayer and Belief* (Cambridge, Mass.: Cowley Publications, 1990), 23.

[22]Ibid., 34.

[23]Ibid., 66.

[24]Ibid., 125–26.

[25]Ibid., 172.

[26]Geoffrey Wainwright, *Doxology: The Praise of God in Worship, Doctrine and Life* (New York: Oxford University Press, 1980), 12.

[27]Words and music by Robert Lowry (1864). See *Chalice Hymnal*, #701.

[28]John H. Westerhoff III and William H. Willimon, *Liturgy and Learning Through the Life Cycle*, rev. ed. (Akron, Ohio: OSL Publications, 1994), 16.

[29]Ibid., 12.

[30]Ibid., 13.

[31]Ronald E. Osborn, *The Faith We Affirm; Basic Beliefs of Disciples of Christ* (St. Louis, Mo.: Bethany Press, 1979), 60.

[32]William H. Willimon, *Remember Who You Are: Baptism, A Model for Christian Life* (Nashville: The Upper Room, 1980), 18.

[33]Westerhoff and Willimon, 18.

[34]Ibid.

[35]Ibid., 19.

[36]Ibid., 20.

[37]Ibid.

[38]Ibid.

[39]This service has been adapted from the baptismal service developed by the editors, in Colbert S. Cartwright and O. I. Cricket Harrison, eds., *Chalice Worship* (St. Louis: Chalice Press, 1996), 26–32.

[40]This paragraph is by Ruth Duck.

[41]Keith Watkins, ed., *Baptism and Belonging* (St. Louis: Chalice Press, 1991), 44.

[42]Westerhoff and Willimon, 21.

[43]A. Roger Gobbel, "An Exercise in Interpreting," in *Education of Christian Living*, ed. Marvin Roloff (Minneapolis: Augsburg, 1987), 148–49.

[44]"In Water We Grow" by Brian Wren (1989). See *Chalice Hymnal* #375.

6
Marriage

Paul F. Feiler

APPROACHING AN AUTHENTICALLY CHRISTIAN MARRIAGE

Introduction

In Thornton Wilder's play *The Skin of Our Teeth*, Mrs. Antrobus says to her husband, "I didn't marry you because you were perfect; I married you because you gave me a promise. That promise made up for your faults and the promise I gave you made up for mine. Two imperfect people got married, and it was the promise that made the marriage."[1]

An authentically Christian marriage is not a perfect marriage. From a Christian perspective authenticity involves commitment, honesty and forgiveness between an imperfect man and imperfect woman, between two people who sometimes make mistakes, who sometimes get angry, feel distant and fall out of love. For this reason, Christian marriage is grounded in the idea of resurrection—resurrection not in the sense of resuscitation, not in the sense that we go back to an earlier time when things were more attentive and passionate, but resurrection in the sense of transformation, in the sense that time holds the possibility that our relationships, even when wounded and dying, can be transformed, re-created into something new and better.

To believe in God's power to resurrect, and to live under the authority or lordship of that power, requires a willingness to live with and work through the tension of unresolved conflict, the state of things before they are transformed, the time, according to the Passion story, between Good Friday and Easter morning. This willingness to suffer ambiguity is at the root of what Mrs. Antrobus in Wilder's play refers to as the promise. In marriage a man and a woman vow to live with one another through the exigencies of life, for better or worse, in poverty or wealth, in sickness and health. The promise makes Christian marriage a broad context in which a Christian man and woman choose to work through whatever they may encounter in life, grateful to God for life's blessing, and affirming always the hope for transformation when life gets hard.

What is God's intention for marriage? As imperfect people of faith, how can we approach and deepen intimacy in marriage? Where do we stand with God when our marriage falls short of God's intention? These questions form the three movements of this section.

A Christian View of Marriage

The creation stories in Genesis suggest that the existence God intends for us is an existence in relationship, a relationship expressed for men and women in marriage. Genesis 1:26–27 affirms that men and women *together* are the image of God. Inherent in this affirmation is the understanding that just as God in God-self exists in relationship ("Let us create…"), so those whom God creates in God's image (men and women) share a capacity for a similar existence in relationship. When God creates a man and a woman and blesses them to procreate, the ultimate paradigm for human relationships becomes marriage (Genesis 1:28). According to the Genesis story, at least one aspect of "being in the image of God" means that the dynamic relationship of a human marriage expresses God's own existence in relationship, that we are what God intends for us to be, like God, when we are living in an intimate marital partnership.

The creation story in Genesis 2 opens with the observation, "It is not good that the man should be alone" (Genesis 2:18). In contrast to the rest of creation which is repeatedly in the story called "good," something here is "not good." Man is incomplete, incapable in his solitude of being what God wants him to be. So God makes a "helper," a "partner," appropriate for him—a woman inherently related to him yet different, so that the relationship might culminate in a true partnership, a marriage (Genesis 2:24). It is significant that the term here used of woman is "helper." The Hebrew term behind "helper" is frequently used of God and is certainly not a designation of a subordinate. It is used in the Hebrew Bible often of superiors and occasionally of an equal, but never of an inferior such as an assistant. The term "partner," which connotes mutuality rather than subordination, is a more accurate understanding of the term. With a partner, the humans that God created become complete— the two become one. Through the intimacy inherent in a marital relationship ("bone of my bone, flesh of my flesh…") the goal of creation is realized. Terms such as "mutuality," "partnership," "intimacy," "oneness," and "harmony" express the dynamic way of being that God intends for us through marriage.

God's beautiful intention for us in marriage expressed in Genesis 1—2 unravels in the events of Genesis 3. With self-centeredness and pride asserted, mutuality and trust are broken. Men and women become aware of their own nakedness and feel a sense of shame. They cover themselves and hide from God. Fear overwhelms them and they blame and accuse one another rather than accepting responsibility for their own actions. Separate from God, ousted from the garden, they are separated from one another. Woman becomes subordinate, man becomes lord. Competition and bondage replace mutuality and freedom as defining marks of their relationship. Over against what God intends for marriage, marriage is now portrayed as we frequently know it today: conflicted, unfulfilling, unbalanced and fractured.

For Christians, the gospel of Jesus Christ provides hope that we can begin to realize in marriage the wholeness and intimacy God originally intended. In his message about the coming of the kingdom of God, Jesus proclaims a new reality. In love God now comes to us to triumph over all that distorts and inhibits life as God intends it: guilt-ridden, we are forgiven; broken, we are healed; grieving, we are comforted; afraid, we are encouraged; even in death, we are made alive. Illustrating this new transforming power by forgiving sinners, exorcising demons, and healing the sick, Jesus calls his followers and us as Christians to words and deeds consistent with this new reality. Confirming Jesus' message through the resurrection, God calls us to a new way of living in response to God's grace. The indicative engenders an imperative. The reality of God's loving presence, the indicative, calls us to work for what God intends, the imperative. Therefore, Jesus could say, "Be perfect, therefore, as your heavenly Father is perfect" (Matthew 5:48); and the apostle Paul could write, "For sin will have no dominion over you" (Romans 6:14), since "in Christ there is a new creation; everything old has passed away; see everything has become new" (2 Corinthians 5:17). While as fallible Christians we may experience the difficulty of attaining a marriage characterized by oneness, mutuality and harmony, there is nevertheless always the potential to move toward this reality as we experience the transforming power of God's love. The creation account points us to the possibilities of marriage as God intends it; the love of God, the good news proclaimed by Jesus Christ, experienced in our lives empowers us to cultivate and to realize those possibilities in our relationships.

There is still the practical question of how we are to reach this God-intended potential for wholeness and mutuality in our marriage. The Bible is not a marriage manual that answers this question with a "how-to" approach. Instead, we are encouraged to move toward God's intention for our marriage through love. Experiencing the love of God, reflecting the effect of God's love on our lives, we are called to love one another, including our spouses ("We love because [God] first loved us," 1 John 4:19). The love that moves us toward mutuality is not the self-possessed, possessed, need-based, romantic love that pervades our culture, but a love lived out of the security we know in God's love, a love which places God and others (our spouses) as the foci of our lives rather than ourselves.

In Ephesians 5:21–33 the apostle Paul supports this understanding of mutual love as the avenue toward God's intention for marriage. Often this passage is misunderstood. Paul's statements "wives submit to your husbands," and "husbands love your wives" are taken to imply that a "submissive" wife and a "loving" husband will ensure an "authentic" Christian marriage. Important elements of the text suggest a different interpretation. Paul uses here a household code borrowed from Stoic philosophy. The meaning of the passage is carried not only in the tradition Paul uses, but in how he uses and modifies it to make his point. Unlike the Stoics who based their understanding of marriage on "natural law," "wives be submissive," implicitly, "because women are inferior," Paul qualifies the Stoic tradition with reference to "Christ" and "Lord." Christ is both the model and the source for accomplishing the kind of marriage God intends and that Paul here describes. Most important, Paul sets a summary preface above the entire passage, "Be subject to one another out of reverence for Christ" (Ephesians 5:21). Mutual submission, therefore, becomes the key for understanding the whole passage. On the one hand, the wife "submits" to the husband (Ephesians 5:22, 24). Within a Christian context, as Paul uses the term here, "submit" clearly means "to love and respect." When the church "submits" to Christ, it carries out Christ's will and desires. Submission in this sense is a synonym for "love," considering another's well-being and desires as of primary importance. On the other hand, similarly, husbands are "to love" their wives (Ephesians 5:25), just as Christ loved the church and gave himself up for her. In this Christlike, sacrificial sense, "love" clearly means "submission." Mutual submission, mutual love is therefore Paul's way for the "two to become one" and achieve what God intended for us in marriage (Ephesians 5:31–33).

The promise to love mutually, to submit to one another, as we love and have been loved by God, holds a marriage together for better or worse. The fundamental affirmation of Christian faith, the resurrection (God's bringing life out of death, God's love transforming us) gives us the confidence to make that promise in the first place and the will to keep it throughout our lives.

While such an approach to mutuality and wholeness in marriage sounds good in theory, how this works out for us personally and practically is more involved. It remains for us as Christians to experience God's love and to apply its liberating, intimacy-building power to our lives and our marriages. The teachings of the Bible suggest the basic principle: "love," "mutual submission," understood in terms of the words and deeds of Jesus Christ. Still, in our experience of this freeing, forgiving, challenging love of God, we must become men and women who are secure enough in God's love that we are able to consider and to work for the well-being of our spouses as much as, and sometimes more than, our own, men and women who are learning practical ways to care deeply. When through time a husband and wife mutually learn practical ways to express their love, and when such words and deeds are experienced as loving by the other, the result is intimacy.

✝Approaching Intimacy in Christian Marriage

Intimacy is an art, not a science. There are many satisfying ways of relating, and many types of constructive relationships. Some are formed between couples who are alike, who are "made for each other," whose life together is quiet and comfortable, whose personalities complement one another. Some are formed between couples who are different, who balance deep passion with frequent and vigorous arguments, whose personalities compensate for what the other lacks. In their book, *The Intimate Marriage*, Howard and Charlotte Clinebell write,

> Intimacy is an art with as many expressions as there are artists to express it. It is often expressed in the sharing of thoughts and ideas and feelings. It is expressed in shared joys and sorrows, in respect for the deepest needs of the other person, and in the struggle to understand

him. Intimacy does not suggest a saccharine sentimentalism; it can be expressed in constructive conflict which is the growing edge of a relationship. Intimacy is not a constant, but is expressed in varying degrees in the ebb and flow of day-in, day-out living. And intimacy is never a once-and-for-all achievement but must be nurtured throughout marriage; with this care, it grows and changes with the stages and seasons of marriage.[2]

Christian marriages, that is, marriages between imperfect men and women who seek to ground their relationship spiritually in God's love and to live out their relationship in mutually satisfying partnership, require work to cultivate intimacy. Certain qualities of a husband and wife individually and of their interaction together, qualities fostered and strengthened through faith, will deepen intimacy. These include *congruence, respect, tolerance, open communication, sexual intimacy, trust, friendship, purpose* and *transcendence.* My description of these qualities is tentative. They are difficult to describe adequately, certainly they are interrelated (e.g., as trust and communication are related to sexual intimacy), and, as was suggested above, they receive various expressions in different relationships. Nevertheless, the general descriptions which follow are useful for identifying the kinds of actions and conditions necessary to keep us close, words and deeds which, taken together, fill out what is meant and felt by the words, "I love you."

1. *Congruence.* Psychologist Carl Rogers uses the term "congruence" to refer to one's ability to be a real person.[3] A congruent person accepts himself as he is. She realizes that she has strengths that can be useful for herself and her relationships, and weaknesses that can be addressed and sometimes overcome. When we are congruent, we know and own our emotions and "ring true" as human beings. There is an inner honesty and consistency about us which makes it possible to know and relate to us. We know we make mistakes. We are able to admit them and to make good use of them as we move along life's journey. Self-acceptance and self-knowledge are, for Christians, products of faith. When we know the unconditional love of God, that our destiny is fixed in this love, life becomes a free educational process. We are able to accept honestly where we are now and hold a vision of what we might become. When self-esteem is weak, we sometimes feel a need to hide behind masks of self-sufficiency and self-justification which can build a wall between us and our spouses and block intimacy. Congruence, honest self-knowledge and self-acceptance is a precondition for our approach toward intimacy.

2. *Respect.* Intimate marriages are built on respect, the ability of each spouse to accept the inherent value and worth of the other both inside and outside the marital relationship. As Christians, respect for others is grounded in the affirmation that all people are God's children, created uniquely in God's image and loved unconditionally by God. Respect involves discovering some quality or ability to esteem in the other. It may be that your spouse is a good parent, or writes beautiful music, or it may be his or her professional competency, or

admiring the way she or he takes care of herself or himself. Respect also involves the recognition of the other's autonomy, for his or her need for solitude and privacy. Intimate relationships are not necessarily ones in which husbands and wives do everything together. Some people do not need relationships in the same way that other people do. Some people may not require as much "togetherness" as others to feel close. People in intimate relationships are able to stand apart from their loved ones and admire, to enjoy the realization that they are connected with spouses who are beautiful and gifted, whether they are present or not. Respect for abilities, autonomy and privacy cultivates intimacy.

3. *Tolerance.* Two persons in an intimate marriage are tolerant of each other. They recognize themselves as fallible, vulnerable human beings and therefore can accept each other's shortcomings. Two ideas out of the context of faith are related to the idea of tolerance: forgiveness and suffering.

Forgiveness is based on the Christian affirmation that as God has accepted us, fallible and finite as we are, we ought also to deem others as acceptable and justified ("just as if they had not sinned"). Dietrich Bonhoeffer concludes his "Wedding Sermon from a Prison Cell" with these words, "In a word, live together in the forgiveness of your sins, for without it no human fellowship, least of all a marriage, can survive. Don't insist on your own rights, don't blame each other, don't judge or condemn each other, but accept each other as you are, and forgive each other every day from the bottom of your hearts."[4]

To understand the meaning of suffering, we must first unlearn our most common definition. Suffering is not the same as pain. Suffering is rather what we do with our pain, what we do with any disruption that seeks to steal our freedom and vitality. The word "suffering" comes from two Latin words: *fero*, which means "to carry" or "to bear," and *sub*, which means "from beneath" or "below." To suffer means to come up under something and bear it, to carry it along toward the point of understanding.

When a relation is disrupted or broken, we have options for dealing with our pain: we can despair before it; we can anesthetize ourselves against pain, with drugs or alcohol, or any number of diversions; we can ignore pain, stoically denying that we are hurting; or we can use our pain as an excuse for feeling victimized, for blaming others for our predicament. But love's way of dealing with pain, love's way of countering the disruptions in relationship, is the way of suffering: to bear it courageously; to keep it in our awareness, using it as an opportunity for an honest exploration of our own souls; to share it with those who love us, who will suffer with us, and so deepen our intimacy; to carry it intentionally, while it carves in us a place for a new self-understanding. Tolerance, forgiveness and suffering aid us in our approach toward intimacy.

4. *Open communication.* Intimate marriages depend on open, honest communication, on the willingness to risk a genuine encounter. No couples agree on everything. Conflict is inevitable in any relationship. Through

communication, by talking through our differences, conflict can lead us to deeper intimacy. Open communication allows us to negotiate quid pro quo's, to come to agreement on common goals and to make progress toward those goals. Further, no relationship remains static. Over time we change, and change requires that we keep working on our relationships, keep talking about our thoughts and feelings until the day we die. Sometimes words or actions once considered loving are no longer perceived as such. Sometimes we need something about which our spouses are unaware. We learn new things. We meet new people. We experience new feelings. Intimacy depends on clear, honest communication about our lives through time. In his book *To Understand Each Other*, Paul Tournier writes this:

> In order to have peace, many couples put aside certain subjects— those that are emotionally charged—those that are important for their coming to a mutual understanding. Thus, bit by bit the transparent window which the relationship of man and wife should be, becomes blurred. They are starting to become strangers to one another.[5]

Open communication, dialogue is a central element as we move toward deeper intimacy.

5. *Sexual intimacy.* From the beginning, God created us for physical intimacy, "the two shall become one flesh." Sexual intimacy is more than sex. It is more than just the physical act of bringing together sexual organs, more than the mutual arousal of partners, more than the sensual-emotional fulfillment of orgasm. It is the merging of two persons, self-abandonment, and the deepest form of sharing. A friend once expressed it beautifully, "When we make love, I feel as if his very soul is coming into me, and my soul is going out to surround him." In this sense, sexual intimacy is an expression of the total experience of love between a man and a woman so prominent in our relationships. In a healthy marriage, sex is enjoyed to such an extent that it gives a warmth and resiliency to the total relationship. In *The Transparent Self*, Sydney M. Jourard writes this, "Sex is that something deeply enjoyed, freely given and taken, with good, deep, soul-shaking climaxes, the kind that make a well-married couple look at each other from time to time, and either wink, or grin, or become humble at the remembrance of joys past and expectant of those yet to be enjoyed."[6] Sexual intimacy enjoyed throughout marriage is a quality central to cultivating oneness.

6. *Trust.* Trust is based on a commitment to faithfulness through time (fidelity and continuity). It is difficult to build intimacy in a climate where one or both spouses are open to an easy dissolution of the relationship when things go bad, or to substitute emotional or sexual intimacy outside the marriage as a solution to a marriage's failure to provide intimacy. Trust is the confidence that we will keep our promises "to stay in this thing together" no matter what crises, conflicts or challenges come along, and that we will use such difficulties

to strengthen our relationships. When things are going well, trust develops as we consistently say and do for our spouses that which makes them feel safe, cared for and secure. Intimacy depends on a feeling of trust, that spouses can be counted on to stay with one another and work with each other in good times and bad, "for better or for worse."

7. *Friendship*. Kahlil Gibran begins his essay "On Friendship" with these words, "Your friend is your needs answered."[7] A marriage approaching intimacy is one that is mutually need-satisfying. It is a friendship in which a man and a woman enjoy each other's company, whether in conversation, activity or silence; it is a friendship in which lovers do fun things together, mutually care for each other and are responsive to each other's wants and needs, whether in conversation, activity or silence. There is an element of mutual self-sacrifice in friendship ("No greater love has anyone than this, to lay down one's life for one's friend." John 15:13) Friends intentionally expend their time and energy to learn to do and enjoy what their friends do and enjoy. Over time such a responsiveness to one another becomes spontaneous. But in the beginning, we learn it. If there is one key approach to intimacy to be emphasized above others, it is the psychological principle behind friendship, "feelings follow behavior." Intimacy between friends deepens to the extent that we learn to treat one another in ways we each perceive to be loving. It is difficult to learn about one another without specific communication about needs and wants. If partners in a marriage could regularly take time to identify words and deeds that would reinforce the other's feeling of being loved, and if partners could learn to speak and act in these ways, they would feel closer. If a newlywed couple took fifteen minutes each week to communicate just one thing they could do for each other that would make each feel loved, by the end of one year each would have a repertoire of more than fifty things known to please the other. These could be updated or changed as each person in the relationship changed through time. Feelings follow behavior. We approach intimacy through friendship when the words and deeds of our relationships, our communications and activities together, are mutually need-satisfying.

8. *Purpose*. Intimacy is strengthened in marriage when a couple shares a common purpose, when they have something to work for together. In the beginning it may be getting one or both of them through school, or working toward making a down payment on a house. For many marriages, family is the primary purpose: having children, providing a secure physical and a loving emotional climate in the home in which they can grow into mature adulthood, providing an education for them from preschool through college, and participating with them in a wide range of nurturing experiences (athletic, artistic, spiritual) in the community and in church. For marriages with or without children, a whole range of benevolent and political purposes can deepen intimacy. In *The Intimate Marriage*, the Clinebells call this "the outreach of intimacy." They caution couples about limiting their purpose to family life alone:

The family which operates on the principle, "We'll make our home an island of sanity and the world be damned," will itself be damned to isolation. Isolated couple or family fulfillment is not full, healthy intimacy. Outreach to the needs of the extended family, to the community, to the world stimulates the family to transcend the confines of the nuclear boundaries. This transcendence is the essence of the wholeness of a family. The healthy closeness of a marriage and a family as social organisms is directly related to the vitality of the relationships and concerns beyond the family.[8]

Together serving meals-on-wheels, together reading for the blind, together working for a political party, together serving in a church as Sunday school teachers, or together coaching little league baseball, couples discover that "the outreach of intimacy" deepens their closeness. A common purpose, inside and outside the home, cultivates intimacy in marriage.

9. *Transcendence.* There is a sense of mystery at the center of intimate marriages. It involves a sense of awe at the complexity of our loved ones, a sense that while we may know them better than we know anyone, we sometimes feel that we know them hardly at all. It involves our bafflement before love, before its profound passion and depth, on the one hand, and its sometimes sudden, wrenching disappearance, on the other hand. Above all, it involves a deep sense of gratitude to God, toward God's ultimate power and love, for bringing into each of our lives this other one who knows us, cares for us and incarnates so much of what God desires to do for us, so much of what makes us whole. For those in intimate relationships, there is a "wow!" hard to experience in any other context of life. We find this mysterious sense of transcendence at the heart of intimate marriages.

Reality

Realizing intimacy in marriage is a profound accomplishment. For this reason throughout this chapter I have used expressions such as "approaching a Christian marriage," "approaching intimacy," or "cultivating intimacy." In reality, many and perhaps most marriages are not intimate, or approach intimacy only in limited ways. They may be stable, satisfying or workable, but fall short of the mutually fulfilling, connected partnership God intends for marriage. In some cases, for a variety of reasons, people feeling broken and hurt by their marriages, not whole and complete as God intends, seek divorce. Sometimes a spouse dies or is physically or mentally incapacitated. Some individuals who want to be married never find a mate with whom to share their lives. God's goal for marriage is beautiful, but often the realities in which we live are bleak.

We end this section where we began. We are imperfect people who live in an imperfect world. What we as Christians have to say to those who are hurting, divorced or single is taken up in other chapters of this book. Here we say at least this: While from the Bible and in the theological thinking of the church we are able to articulate God's intention for marriage, imagine an intimate marriage, work toward intimacy and sometimes achieve it, God stands with us wherever we are. For us imperfect people in hurting relationships, God sets out ways to deepen intimacy, to make us as individuals and partners more whole and better related than we would otherwise be. For us as imperfect people, God stands with us when we are conflicted, despairing, and alone, even when we give up, so that we might have second chances and new beginnings, discovering intimacy in unexpected places and at unpredictable times.

Intimacy in marriage is a profound accomplishment, requiring careful attention and grace through time. As pastors we are invited into the lives of engaged couples at the beginning of their journey. How we get them started, aware of God's intention for marriage, aware of their imperfections, aware of potential barriers to intimacy and how they can overcome them, and, most important, how we fill them with an enthusiasm for the beautiful possibilities of their future partnerships together, is the subject of the following section.

PREPARATION FOR A MODERN WEDDING SERVICE

The First Session

Of all the couples I have married, I can count on one hand those who were enthusiastic about the prospect of premarital counseling. In fact, one of the first questions many couples ask is, "Do we have to have premarital counseling?" I always answer "No." Coerced counseling, in my experience, is seldom productive. Hearing this, couples are immediately relieved. By the end of the first session, however, they almost always agree to meet for several hour-long sessions in the months before the wedding to explore their relationship (if not in my office, then over lunch at a nearby restaurant). Moving from reticence to openness about exploring the relationship during the engagement period is a goal of the first session.

I begin by expressing my gratitude to the couple for inviting me into their lives during this special time. What I love about being a pastor is the great privilege of being invited into people's lives in ultimate moments, at times when we clearly recognize our finitude and our need for God—at birth and baptism, at confirmation, graduation and leaving home for college, in marriage and divorce, in worship, in times of celebration and trouble, in sickness, and in death (and for an occasional golf game!). A wedding is an ultimate moment, a transition from living alone to living together in a committed partnership, a transition that raises many questions about who we are individually and as a couple, about who we were in the past and who we will be in the future. I tell the couple that I am committed to them, that I will pray for them, that I will do my best to help them with any difficulty they might face before and after they are married, and that if I am not available or if what they are facing is over my head, I have phone numbers of counselors I know who can help. I give them my home phone number and tell them that they can call me there if they cannot reach me at church. I tell them that for me one goal of the engagement period is our friendship—that they might know on the day they are married that the person who is conducting the service knows them, cares about them, and is someone they can turn to in the future should they need to talk.

To emphasize the importance of exploring and deepening their relationship during the engagement period, I sometimes tell the couple an African folk tale taken from Robert Johnson's book, *Lying with the Heavenly Woman*:

> A father tells his son that one night a heavenly woman will come and ask to lie beside the son. The father describes her beauty and seductiveness and tells the son that he will be dead in the morning if he agrees to the offer of the heavenly woman. As time goes by the father becomes increasingly worried about this danger to his son and moves to another village so that the heavenly woman may not find the son (perhaps he knew the heavenly woman earlier in his own life?). But one night, when his parents are away, the heavenly woman comes to the son and asks to lie with him. Though he had been warned, the son is so dazzled by the beauty of the maiden that he agrees to let her lie beside him for the night. In the morning the son is dead. The heavenly woman is horrified, since she had no wish to harm the youth. She goes quickly to an old shaman who lives nearby and asks for help. The shaman comes and after some time builds a huge fire and tosses a lizard into the hottest part of the fire. He says that anyone who loves the dead youth enough to walk into the fire and retrieve the lizard will return the youth's life to him. The heavenly woman tries, but fails; the fire is too hot. The boy's mother fails, his father fails; the fire is too hot. Then a plain girl from the village who loves the boy but has never let it be known walks into the fire and retrieves the lizard. Her ordinary human love has the power to bring the boy to life. The boy awakens and we might wish that the story ends here in so much happiness, but there is one further episode. The old shaman tells the celebrating villagers that one decision remains. He builds the fire again, throws the lizard back into the middle of the flames and tells the boy that he must make a decision. If he retrieves the lizard from the fire (a power he now has), the plain maiden will live, but his mother will die. If he leaves the lizard in the fire, the plain maiden will die but his mother will live. The story does not tell us which decision the youth makes.[9]

I use this story at the beginning of my relationship with an engaged couple to point out that it will take intentional effort (walking into the fire) for them to know one another and to nurture their marriage. The story raises the possibility that our understanding of our partner might be limited or distorted by a set of hopes, expectations, and projections that we bring to the relationship out of our own personal histories. It is interesting that often at the beginning of a relationship our friends and family members are able to see the weaknesses in our partner while we cannot. This is because this one with whom we have a romantic attachment has become for us the heavenly woman or man, the projection of all we have hoped for, all we have ever wanted, able to meet our every need, the most handsome, the most beautiful, the most sensitive, honest, creative, caring man or woman in the world. When we marry this heavenly man or woman, this idealized, romanticized understanding of our partner, we are headed for trouble (dead by the next morning). No man or woman can live up to the level of our romantic projections.

If the marriage is going to work, each person in the relationship must be willing to "walk in the fire and get the lizard," to do the hard work of getting to know, in a real way, the "plain" woman or man who loves him/her. The engagement period is a time for a couple to separate understanding of each other's partner from that of mother or father. It is a time to distinguish how they will relate to each other from how their parents related. It is a time for each to identify what is needed and wanted and what each will be able to give to make his or her partner feel loved. At the beginning of this process I hold out for a couple a goal: that on the day they marry, as they face each other to say their vows, they will both carry a full confidence that they are each individually known and accepted by the other, that they each have the ability to love the other in ways that will be experienced as loving, and that they will be able to deepen their intimacy through time. The Bible's version of the story of the heavenly woman is this: "Leave your mother and father and cleave to your husband or wife" (Genesis 2:24, paraphrase).

We usually talk together for a few minutes about the story, about how it relates specifically to their relationship and their hopes for the engagement period. We then discuss a potential agenda for the engagement period. I show them a list (see next page) of some topics we could cover if they would commit to a series of sessions to explore their relationship. I ask them what on this list interests them and whether they have other concerns they might like to discuss. If they agree to meet, we set up a schedule. On occasion, when a couple is ambivalent or refuses, I ask them if they would have lunch with me a few times before the wedding "just so we can get to know one another a little better." If they agree to this, we set up those dates. One way or another we will usually find a way to talk about their present relationship and future marriage.

I usually close the first session with two pieces of advice. First, I encourage the couple to plan a great honeymoon: "The longer the better. If you have to go into debt to pay for it, do so. If you need me to call your employer, let me know. Get in the habit of creating and regularly contributing to a repertoire of great memories that you share together." Second, I encourage the couple to find friends who will do the little jobs and handle the emergencies that usually pop up on the wedding day (e.g., going to the airport to pick up your stranded uncle after you have just returned from the airport with your grandmother): "I want you to have enough energy to enjoy the service, the reception, and the rest of your evening together." At the conclusion of the session, I give the couple a brochure that outlines our wedding policies and procedures (96–98).

A Potential Agenda for Premarital Counseling

During the first session, I give the couple a list of topics we could explore together during the engagement period. I ask each of them to check their preferences. On the basis of their responses we establish an agenda, usually a five- to ten-week course:

_____ personality types and conflict in marriage

_____ compatible vs. complementary relationships

_____ premarital medical examination

_____ overcoming barriers to intimacy and building trust

_____ skills for keeping communication open

_____ skills for resolving differences and compromise

_____ the wedding itself

_____ finances

_____ work-related issues

_____ issues arising out of your parental home or your parents' marriage

_____ potential in-law problems

_____ sexual adjustments in marriage

_____ faith and worship

_____ different faith traditions and marriage

_____ the outreach of intimacy and the purposes of marriage

_____ attitudes about divorce, issues emerging from previous marriage(s)

_____ merging two families

For each of these topics I have handouts or readings I give the couple the week before we discuss them. In the beginning, I often ask the couple to take the Myers-Briggs Type Indicator, which a psychologist scores and analyzes, to which we refer in connection with a number of different subjects. In each session I encourage the couple to talk through their particular issues or concerns. When a particular subject needs more time, we are flexible with the agenda. In fact, several times when a couple thought they were not through with the process by the wedding day, we continued to meet during the weeks following the wedding.

For couples who prefer to meet outside my office over lunch or for those who hesitate to identify specific areas to explore, I have found the following "Lunchtime Questions" to be helpful discussion starters:[10]

- How did you meet?
- How long has your love been developing?
- How did you come to the conclusion that he/she was the one?
- What qualities originally attracted you to each other?
- What is your concept of the ideal wife/husband?
- Who will be the president and secretary/treasurer of this organization?
- What can you get from being married that you can't get from being single?
- If neither money nor training were an issue, what would you do with your life?
- What is your greatest fear as you approach marriage?
- Why will your marriage succeed when so many are failing?
- What are your parents like?
- What are your parents' attitudes toward their marriage?
- What are your parents' attitudes about your marriage?
- How do you handle conflict, individually and together?
- What makes you angry and how do you handle it?
- What changes are you willing to make that will benefit your relationship?
- What gets on your nerves?
- What pleases you the most about your partner?
- What are your plans about children and family?
- How do you see the church contributing to your marriage?
- What do you do together for fun?

Most of the time, by the end of this process, we are close to achieving the goals set out at the beginning. We are friends. I have a good sense of who they are. They know that someone is conducting the wedding who cares about them. They have learned a lot about each other, they know potential sources of conflict in their relationship, they know specific ways to love each other that their partner perceives as loving, and they are confident about their future together.

Sometimes, however, pastors who take seriously their responsibility to the couple may come to the end of this process and refuse to conduct the service because of their ambivalence about the viability of the relationship, even though the couple does not share such doubts and still desires to be married. This situation has not yet arisen in my ministry, but if it did, I would feel obligated to communicate my reservations to the couple and not conduct the service. In one case, both the couple and I shared serious reservations. We mutually agreed to postpone the service. I referred them to a professional counselor while we continued to meet monthly. They were married a year later and still have a strong marriage. In another case, I refused to marry a particular couple, not because I felt their marriage would not work, but because I was aware that for me to conduct the wedding would be hurtful to a number of people in our congregation who were still grieving over the recent dissolution of both of their previous marriages and who still had strong relationships with each of their previous spouses. After dialogue with the couple and the families involved we reached a compromise. The couple was married in the parlor of our church, not the sanctuary, by another minister.

What to do in situations like these entails difficult pastoral issues which can have churchwide ramifications. Each circumstance merits special consideration. It helps if a pastor has developed beforehand some general guidelines for situations such as these with the session, church board or worship committee.

In all cases I try to keep in touch with couples in the months and years following the wedding. I regularly see members who married at the church. Also, a number of non-members who were married at the church have since joined our congregation. If specific concerns have been discussed during the engagement period, I call to check up on these several months down the road. I know some pastors who send cards or call the couples on their anniversaries. It is especially enjoyable, as years go by, to see the couple back in front of the church, there to baptize their daughter or son.

Preparation for the Wedding Service

From the perspective of the pastor, beyond premarital counseling, preparing the couple for the wedding service itself involves helping the couple with plans and arrangements for the wedding and conducting the rehearsal.

Making Arrangements—the Wedding Brochure

I am the pastor of a Presbyterian church. Our church polity gives the Session (elders and pastors) the oversight of all worship services. Accordingly, the elders of our church and I have prepared a wedding brochure which sets forth approved policies and procedures for weddings at our church and which guides a couple as they make arrangements for their service. By the end of our first meeting each couple is given a brochure.

The brochure begins with a letter I have written which defines briefly a Christian marriage, describes the wedding as a service of worship, and admits our willingness through dialogue to be flexible about the policies and procedures outlined in the brochure. The brochure is organized under the following categories:

1. *Scheduling*. Here we describe how to reserve a date and a time for the wedding; the importance of scheduling a premarital conference with a minister;

church policies regarding weddings on holidays, holy days, or Sundays; and special procedures for nonmembers who desire to schedule a wedding.

2. *The Minister.* This section sets out our understanding of a pastor's responsibility to use discretion in marrying a given couple: "Whether a couple may be married at St. Philip is a decision for the minister to make. The Presbyterian Church does not require its ministers to marry anyone but expects them to serve the people in a responsible and 'pastoral' manner." The church's requirement that one of our pastors be present at every wedding held in our sanctuary, and procedures for inviting other pastors, priests or rabbis to participate in the wedding, are also described here.

3. *The Church Wedding Coordinator.* Our church's wedding coordinator helps the couple with the details of the wedding. She is knowledgeable about local florists, a range of locations at which receptions may be held and other details which ensure a smooth and carefully planned wedding. Her name and phone number are included here.

4. *Wedding Music.* Since a wedding is a service of worship, the music chosen must be appropriate to the sanctity of the occasion. The church organist meets with the couple to plan the processional, recessional and supplementary selections. This section describes how to make an appointment with the organist, the procedures to follow if an outside organist is desired, and how to find qualified instrumentalists and vocalists.[11]

5. *The Rehearsal.*[12] Here we answer these questions: Who is in charge? When does it usually begin? How does one schedule rehearsals for vocalists and instrumentalists?

6. *Services, Fees and Facilities.* This section of the brochure sets out our fees for members and nonmembers. For members, fees are charged only for the wedding coordinator, the organist and the custodian. For nonmembers these fees are increased and, in addition, a fee is included for building use and for the minister. Here also is described when fees must be paid (at the time the church is reserved for the wedding) and to whom checks are payable.

7. *Decorations.* Procedures regarding flowers, decorations, candles, treatment of the woodwork in the church, ribbons, communion elements, rules about the throwing of rice and birdseed, and policies about post-service inspection of the church facilities are included.

8. *Photography.* Since a wedding is a worship service, it is contrary to our procedures for flash pictures to be taken during the ceremony. Time exposures are permitted from the balcony or rear portion of the sanctuary. Other policies about photographs and videos are set out here.

9. *Deliveries.* To which part of the church should the delivery of dresses, flowers, and decorations be made? When will someone be at the church to receive them? How can arrangements be made with the Wedding Coordinator for deliveries? What is the church's responsibility for these items before, during, and after the service?

10. *Marriage License.* Laws regarding marriage vary from state to state. This section sets out the legal requirements for marriage in our state and county, how a couple may obtain a marriage license, the cost of the license, the requirements for a premarital blood test, the pastor's responsibility for filling out and returning the license to the County Clerk, and how copies of the license can be obtained by the couple at a later date.

11. *Receptions.* A couple can secure a place to hold the reception on their own, the church can help them find a suitable place, or the reception can be held in the church fellowship hall or parlor. The procedures and fees for holding receptions in church facilities are set out here.

The Wedding Rehearsal

To adapt a familiar Bible verse, "Information casts out all fear." We have a wedding rehearsal to prepare and reassure participants in the service. The rehearsal also gives the pastor an opportunity to interpret for the whole wedding party the character of the ceremony as a service of worship.

When everyone arrives and is seated in the front of the sanctuary, I greet them with a prayer and some introductory words about the couple and their love for one another. I tell them that I am happy to be participating in the service. I describe the nature of the service as a service of worship and tell them what we are about to do in the rehearsal.

I normally begin the rehearsal by placing everyone in the front of the church in the positions they will be in after the processional. We then move through the entire service, we practice the recessional, practice the processional, go through the service again, practice the recessional, and conclude with a second run through the processional. Along the way, the Wedding Coordinator and I give stage directions about where to stand, about handing flowers to the maid of honor, buttoning coats, adjusting the veil, about where men should put their hands (at their sides or folded behind their backs), about chewing gum, about what happens if someone comes to the wedding drunk, and about what happens if the ring falls to the floor and rolls down into the air conditioning vent. The most important of these is my instruction to the bride and groom that they are expressing their vows to and exchanging rings with one another and therefore should face, look at, and speak to one another rather than to me. I like to create an atmosphere that is light, fun, and inspires confidence.

I conclude the rehearsal with a humorous anecdote about a wedding I attended twenty years ago in which several catastrophic things happened—a true story in which a fight broke out between the mothers-in law, the groom and a bridesmaid fainted, the minister brought in chairs for the whole wedding party, and the flower girl..., well let us just say that there was a small yellow puddle under the feet of the flower girl that worked its way up the left side of the bride's dress. I assured them that even this couple was still happily married and that nothing like this could possibly happen at this wedding. What makes the wedding beautiful is the love being expressed between the bride and groom, not a perfect performance from every participant. We check the times when everyone should arrive for the wedding, and we make sure that everyone is informed about when pictures are going to be taken. Then I offer a prayer, and we are off to the rehearsal dinner.

The Wedding Service[13]

The church has not always conducted wedding services. The first Christians married according to the laws and practices of the Roman Empire. Civil ceremonies were normally performed in the home and contained customs still observed today: the giving of consent, the joining of hands, the exchange of rings, and the wedding feast with a wedding cake.

With time, the influence of the church on the marriage ceremony grew. At first, pastors simply encouraged fellow Christians to marry within the faith and provided guidance to betrothed couples. Later, a Christian blessing was added to the end of the civil ceremony. By the end of the twelfth century, the Catholic Church developed a full marriage rite, which took place at the front door of the church. During the Reformation, the service moved inside the church building itself. The Reformers modified the Catholic service, translating it into the language of the people and simplifying it. Recently the church has reexamined and revised the language and theological purposes of the service consistent with an understanding of marriage as a steadfast covenant between two people—a partnership rather than the property contract that marriage had been considered in past centuries (e.g., changing the action of the "giving away" of the bride to that of giving a blessing). In recent years, several denominations have sponsored and published their own revisions of the marriage service.

Our church encourages a healthy balance between tradition and order, on the one hand, and liturgical freedom and flexibility on the other.[14] The wedding ceremony is first a service of worship that reflects a Christian understanding of marriage for a Christian congregation (see the previous section). In God's presence, we voice certain claims, promises, prayers, and blessings that embody the Christian faith, express thanksgiving to God for the gift of marriage in general and the love that joins this couple in particular, and ground their vows in God's word. While the ceremony is first a service of worship, it is also very much a personal and family event. Within a general liturgical framework we encourage a couple to compose certain elements of the service in a way that reflects their personal faith, the nature of their commitment to God, and their love for each other. Certainly the service should also reflect the couple's ethnic and cultural background, and if either the bride or groom comes from a different faith tradition, it is important to have some way to acknowledge this (e.g., an invitation to a priest or a rabbi to participate in the service).

For the weddings I conduct I use *The Marriage Service*,[15] an older, beautiful, and dignified service taken from The Book of Common Worship. The structure of the service follows its logic: (1) with reference to scripture, the opening sentences set out God's intention for marriage and our corresponding responsibilities; (2) the invocation asks God to be present with the couple as they now make their vows and to bless them as they seek throughout life to fulfill their responsibilities to each other; (3) the couple expresses to their family and to the congregation their intentions to commit themselves to one another; (4) speaking for the family and congregation, a representative, often the bride's father, either gives a blessing or "gives away" the bride, affirming the couple's intention to wed; (5) with the bride and groom, family and congregation now in agreement about this potential marriage, the bride and groom exchange vows; (6) the making of vows is symbolized by the exchange of rings; (7) a prayer asks God to bless the couple and to help them keep the vows they have made; (8) in the declaration, the pastor declares that the man and woman are now husband and wife; (9) the pastor faces the couple and gives them a blessing.

At the discretion of the pastor and the couple, other elements may be inserted into this basic structure. These include scripture lessons, a homily, vocal or instrumental selections, and a unity candle. In traditions that do not include a brief wedding homily, pastors sometimes write a personal "wedding letter" to the couple expressing their love and hopes for them. The letter is either sent or given to the couple following the service. It is also appropriate for the service to include a celebration of the Lord's supper. The eucharist was one of the first ways the early church connected marriage to worship.[16] As an expression of Christ's presence, it represents for us the source of the strength that empowers us to keep and fulfill throughout our lives the responsibilities of marriage.

The wedding service is a deeply personal, tender moment that pastors are privileged to witness. On the day of the wedding I usually arrive about an hour before the service. I meet both the bride and groom individually and then their parents to ease any general pre-service jitters and to resolve the specific concern about "whether or not the minister will forget to come." I also pray with them. A few minutes before the service I meet with the groom and groomsmen, and at the appropriate time we walk into the sanctuary together. Having established a relationship with me during the engagement period, several brides and grooms have reported that they have been able to draw strength from our friendship to keep their composure during the service. Eye contact, a smile, a slight nod keep us focused and centered.

I have felt a deep affection for each couple I have married, whether they were young or old, getting married for the first time or entering a second marriage and merging two families. To see a couple confidently in love hold hands, look each other in the eyes and say, "I take you to be my wife," "I take you to be my husband," is to witness one of the great triumphs of life.

[1]Thornton Wilder, *Three Plays* (New York: Harper and Brothers, 1957), 200.

[2]Howard J. and Charlotte H. Clinebell, *The Intimate Marriage* (New York: Harper and Row, 1967), 24–25. In addition to this book, the following have been helpful in formulating my thoughts on developing intimacy in marriage: Morris Fishbein and Ernest Burgess, *Successful Marriage* (Garden City, N.Y.: Doubleday, 1963); William Lederer and Don Jackson, *The Mirages of Marriage* (New York: W. W. North, 1968); Thomas Moore, *Soul Mates* (New York: HarperCollins, 1994); Ethel Person, *Dreams of Love and Fateful Encounters* (New York: Penguin, 1989); Gibson Winter, *Love and Conflict* (Garden City, N.Y.: Doubleday, 1961).

[3]Carl Rogers, *On Becoming a Person* (Boston: Houghton Mifflin, 1961), 47–49.

[4]Dietrich Bonhoeffer, *Letters and Papers from Prison* (New York: Macmillan, 1971), 31–32.

[5]Paul Tournier, *To Understand Each Other* (Richmond: John Knox Press, 1967), 14.

[6]Sydney M. Jourard, *The Transparent Self* (Princeton: D. Van Nostrand, 1961), 31.

[7]Kahlil Gibran, *The Prophet* (New York: Alfred A. Knopf, 1940), 64.

[8]Howard and Charlotte Clinebell, *The Intimate Marriage*, 204.

[9]Robert A. Johnson, *Lying with the Heavenly Woman: Understanding and Integrating the Feminine Archetypes in Men's Lives* (San Francisco: HarperCollins, 1994), 48–49. Johnson uses this story to distinguish between the light anima (the heavenly woman), which can incapacitate a man for ordinary life and the dark anima (the plain girl), which represents the human capacity for relationship. As I use this story, I make clear that the gender roles can be interchanged; the story works for both men and women: women often come to marriage with their visions of a heavenly man, men often come with their visions of the heavenly woman, while in both cases the real person (the plain man or woman) stands there ready and willing to love them.

[10]This list of questions is adapted from one I found in an article titled, "Questions I Ask Engaged Couples," *Eternity* (June 1977), 19–20. One thousand ministers from 25 denominations were asked, "What are the four most important questions that you ask couples during premarital counseling?"

[11]*Christian Marriage: The Worship of God* (Supplemental Resource 3), prepared by the Office of Worship for the Presbyterian Church (U.S.A.) and the Cumberland Presbyterian Church (Philadelphia: Westminister Press, 1986), 103–11, lists music appropriate for the wedding service, including pre-service music, processionals and recessionals, hymns, music from Black, Hispanic, and Asian American sources, musical settings from the Psalms, and selected vocal repertoire.

[12]A more complete description of the wedding rehearsal follows below.

[13]Resources on the history of, the theology behind, and the various rites of a Christian wedding service include: *Christian Marriage*, 81–102; "Marriage," in *The New Westminster Dictionary of Liturgy and Worship* (Philadelphia: Westminster Press, 1986), 349–64 (includes a summary of marriage rites and practices in fourteen different Christian traditions plus bibliography); Kenneth Stevenson, *Nuptial Blessing: A study of Christian Marriage Rites* (London: Oxford University Press, 1983); James White, *Introduction to Christian Worship*, chap. 8, "Passages" (Nashville: Abingdon Press, 1980); Geoffrey Bromiley, *God and Marriage* (Grand Rapids: Eerdmans, 1980).

[14]*Christian Marriage*, 83.

[15]*The Marriage Service* (Philadelphia: The Board of Christian Education of the United Presbyterian Church in the U.S.A., 1945). See *Book of Common Worship* (Louisville: Westminster John Knox Press, 1993), 841–81. Other denominations have recommended wedding services in their respective books of worship, such as *Chalice Worship* (St. Louis: Chalice Press, 1996), 34–45; *Book of Worship* (New York: United Church of Christ Office for Church Life and Leadership, 1986), 323–46; *The United Methodist Book of Worship* (Nashville: The United Methodist Publishing House, 1992), 115–33.

[16]*Christian Marriage*, 85.

7
Divorce

J. Earl Thompson, Jr.

MINISTRY TO THE DIVORCED

Divorce is a trauma, precipitated by the acids of alienation, which disrupts and derails both individual and family life cycles. There is nothing natural or inevitable about this transition that strikes one-half of all those who marry; on the contrary, it is an "unscheduled"[1] transition that can happen at any point in the adult life cycle. "It marks the end of one distinct stage in one's personal life and the beginning of another."[2] The anxious and threatening question confronting every divorcing person is in what direction this transition will go. Will it become the gateway to greater emotional and spiritual maturity, or a dead end of depletion and despair?

This essay discusses the primary emotional and spiritual factors that lead to divorce, some of the major consequences of divorce for the divorced and their families, and how the church's ambivalence about divorce interferes with its ministry to the divorced. I conclude with some thoughts about the church's mission to the divorced. I believe that, if the church shoulders its pastoral responsibilities to those who are divorcing and divorced, it can facilitate their healing and the reintegration of their fractured lives.

In order to understand divorce, it is necessary to say a word about marriage. I believe that marriage is a covenant made before God and the community, a sacred bond which has the capacity to develop enduring solidarity or to degenerate into unbridgeable alienation. "All social bonds are at risk"[3]; marriage is no exception. All couples have to decide what kind and quality of marital bond they will create. "In all interaction, either the social bond is being built, maintained, or repaired, or it is being damaged."[4] In my clinical practice, I have been amazed at how many people assume that marital satisfaction is virtually automatic, and therefore that the relationship needs little or no care and attention. If the covenantal bond is to be strong, resilient, and durable, however, it has to be cultivated and maintained on a regular basis.

What is divorce? It is a relational failure, the irretrievable breakdown of the sacred bond of marriage. What leads to this breakdown? It is usually the result of many and varied injuries. John Gottman, a cognitive behavioral psychologist, concluded after two decades of longitudinal studies of couples that these hurts are inflicted by the "four horsemen of the apocalypse," namely, criticism, defensiveness, stonewalling or withdrawing, and contempt.[5] Couples who feed each other a steady diet of these negative behaviors starve the relationship of life-giving nutrients. In order for a marriage to sustain a viable and satisfying bond, the couple will have to maintain a balance of five positive benefits for every injury they inflict upon each other, Gottman claims.[6]

Thomas Scheff and Suzanne Retzinger, sociologists of emotions, contend that shame and genuine pride are the primary social emotions which are communicated verbally and nonverbally between spouses, and therefore signal the state of their social bond. Shame undermines the social bond; genuine pride strengthens it. When couples intentionally or unintentionally shame each other by gesture, word, or action, they injure the emotional and spiritual connection between them and sow the seeds of estrangement. When they affirm and acknowledge each other, they increase genuine pride and strengthen their covenantal tie. Couple communication determines the quality and character of the marital bond. If spouses are to foster genuine pride in each other, they will have to communicate in a clear, candid, and direct manner. Attunement and solidarity occur when "each party understands and ratifies not only the other's present thoughts, feelings, and actions but also their intentions and character—their being, so to speak."[7] Shame is triggered when there is little or no understanding or ratification of one another, and when criticism and self-justifying stonewalling prevail. "Shame is the emotional aspect of disconnection between persons."[8]

It is important to realize that all marital relationships generate some measure of shame in the give-and-take of everyday living. What is critical is whether the shame is acknowledged and processed constructively by the couple. If so, occasional acts of shaming can actually increase attunement between the spouses and cement their bond. What poisons relationships and activates alienation is unacknowledged shame, which, in turn, triggers anger and rage as defenses. The outcome is often a spiral of shame-rage between the spouses which can escalate to a level of emotional abuse, physical violence, and even the end of the marriage.

Divorce is usually traumatic to individuals and devastating to families. Divorce is like death—the death of the intact family. Relationships end or are profoundly altered. The family dies in its recognizable, familiar form and will have to be reconstituted in a different form, namely, a single-parent family or a stepfamily.

The most comprehensive model to describe this transformation has been stage theory. The underlying premise of stage theory is that the family, fractured by divorce, will move over time from a phase of disequilibrium and disorganization to one of restabilization and reintegration. Mavis Hetherington argues that this process can take from one to three years, but there is seldom anything smooth or uniform about it.[9] Divorce catapults individuals into a crisis of mourning, radically disrupting their personal lives and their family life.

Constance Ahrons has developed the most cogent and illuminating stage model based upon a longitudinal empirical study of families going through divorce.[10] In Stage One, Individual Cognition, at least one spouse is disillusioned with the marriage and is seriously considering divorce. This can be a period of intense conflict, emotional distancing, mutual shaming, bitterness, depression, and extramarital affairs. In Stage Two, Family Metacognition, the initiator discloses that she/he wants a divorce, precipitating a serious crisis. The non-initiator, often caught off-guard by his/her partner's decision, is thrown into great anxiety and distress. Stage Three, System Separation, is when the actual separation takes place. In this phase the spouses are thrown into "tremendous emotional upheavals"[11] and are vulnerable to a frightening emotional roller coaster ride of highs and lows and sharp, unexpected curves. Stage Four, System Reorganization, involves the restructuring of the family, which requires the recasting of boundaries, rules, roles, and routines. If there are children, the divorcing parents will be faced with the critical and demanding challenge of working out collaborative approaches to co-parenting. System Redefinition defines Stage Five. In this phase, the family completes the tasks of the previous stages and attains a "new self-definition."[12]

Throughout these stages what does divorce do to people? What are some of the emotional, spiritual, economic, and parenting consequences of divorce?[13]

As is the case with any profound and disabling loss, divorce precipitates a time of seemingly endless suffering. Although people going through a divorce experience an increase of anger and depression, they are troubled far more by emotional peaks and valleys. In addition, they are buffeted by hurricane force winds of anxiety, rejection, failure, and social and sexual incompetence especially during the first year after the divorce. The most painful period for women, who in two-thirds to three-fourths of the cases are the initiators of divorce,[14] is the time of decision making when they are wracked by ambivalence, guilt, and shame. During this time of anticipatory grief, their immune systems are likely to be weakened, and they are more vulnerable to becoming ill or contracting diseases. They are also more likely to depend upon their families of origin for solace and support. Six years after the divorce some women are still troubled by feelings of low self-worth and incompetence. In contrast, the hardest time for divorcing men is after the separation-divorce when they realize what they have lost. Haunted by confusion and rootlessness, they often throw themselves into compulsive work, sexual escapades, or both. Their former wives are much less likely to become sexually promiscuous.

The first anniversary of the divorce is very painful. Both men and women reported a resurgence of distress and anguish around this time. Yet Hetherington learned that most men and women do adjust to divorce within two to three years unless they are hit by more stressors. What was the most significant factor in restoring and "enhancing self-esteem and personal well-being in divorced people" was establishing "a new, intimate and satisfying personal relationship" in which they felt accepted and cared for.[15] In other words, when they were able to restore a secure bond of genuine pride and resolve some of their debilitating shame from the previous marriage, they experienced an emotional and spiritual recovery.

For women, divorce opens the door to financial hardship, if not poverty. This has not been the case for the majority of divorced men who report being financially "'well off.'"[16] In contrast, Weitzman, who studied the effects of no-fault divorce in California over ten years, asserted that women and children were "'the victims of the divorce revolution'" and that in most cases women were "unprepared financially or occupationally for divorce."[17] According to the U. S. Bureau of the Census (1983), 47 percent of financial support agreements between former spouses were not fulfilled. The annual income of women receiving child support was $9000, and for those without support, $6500. As a result, more than 50 percent of mother-headed families were living in poverty.[18] On the basis of her study, Hetherington concluded that divorced women had a 22 percent decrease in income after one year and a 31 percent decrement after five years. In her sample, 50 percent of noncustodial fathers paid the full court assessment; 25 percent paid less than the full amount; and 25 percent paid nothing at all. In most cases, custodial mothers had to return to work, live in poorer neighborhoods, and put their children in weaker schools. The conclusion is clear: divorce has led to "'the feminization of poverty.'"[19] On the brighter side, women generally have more control of what money they do have than they did during their marriages.[20]

Divorce also tends to weaken and compromise the capacity of parents to parent, according to Hetherington. Single-parent mothers (about 90 percent of custodial parents are mothers) are overloaded, even overwhelmed, with responsibilities, and have little time and energy for parenting, particularly the more satisfying aspects of that role. In the first year after divorce, their parenting deteriorates markedly as evidenced by inadequate control and inconsistent discipline of children, less communication with them, and less attention and nurture. In addition, household disorganization is likely to occur with a break-down of family rules, roles, and rituals. Six years after the divorce, reported Hetherington, divorced mothers were less effective in controlling their children than non-divorced mothers. For their part, noncustodial fathers have a serious problem sustaining a relationship with their children and parenting effectively outside marriage. Actual contact with their children is likely to fall off dramatically. Hetherington learned that 50 percent of noncustodial fathers had not seen their children in one year or longer. In a 1990 study by Professor Kathleen Harris of the University of Pennsylvania, 60 percent of black non-custodial fathers had not seen their children in one year, while 47 percent of white noncustodial fathers had not seen theirs.[21] In many cases, divorce leads to the distancing, if not the complete cutoff of fathers, and the virtual end of effective parenting by them.

The primary spiritual result of divorce, I believe, arises from the crushing realization on the part of the divorced that they have experienced probably the most profound and painful failure of their lives—a failure which has left most of them emotionally shattered and spiritually depleted. They have bro-ken their marriage covenant and betrayed the hopes of their former spouses, friends, families, and themselves. As a result they find themselves trapped in a pit of shame and sin. Bearing the social stigma of divorce, they often end up feeling alienated from God, others, and themselves. It is not unusual for divorced people to be ostracized by some friends and family members. Since divorce is an assault upon people's sense of self-worth and self-confidence, they are tormented by self-doubt and feelings of personal and relational in-competence, agitated by anger and fantasies of revenge, and incapacitated by despair and hopelessness. In the wake of divorce, they can often be confused and disoriented about the purpose and direction of their lives. Burdened with these debilitating feelings, they will also be struggling for the first year or two to reorganize their lives and to restructure their families, usually in the case of single-parent mothers with inadequate financial and social resources. The tragic irony of the divorced is that when they have the most need for an abundance of internal and external resources, they are least likely to be able to marshal them. To be divorced is to be thrown into emotional distress, spiritual confu-sion, social isolation, and financial stringency. If these people faced the same plight as a result of the death of a spouse, the church would surely rally to support and sustain the surviving spouse and his/her children. Those who are divorcing or divorced, however, have not been able to count on the church's embrace.

What is the church's mission to the divorced? I think that the church is conflicted about divorce itself and divided about whether to treat the divorced as sinners who need to repent, or as casualties of emotional and spiritual warfare who need comfort, healing, forgiveness, and guidance for post-war renewal and reconstruction. Is divorce a sin or a courageous act of faith? William Willimon writes, "Divorce is a sign of failure and of the presence of evil. A union was severed; love was overcome; a promise was not kept." He con-cludes, "There will always be a note of judgment in the church's dealings with divorce. If it is not there, we run the risk of dishonesty and unfaithfulness."[22] In contrast, Robert Sinks asserts that not all divorces are sinful. Some divorces "are responsible decisions reached in the context of tragic and limited circum-stances. Such actions are not to be repented…but affirmed as thoroughly jus-tified if destructive relationships are to be escaped and the possibilities of new growth achieved.'"[23] Richard Lyon Morgan seeks a middle ground where di-vorce can be recognized as a sin and as "a responsible act of faith and con-science."[24] He asks:

> Is divorce a sin? Yes; divorce means falling short of God's intention for marriage. It means breaking God's covenant and becoming alien-ated and estranged from one's spouse.

> Is divorce a sin? No; divorce is not always wrong or unchristian. Some-times it may be a necessary journey to wholeness.[25]

I think that the church's confusion and uncertainty about how theologi-cally to assess divorce has let to several inadequate pastoral responses to the divorced. First, the church has tended to avoid and deny divorce and the suffering of the divorced. In my experience, it is a rare minister who initiates contact with parishioners who are separated or going through a divorce to offer pastoral support and guidance. In most cases, these church members are not given moral guidance and spiritual encouragement but are left to work out their own problems. They are likely to be ignored by their pastor and other parishioners and offered little, if any, consolation and concern. Moreover, in my lifetime as a worshiper in mainline Protestant churches, I can count on one hand the occasions when I have heard a sermon on the subject of divorce or heard clergy pray publicly for divorcing Christians and their families. Only the most resourceful and farsighted churches offer support groups and educational programs for divorced people and their children. Divorce continues to be an embarrassment to the churches—so much so that the church has even deluded itself about the extent of divorce among its own members.

Second, in other situations the church has condemned divorce as an unmitigated evil and shunned the divorced. In some cases, this is done in an outspoken, direct way, and in other situations it is carried out subtly. In both scenarios the result is the same: divorced Christians are often frozen out of their churches by being ignored in everyday social intercourse and even excluded from leadership responsibilities. When the pain of their loss goes unacknowledged and their brokenness uncared for, the divorced feel like outcasts, modern lepers, and they end up feeling more ashamed, stigmatized, and unqualified for participation in the church. In this context of exclusion, divorced Christians and their families frequently leave the church and remain in exile.

Third, the church has at least unwittingly colluded with the social forces contributing to divorce. By this I mean that the church in some quarters has accepted and defended patriarchal norms for marriage which seriously disadvantage and injure women. This has empowered husbands to treat their wives in inequitable ways and has contributed to their wives' disillusionment and disaffection. I sometimes wonder if the church has given up its mandate to teach young people and adults basic ethical principles of being-in-relationship. Until the church invests significant time and imagination in undermining patriarchal principles and relational structures, and in inculcating the principles and practices of relational equity, it will continue to be a part of the problem instead of the solution.[26]

What are some of the church's responsibilities to the divorced? Two of the essential historical marks of the church, unique aspects which set the church off from other communities and institutions, are unity and holiness. When the church condemns, shuns, and avoids the divorced, it endorses holiness as its essential mark and becomes an exclusive group of the righteous, that is, married or soon-to-be married people, and certainly not the divorced. In contrast, I believe the church is defined primarily by unity, by its mission to be an inclusive community of sinners seeking forgiveness and transformation. Thus the church's divine purpose is to provide a fellowship of forgiveness, support, guidance, and healing for divorced persons and their families, a community where all can work toward the clarification and resolution of their personal and relational issues in the wake of divorce. I agree unreservedly with Lewis Rambo's position that "the church is a community of forgiveness and healing, not a jury to judge the guilt or innocence of anyone."[27] The challenge confronting the church is "to learn to minister to the divorced."[28]

This mission is especially imperative because our society lacks social norms for the divorce process and social supports for the divorced. There are no widely accepted social or moral principles to guide the divorced in their recovery process. With the exception of the legal system, divorcing persons have no clearly identifiable and socially sanctioned blueprint to follow in rebuilding their shattered lives. All the more reason for the church to be a fellowship intentionally and actively holding, sustaining, and guiding the divorced to a firm foundation of personal renewal and the reintegration of their lives.

In order for the church to be of the greatest help to the divorced, we have to coax and encourage the divorced to ask the following questions: How can they learn from their experience of failure and shame instead of being trapped "in endless self-mutilating battles of self-hatred"?[29] How can the divorce process be converted into an experience which ultimately leads to emotional and spiritual growth and development? How can the trauma of divorce become "a redemptive process in which God's grace and truth are manifest"?[30]

In order for the church to be of the most assistance to the divorced, we must be cognizant of their formidable developmental tasks, and support them as they confront and work through these challenges. First, those divorcing must thoroughly mourn their many losses if they are constructively to reorganize and redirect their lives into creative ventures and fulfilling relationships. Beginning with the loss of an intact family, divorce leads to many other destabilizing losses. Divorce represents the loss of the familiar and the customary in the couple relationship: roles and responsibilities, rules governing how to interact with one another, and daily rituals. In addition, the divorced often have to give up house, job, school, neighborhood, friends, church community, and in-laws. The list is potentially endless. Effective mourning also enables people to work through and move beyond their negative emotions, particularly shame, guilt, and anger, which have the power to keep people stuck in self-recrimination, blame of the former spouse, and depression. As long as the divorced are mired in these emotions, they cannot move forward in their recovery.

Second, the divorced have to find ways to end their marriage in a constructive manner. This is far from easy because of the firestorm of emotions attendant on divorce. People going through the first year of divorce are seldom in a frame of mind in which they can make judicious decisions that are in the best interests of all concerned. Judith Wallerstein has pointed out that the divorced have two temptations in this regard.[31] The first temptation is that one spouse, motivated by shame and guilt, or by the desire to entice the mate to change his/her mind, will give up all or too many of his/her legal rights. The second temptation is that one or both of the former spouses may devote his/her life to extracting revenge by prolonging the divorce process, refusing to follow through on the child support agreement, and sabotaging efforts to cooperate in co-parenting. When people can genuinely mourn their losses, they are much better able to resolve their divisive issues with each other and to end their marriage.

Third, when children are involved, their parents must transform their former marital relationship into a partnership of co-parenting. Unresolved spousal issues which foment antagonism and hostility have to be separated from parenting issues which demand collaboration for the sake of the children. The temptation is great for former spouses to use their children as pawns in a never-ending struggle to settle the score. In some cases, children are used as sounding boards for parents to degrade one another. In other cases, children are recruited by one or both parents to carry messages from one to the other or to become spies on the former spouse's new life. In all of these situations, children are pressed into inappropriate roles and are exploited. What is in the best interest of children is to have two divorced parents cooperating in furnishing them guidance, protection, and security.

Fourth, the divorced must subject their participation in the marriage to a candid, critical, and compassionate assessment. Since the initial, almost reflexive reaction of divorcing and divorced people is to blame their partners, this self-scrutiny is a tall order indeed. It takes enormous courage and resolve for the divorced to ask themselves such questions as: What did I do that contributed to the dissolution of the relationship? Why did I choose this person as a spouse? What could I have done to prevent marital disaffection from reaching the point of no return? These inquiries are essential if they are to develop a balanced and meaningful understanding of their marriage and the part each one played in its dissolution.[32] Honest and searching self-analysis can eventually prepare former spouses to exonerate each other for the hurts they have endured and can empower them to forgive themselves and each other for breaking the sacred covenant of marriage.[33]

The church is called to be a community of healing for divorcing and divorced persons and their families. Those traumatized by a severed marital relationship need a faithful fellowship of support. Those grieving their numerous losses need care. Those burdened with the stigma of a failed marriage long for understanding, acceptance, and forgiveness. The church needs actively to embrace these suffering ones with the assurance of God's steadfast love. This ministry can be carried out in many ways. In the weekly liturgy, the minister can address the subjects of marriage and divorce by means of an occasional sermon and can regularly lift up the anguish and struggles of the divorced in pastoral prayer. This concern for the divorced would go a long way to persuade them that their minister is a compassionate shepherd to whom they can safely go for support and guidance and that the congregation is an inclusive and accepting community. The divorced have often been strengthened in their recovery by coming together in an ongoing support group guided by a sensitive and skillful pastor. This group approach has also been used effectively with children of divorce.[34]

Another resource that the church might consider offering to those struggling to live with the alienation and stigma of divorce is a liturgical ceremony marking the end of their marriage and assuring them of the compassion, forgiveness, and healing of God. This liturgical possibility will be explored in the next section.

A Liturgy Marking the End of a Marriage

Divorced and divorcing people often feel alienated from themselves, each other, the community of faith, and God. They long for God's healing of their personal brokenness and shame, and of their resentment and bitterness toward their former spouses. Can a liturgy marking the end of a marriage minister to the emotional and spiritual needs of former spouses, their children, their families, and their friends? Can it help them to conclude their marriage in a more civil way and to move forward in their lives in a constructive manner? Can it encourage them to take fair and balanced responsibility for what they themselves did to sow the seeds of marital discord and to lessen their tendency to blame and demean each other? Can it increase the likelihood that the former spouses can join amicably in co-parenting their children? In a word, can this rite contribute to the reconciliation of divorced persons so that they can be freed from the bondage of their angry, hostile, and vengeful feelings?

A divorce ritual has the potential for both healing and hurt. It is not an unambiguous good. By bringing the former spouses together in such a highly charged face-to-face encounter, the service could reopen old wounds, stir dormant angers and antagonisms, and provoke needless accusations and retaliations. It could interfere with and complicate the process of mourning, and make it doubly difficult for the former spouses to continue their movement toward separate lives. It could also reawaken in the children the false hope that their estranged parents would reconcile and reunite, and thus subject the children to a fresh wave of disappointment and hurt.

Like other rituals of the church, a service recognizing the end of a marriage could be in theory one of healing and empowerment for the participants. This could happen in four ways. First, the service could uphold and sustain individuals caught in a maelstrom of negative emotions, triggered by the dissolution of the marriage and the divorce, and provide them a context in which some of the intensity of these emotions could be contained and moderated. Second, the divorced, going through many uncertain and confusing transitions, could receive communal support from the congregation and the assurance that they are not alone as they seek to rebuild their lives. Third, the liturgy could highlight the changed structure of the former intact family and the new structures which have replaced it. This boundary clarification could enable adults and children to face and be clear about who belongs where and to whom. This is of first importance for children who often have to manage in the space of a week or two a movement from one household to another. Fourth, there are some divorced persons, especially those who did not initiate the breakup and who have resisted coming to terms with it, who could gain greater clarity about and acceptance of their new, if unwelcomed, identity as unmarried persons. There are no guarantees that any of these benefits could be gained by entering into a ritual of divorce. Great pastoral sensitivity and skill will be required to prepare the divorced for realizing emotional and spiritual benefits from the service and to guide them through it.

What, then, are the primary pastoral concerns that ought to be addressed in this preparation? If a divorce ritual is to be a service of healing and hope, the pastor and the divorced individuals will have to explore the following questions in a careful, candid, and compassionate manner.

Given that most divorced persons are wounded to the core of their being, to what extent can a liturgy of divorce lead to their emotional and spiritual healing? This is the paramount pastoral question.

- Can this service enable former spouses to grieve their losses as a result of the divorce and be comforted in their anguish and sorrow?

- Can it diminish the enervating sense of shame and guilt that usually accompanies a failed marriage?

- Can it pave the way for the couple to forgive one another and themselves for their many unfulfilled expectations, broken promises, and the numerous unintentional and deliberate injuries inflicted upon each other?

- Can it assist them to disengage emotionally from each other, and to move on with courage, creativity, and hope to the next phase of their independent lives?

- Can it help them renew and restore their fractured self-esteem?

- Can it lessen their cynicism and bitterness about intimate, committed relationships and temper their fear of being hurt again in a close relationship to the degree that they can, if they choose, enter such a relationship with confidence?

- Can it assist them in sorting out their divisive spousal issues from their parental concerns so that they can cooperate in a constructive spirit in the ongoing tasks of co-parenting?

- Can it reduce the sorrow and anxieties of the children of divorced spouses and assure these children that they will be cared for, guided, and protected by both of their parents?

- Can it aid the former spouses' parents, relatives, and friends to accept and mourn the reality of the divorce, keep from choosing sides, and redefine their relationships with the divorced individuals?

- Can it enable the community of faith to come to terms with the fact of this divorce, reaffirm their care and support of the divorced persons, and assure them that they are still welcomed in the church fellowship?

The interest in the development and use of divorce liturgies is a recent and controversial innovation in Protestant Christianity. To my knowledge, the United Church of Christ is the only mainline Protestant church that has included a liturgy to recognize the end of a marriage in its official book of worship.

Constance Ahrons contends that the social stigma of divorce has impeded the creation of such liturgies and has cast divorce into "a zone of ritual ambiguity."[35] Evan Imber-Black and Janine Roberts regret that divorce remains one of the most disabling, painful losses without a ritual to acknowledge it.[36] What an irony it is that one of the most devastating losses people can experience has found so little pastoral support in the ritual life of the church! Elaine Ramshaw attributes this to the fact that the church lacks "any clear normative understanding of divorce on which to proceed."[37] This was illustrated by a conflict in the United Methodist Church in the 1970s about what is a defensible theological foundation of a divorce liturgy.

In the early 1970s the Alternate Rituals Project of the Section on Worship of the Board of Discipleship of the United Methodist Church set itself the task of creating some alternative rituals that were "more contemporary and ecumenical" than those then in use.[38] One outcome of this venture was a collection of experimental liturgies entitled *Ritual in a New Day: An Invitation,* developed by the Task Force on the Culture Context of Ritual. This Task Force, sincerely concerned about effective pastoral care for the divorced, issued a call for the creation of "personalized" rituals for the divorced.[39] The hope of the Task Force members was that the use of these services would be public and that the choice of "a private ritual would be the rare exception."[40] Moreover, their idea was that the whole congregation needed to join the divorced in repenting their own failures, their broken promises and agreements. "What is needed is a liturgy—honest, penitential, and sober in tone—which enables the entire gathered community to reclaim the act of repentance and also face up to failures in their own lives."[41] They made allowances for the fact that in some circumstances only one of the former spouses might choose to participate in the service, and they also entertained the novel idea that some parts of the ritual might be included in a service of remarriage.[42]

Fellow Methodist William Willimon confronted this experimental divorce liturgy with sharp, incisive criticism. He branded it "'cheap grace'" and an example of "irresponsibility and unfaithfulness" because it lacked an essential "note of judgment" about "the presence of evil" in divorce.[43] Three years later Willimon, in conjunction with Episcopalian John Westerhoff III, ventured forth with an alternative "trial liturgy" of divorce.[44] They argued that this service ought to sound a resounding note of reconciliation. Its overarching purpose should be "to make a bold, either public or private, statement of the presence of sin and an equally bold statement of the availability of grace."[45] Then it can fittingly give "a more-or-less public recognition" to the end of a marriage.[46] In no way, concluded these two writers, should this liturgy be "a blessing, a celebration, an announcement of making of a divorce."[47]

In her research Elaine Ramshaw discerned four types of rituals of divorce or "four major metaphors or paradigms."[48] The first type sees divorce as "freedom" from the bondage of a relationship that is sapping the vitality and purpose from one or both spouses.[49] The second is a "repentance and grace" paradigm, grounded in the need to confess the sins of omission and commission which led to the divorce and to receive absolution.[50] The "metaphor of death and resurrection" undergirds the third type.[51] In this type of service, the death of the marriage is acknowledged and renewed and redirected life is prayed for. The final form of divorce ritual is "a rite of healing."[52] Ramshaw declares,

> The advantage of this pattern is that it allows for a healing also of guilt, for forgiveness, without focusing the guilt and seeming to "rub it in." People who participate in the new rites of healing are often seeking a generalized healing of their brokenness, the forgiveness of sins as well as the alleviation of suffering.[53]

Ramshaw overlooked another liturgical possibility that is rooted in the biblical metaphor of covenant[54] or, more precisely, the renewal of the covenant. In 1986 the United Church of Christ issued a liturgy of divorce called, "Recognition of the End of Marriage."[55] The creators of this rite describe it as "penitential in nature" and in no way intended to "encourage" divorce on the one hand or to be regarded as "a deprecation of marriage" on the other.[56] Their hope was that the service would help the divorced "reorder their lives in a wholesome, redemptive way."[57] The creative core of this service of worship is an explicit renewal of the covenant between the former spouses.

This liturgical approach has several distinct theological and pastoral advantages. First, the former spouses can acknowledge and confess in either general or specific terms the ways in which they have contributed to the breakdown of the marriage. Second, having accepted God's forgiveness, the divorced persons are invited to put their past failures and sins behind them and to turn toward God's promising future for them. The overarching purpose of this liturgy is to empower them to define in clear, concrete, and unambiguous ways their responsibilities to each other and to their children, if any. I believe that reconciliation and healing are most likely to flow from a worship service that inspires people to move into the future in the confident hope that God can guide them into a different but responsible relationship with one another.

A Liturgy Marking the End of a Marriage

CALL TO WORSHIP
Bless the Lord, O my soul, and all that is within me, bless his holy name.
Bless the Lord, O my soul, and do not forget all his benefits.
Who forgives all your iniquity, who heals all your diseases,
Who redeems your life from the pit, who crowns you with steadfast love and mercy,
Who satisfies you with good as long as you live so that your youth is renewed like the eagle's.

INTRODUCTION
We have gathered together before God and as a community of faith, hope, and love to acknowledge and mourn the end of the marriage between *name* and *name* and to witness their commitment to a new covenant between them.

The purposes of this new covenant are to restructure their relationship and to guide the ways they will treat each other in the future. Above all, this new covenant represents their promise to live apart but to relate to one another in the spirit of reconciliation, peace, and cooperation.

GENERAL PRAYER OF CONFESSION
    If we confess our sins, God who is faithful and just will forgive us our sins and cleanse us from all unrighteousness. Therefore, I announce in God's name that we are forgiven.

HYMN (*A hymn of gratitude may be used here.*)

READING OF SCRIPTURE (*One or more selections may be read.*)
Psalms 13; 31: 1–2, 9–10, 14, 16; 46: 1–3; 91: 1–6, 9–12; 103; 130: 1–7
    Isaiah 43: 18–21, 25
    Matthew 5: 3–10; 7: 1–5, 7–11
    Mark 4: 35–41; 9: 33–37 (*if children are involved*)
    Romans 8: 35, 37–39

RENEWING THE COVENANT
    Here may follow personal words spoken by the woman and man. The words may express some of the agreements they have made with each other after much work, anguish, and counseling. Areas that may be included are:

regret, apology, and confession related to unfulfilled intentions;
mutual care and respect;
support and care for their children;
the need for supportive friends;
affirmation of good continuing from their new relationship.

    The leader may invite words of support and love from those present or from a representative among them.[58]

AFFIRMATION OF THE CONGREGATION
    We have heard the promises you have made to one another, and with God's help we pledge to encourage, support, and strengthen you in fulfilling these commitments.

PRAYER
    O God of everlasting mercy and unfailing hope, embrace *name* and *name* with your unconditional love so that they may forgive themselves for their mistakes, failures, and sins in their marriage and pardon one another for the injuries they have inflicted upon each other. Heal their painful memories of unfulfilled expectations and betrayed hopes. Help them appreciate what love and companionship they have shared in the past. Comfort them in their sorrows and uphold them in the wake of their many losses. Scatter the dark clouds of their disillusionment and despair. Teach them to respect the separateness of their lives in the future. Bring them together in a spirit of goodwill and cooperation so that they can creatively co-parent their children. Fill them

with the hope of a promising future lived under your guidance and in your peace. In the name of Christ. Amen.

Hᴙᴍɴ

Bᴇɴᴇᴅɪᴄᴛɪᴏɴ
Go in peace and may the God of peace go with you. Amen.

Divorce is a trauma that deeply shakes and sometimes crumbles the foundations of people's lives. Recovery from it can be a long, arduous, and painful process. The church is called to embrace those who are divorcing and are divorced in the arms of an inclusive community of reconciliation and hope. For some divorced couples, a liturgy of divorce could be one ministry of support and guidance through which they could accept God's forgiveness and healing, and relate to each other as friends rather than enemies.

---

[1]Constance Ahrons, *The Good Divorce: Keeping Your Family Together When Your Marriage Comes Apart* (New York: HarperCollins, 1994), 76.

[2]Ibid.

[3]Thomas J. Scheff and Suzanne M. Retzinger, *Emotions and Violence: Shame and Rage in Destructive Conflicts* (Lexington, Mass.: Lexington Books, 1991), 14.

[4]Ibid., 64.

[5]*What Predicts Divorce? The Relationship between Marital Processes and Marital Outcomes* (Hillsdale, N.J.: Lawrence Erlbaum Associates, 1994), 110.

[6]For a succinct summary of Gottman's ideas, see John Gottman, "Why Marriages Fail," *The Family Therapy Networker* (May/June 1994), 40–48.

[7]Scheff and Retzinger, 24.

[8]Ibid., 27.

[9]For a succinct summary of Hetherington's findings, see E. M. Hetherington and A. S. Tyron, "His and Her Divorces," *The Family Therapy Networker* (Nov./Dec. 1989), 58–61. Other seminal essays by Hetherington are: E. M. Hetherington et al., "Beyond Father Absence: Conceptualization of the Effects of Divorce," in *Contemporary Readings in Child Psychology* (New York: McGraw-Hill, 1977); E. M. Hetherington et al., "The Development of Children in Mother Headed Households,"in H. Hoffman and D. Reis, eds., *The American Family: Dying or Developing* (New York: Plenum, 1978); and E. M. Hetherington et al., "Divorce: Challenges, Changes, and New Chances," in F. Walsh, ed., *Normal Family Processes*, 2d ed. (New York: Guilford Press, 1993).

[10]Constance R. Ahrons and Roy H. Rodgers, *Divorced Families: A Multidisciplinary Developmental View* (New York: W. W. Norton, 1987), 43. See also Judith Stern Peck and Jennifer Manocherian, "Divorce in the Changing Family Life Cycle," in Betty Carter and Monica McGoldrick, eds., *The Changing Family Life Cycle: A Framework for Family Therapy*, 2d ed. (Boston: Allyn and Bacon, 1989), 338–43.

[11]Peck and Manocherian, 340.

[12]Ibid., 343.

[13]The most reliable resource for these outcomes is the research of Mavis Hetherington, who conducted a ten-year study of 144 white families, 50 percent of whom were divorced and 50 percent of whom were not. I am deeply indebted to her. See footnote 9.

[14]Ahrons, *The Good Divorce*, 35.

[15]Hetherington, *The Family Therapy Networker* (Nov./Dec. 1989), 60.

[16]Peck and Manocherian, 342.

[17]Ibid.

[18]Ibid., 342–43.

[19]Ibid., 343.

[20]Ahrons, *The Good Divorce*, 15.

[21]National Public Radio, June 5, 1990.

[22]*The Christian Century* (June 20–27, 1977), 669.

[23]Quoted by Richard Lyon Morgan, *Is There Life after Divorce in the Church?* (Atlanta: John Knox Press, 1985), 77.

[24]Ibid., 61–81.

[25]Ibid., 78.

[26]For a creative and compelling discussion of equity from the perspective of family therapy, see Barbara R. Krasner and Austin J. Joyce, *Truth, Trust, and Relationships: Healing Interventions in Contextual Therapy* (New York: Brunner/Mazel, 1995).

[27]*The Divorcing Christian* (Nashville: Abingdon Press, 1983), 59.

[28]Ibid., 93.

[29]Ibid., 23.

[30]Morgan, 3.

[31]Judith S. Wallerstein and Sandra Blakeslee, *Second Chances: Men, Women, and Children a Decade after Divorce* (New York: Ticknor & Fields, 1989), 278. See chapter 17 for instructive ideas about the psychological tasks confronting the divorced.

[32]Ahrons, *The Good Divorce*, 91–92.

[33]For useful distinctions between exoneration and forgiveness, see Terry D. Hargrave, *Families and Forgiveness: Healing Wounds in the Intergenerational Family* (New York: Brunner/Mazel, 1994).

[34]David C. Bowling, "A Church Support Group for Adolescents Whose Parents Are Divorced," unpublished Doctor of Ministry Project, Andover Newton Theological School, 1989.

[35]*The Good Divorce: Keeping Your Family Together When Your Marriage Comes Apart* (New York: HarperCollins Publishers, Inc., 1994), 69. See 69–72.

[36]*Ritual for Our Times: Celebrating, Healing, and Changing Our Lives and Our Relationships* (New York: HarperCollins Publishers, Inc., 1992), 45.

[37]*Ritual and Pastoral Care* (Philadelphia: Fortress Press, 1987), 51.

[38]*Ritual in a New Day: An Invitation* (Nashville: Abingdon, 1976), 6.

[39]Ibid., 83.

[40]Ibid., 84.

[41]Ibid., 83.

[42]Ibid., 86–87.

[43]"The Risk of Divorce," in *The Christian Century* (June 20, 1977), 669.

[44]*Liturgy and Learning Through the Life Cycle* (New York: The Seabury Press, 1980), 123.

[45]Ibid., 131.

[46]Ibid.

[47]Ibid., 124.

[48]Ramshaw, 51. See 51–54.

[49]Ibid., See 51–52.

[50]Ibid., 52.

[51]Ibid.

[52]Ibid.

[53]Ibid., 52–53.

[54]For an exposition of marriage as covenant, see William Johnson Everett, *Blessed Be the Bond: Christian Perspectives on Marriage and Family* (Philadelphia: Fortress Press, 1985), 44–49.

[55]*Book of Worship: United Church of Christ* (New York: United Church of Christ Office for Church Life and Leadership, 1986), 289–95.

[56]Ibid., 289.

[57]Ibid.

[58]Ibid., 294.

8
Women Entering Midlife

Marie Johnson

WOMEN CAN CELEBRATE SO MANY THINGS

We can celebrate so many things as women. We can celebrate that there are so many women writing about women's experiences, affirming, exploring, understanding, and validating women's ways of being. We can celebrate all the voices and discoveries about women, even the painful ones, because speaking out is self-validating and because telling our stories and being heard can be healing. However, before the church can participate in celebrating women's midlife passages, the church needs to listen to the experiences of women. Wanting to listen to women rather than assume from my experience or rely upon traditional authorities, I designed a simple questionnaire[1] about women, midlife and the church, and sent it to my friends, colleagues, and acquaintances. It was a small attempt to hear their voices. I appreciate the opportunity to write this chapter and am indebted to ten women who shared their words. Their ages ranged from 40 to 71. Two were Roman Catholic and eight were Protestant. Their material was treated anonymously.

Story as Container of Wisdom

Many years ago I attended a "last minute" Kansas family reunion, last minute because we had not reached a time when the reunions were scheduled at least a year in advance, as they are now. My three children and I were driving an ambitious trip from the East Coast to the Midwest, including a touch of Mexico and a swing back through Canada. There is an unstated family assumption that if you get near Kansas you stop. We stopped and sixty of "the clan" were able to gather.

Mother could not come, but because of her and her large family, I have had deep ties to my Kansas relatives out of all proportion to the actual time I had lived there. One night, sitting in the dining room of the farmhouse, I could see aunts and uncles and cousins and in-laws spread throughout the downstairs, talking, eating, drinking and laughing. They had come because I was in town, as they always had when my family was "home again." This was my second visit back as a married woman with children. The first time, when Grammy was still alive, I had experienced a wonderful warm glow inside when I realized that the gathering was because I was in town and that it did not require my whole family of origin to actually be present. I had become young adult enough to represent them. Then, I was twenty-five years old and I felt satisfaction for being an important part of this large family.

This time, ten years later, there was a very different metamorphosis, as I sat in the midst of my relatives. The humid air crept heavily through the open windows and screen doors, carrying the conversations of the young adults and the noises of the children of my cousins and even the children of some of those children. I recognized the night laughter and the games and the occasional fighting of the young outside on the farm, and suddenly, I was someone else. I had lost something, and yet I was the same. I was outside my body in the dark in what had been my playground, observing from afar, yet at the same time being very alert to my body in the dining room. Then a feeling of loss descended upon me. I realized I could not go back. Another metamorphosis had occurred in the space of a breath. My youth was gone. I belonged with the middle aged adults. I was thirty-five years old.

A mantle of middle age had been passed on that night. Perhaps no one else noticed because they lived there and I was the visitor. My grandmother had been alive eleven years ago. Now my aunts and uncles were her generation and I had replaced my aunts' and uncles' generation, and all of us were the "grown-ups" who sat in the house. The cycle of life, continuing without my choosing, was given to me in a special place of extended family, childhood memories, and missed loved ones.

At that clear moment of passing into another generational space, there was no ceremony to acknowledge it, no ritual to honor such a powerful transition. On the one hand, that would have been special, and on the other hand, I am not sure I would have been ready for such an acknowledgment. But, after young adulthood, are we eager or ready for the next passage? Over time I realized that the family reunion experience was a foretaste of what was to come experientially over the next twenty years. At the time, my attempts to communicate my experience of some internal change met with lighthearted joking, and when I persisted, with heavier dismissal about the obvious fact of aging. This experience made me feel that my attempts to share were unimportant, too serious, and of little interest to others. Understanding that humor is often a protection from the discomfort of acknowledging age and mortality did little to assuage the lost opportunity to share my inner experience.

Listening to the Culture of Women

While the satisfactions and struggles of maturity have come gradually to me over the last twenty years, I realize my particular experiences are not normative for every woman. Even less can traditional core theories of cognitive development, moral development, identity development, and adult development be automatically applied to understand women since they have been based on the study of male subjects. No matter how creative, insightful and heuristic these theoretical paradigms of human development may be for men, women's experience must be the focus when creating paradigms for understanding women. Carol Gilligan's[2] early article challenged the prevailing assumption of the traditional core theories that women view the world as men do and that women's development is identical to men's development. This article, published in 1979, was like a breath of pure oxygen giving renewed life to my experiences the year I started graduate school, which was another marker for entering midlife.

Is this really such an astounding idea, that women relate to and view the world differently than men do? After all, the traditional core theories suggest that a major sign of growing up is the ability to distinguish oneself from another. Women are differentiating themselves from men as well as from other women openly and for publication. Women's ways are being affirmed by women's studies programs in colleges across the country. In *Women's Ways of Knowing*[3], women who rely upon "received knowledge" as the only truth are simply regurgitating information that has been already given. To take in information and not react to it as a self is neither learning nor growing. Reading this book reminded me of the single most important experience I had in college. My literature professor, a man, gave me a B+ and wrote on my paper about the interpretation of a poem, "This is very good, but I do not agree with one word of it." This was amazingly exhilarating to my young self to be so confirmed for who I was and how I thought, but unfortunately it was, also, a rare college experience.

Women organize their experiences of reality around relationship, seemingly from the beginning of time. Thus, women arrive at midlife by a different path than men, who, according to the traditional core theories, have been working on autonomy issues, which involves separating out from others and achieving on one's own, attitudes and behaviors that our society rewards.[4] The "self-in-relationship" model of development has come out of the exciting work done at the Stone Center[5] and is in such stark contrast to the self-differentiating-from-others model that it sounds as if we are talking about cross-cultural differences. The culture of men and the culture of women are different. Like the Sufi story where in order to find God one must first stand on one's head to see the world upside down, the church needs to turn itself upside down in order to make a paradigm shift from hierarchical relationship to mutual relationship. To listen to women's experiences about midlife, the church needs to acknowledge the culture of women from the woman's perspective.

Recognizing Midlife and Its Life Issues

It is hard to define midlife precisely. It is in the middle somewhere between youth and old age, between birth and death. We can define it chronologically by age, descriptively by tasks and transitional events, and existentially by one's interior experience. What we do know is that more and more people are getting older and it seems aging is coming of age. With modern advances and social changes, there is a substantial amount of midlife time and a multitude of lifestyles that defy over-simplifying the complexity and richness of this time.

There are several reasons why the church should be acknowledging and celebrating this transitional period for women. The first two are rather obvious. First, the church members are primarily women, especially older women.

Second, the church is about the business of the development of a spiritual life, that is, a relationship with God, with ultimate reality. Third, the second half of life involves a search for meaning, which at its core is a spiritual quest. Fourth, women experience reality relationally. Fifth, there is a great deal of wisdom accumulated in the experiences of women. Sixth, women will go elsewhere if their voices are not heard, and the younger women seem to be doing so.

The first three questions on the questionnaire were designed to solicit the individual's experience of where she was on her own time line, if there were any marker events that heralded the beginning or ending of midlife, and what her issues were at midlife.

If one is to divide up life into periods, Lee at 52 saw herself probably closer to the end of midlife. Her decade of the 40s was a critical time for many life events involving family, friends, work, school, and her body. Intuitively anticipating significant happenings to come, Lee thought it was important to celebrate with lots of people and to be happy about being forty. In retrospect it was an unnamed initiation ritual, helping Lee into midlife.

> I celebrated both its entrance and exit in very different ways. For my fortieth birthday, my husband and my oldest daughter had a big party at my request. I invited all the people from the various aspects of my life, family, church, work, school, parent volunteer groups, lifelong friends. It was important to bring all these various people together in one place.

In contrast, Lee celebrated turning 50 in a very different way—with a quiet dinner out with her husband and college daughter. A nodal event, the death of her mother, had just occurred.

> I told myself that I didn't want a party because my mother had just died and I was grieving the loss of what that relationship had never been able to become. I think I was also grieving what would never be in my life as well. I had a sense that I already was the person I was and not someone I sometimes imagined I could become.

Looking back from the vantage point of 62 , Joanne also experienced the middle years as extremely busy. Her surprise at finding herself almost a senior citizen is reminiscent of Sarah F. Pearlman's phrase, "late midlife astonishment,"[6] which captures the surprise we sometimes experience with our own aging.

> I was so busy letting go of our children and making my place of identity in social work, I hardly noticed [time] passing and suddenly I am almost 62 and about to become a senior citizen legally.

A decade older than Lee, Joanne is concerned about changes in ability, retirement decisions and different spousal needs:

> Will I be able to continue doing what I like to do, and doing it as well as I like to, for four more years? I may reevaluate plans and stop sooner, or perhaps my husband and I will retire together in two years.

Sheila at 40 experienced "being on the way in" to midlife, an approach that was triggered by two events, her first mammogram and her twentieth wedding anniversary. Because she had already worked as a professional for more than a decade and had a new child, her current life issues revolved around taking time off from work and staying home for the children but also for herself, to do some writing.

A heart attack in her early 40s signaled the entry into midlife for Maureen, who at 56 felt well into the transition and hoped she was more than halfway through. The life issues she faced were:

> Understanding my limitations, physically and psychosocially and in terms of idealism. Understanding that what I wished for, or longed for, could not always be accomplished.

Susan at 55 felt she had completed the midlife transition, and although she felt wiser and more experienced she did not feel older. Retrospectively Susan identified the involvement in an affair as the beginning of midlife and the subsequent losses of the men in her life as shaping the middle years: her father died, her husband became seriously ill, her son went to college, and the affair ended. Susan's reflection on the first half of her life was poignant:

> My upbringing and life had influenced me to become a passive, outer-directed person, dependent on the men in my life for direction and decision. Because these men were not there as time went on, I was forced to develop my own coping skills, to find my own inner strengths and to explore my own belief system.

Chronologically, Carolyn thought she was at the end of her midlife at 58, but experientially, she still felt she was living in the middle of the transition. Two events brought her into the beginnings of this period: reading Betty Friedan's classic book, *The Feminine Mystique*,[7] and participating in encounter groups sponsored by the church.

> I was convinced that her book was written just for me. I had long felt vaguely dissatisfied and trapped in the wife-family-homemaker-volunteer roles—yet guilty at the same time, feeling something surely must be wrong with me to want more. The women's movement began to open the doors and windows for me. I had a right to want a full range of choices in life! A revelation.

> Encounter group experiences of shared self-explorations and deeper aspects of love and friendship relationships. This group gave me a safe and regular weekly framework to begin growth work with men and women.

Entering and finishing graduate school, obtaining work and becoming involved in many new community issues during her 40s was a great boost to Carolyn's self-esteem. Not incidentally, she added, "It also took some pressures off the marriage to discover I could get significant psychological and emotional needs met elsewhere."

Jeanette's transition into middle age took five years:

> I identify the beginning of this transition with the death of my father (I was 40), a crisis which made me realize that I could not identify or claim a real Self—I had little sense of inner selfhood which would carry me into middle age when generativity is called for.

Beverly at 71 was past middle age. She recalled that premature menopause due to a hysterectomy at age 42 began a period of fighting depression. In addition to physical stress, Beverly experienced much hurt and rejection when one of her three teenagers cut off emotionally from the family during these years.

Alice, 55, identified her late 40s experientially as the midlife for her. She had returned to school at the very beginning of midlife chronologically, 39, and had had her first full-time job for five years when her husband's job uprooted the family when she was 47. Two of their three children were in college, the youngest was starting tenth grade.

> I certainly did not see my life as half over when I started graduate school. My 40s were very energizing. There were many new beginnings. While I was willing to make a major move, I was not ready to leave my work and I wanted my daughter to accept her junior year of college in England, which we couldn't afford if we moved across the country. That move was very difficult, but we were adjusting. However, after the first two years my husband turned 50 and ended the marriage. This trauma threw me to the end of my middle years and at 50 for the first time I felt old and anxious because of age. It was like a death deep within me.

Midlife: Beginning the Second Half of Life and the Spiritual Journey

The need to develop and nurture the spiritual side of our human nature is as real as the need to develop the rational mind, emotional life, or physical body. We can celebrate that many people have heard the wisdom of Carl Jung, one of the fathers of modern psychology, who experienced the unconscious as a positive force that can help us to individuate, to become more fully who we are, our self, by exploring our dreams and especially by coming to terms with the unknown parts of ourselves. While the individuation process is a lifelong process, Jung believed that the second half of life was the time of the deepest journey into the soul, the inner journey into the unconscious. Women theorists[8] are now revisioning Jungian thought. There is now the clear necessity to listen to women, to hear from them directly concerning their experiences of their souls' journey in midlife, and to identify symbols and images that are empowering for them. The fourth question was an attempt to touch upon the midlife transition as a door into this spiritual space.

"I am trying to relate to the God who is other than phallocentric and authoritarian." Unfortunately this statement was all that Sheila could say at the time. It is very difficult to listen to women's experience in a patriarchal society because any difference often is perceived as a threat to the establishment or as inferior. Listening to male-gendered language about God is not all there is to say about God, unless we have a very limited God. How can women be heard in a society that overvalues the masculine and undervalues the feminine and especially the aging feminine? How can women ever hear themselves when they have grown up in such a society: Mantecon[9] asks pertinent and powerful questions about such dilemmas. What does it mean to women's souls to grow older in a society that values masculinity and youth? When a culture's language has no word to connote "wise elder woman," what happens to the women who carry the "Grandmother" consciousness? This kind of deep pain is echoed in the words of Jeanette:

> …I must say that the institutional church was the cause of much of my pain, due to its rigid patriarchalism and misogyny. Many of the women, in turn, have internalized this misogyny and used it against other women. I have experienced oppression, rejection, and marginalization from my church all of my life; I have been silenced, ignored and laughed at. I have experienced that there is no place for women to express vocation in this church other than in positions of inferiority and dependence. To continue to claim this church was a moral dilemma.

The journey of the soul has had other descriptions that give more of a flavor of the turmoil, struggle and agony involved in such a fearful undertaking, for example, the dark night of the soul and the void. Jeanette further elaborated her dilemma:

> I value greatly the richness of the sacraments as encounters with God through which I have had many religious experiences. To leave the church would be to throw the baby out with the bathwater. After much pain, which continues, and I expect always will, I have come to be able to articulate that my vocation concerns helping to heal the church. Thus, I have come full circle: the church has helped to heal me from the pain which it caused, and now I must respond to the call of the Spirit as a faithful member to help heal its own brokenness.

When we are suffering it is so natural to want a miracle. Beverly simply stated this truth:

> What I wanted was a minor miracle, which neither God nor my husband could or did provide. Instead, I saw two older kids off to college,

went back to work part-time, joined a group at church, and finally came to see that we had done our best—and kicked the guilt.

Beverly did not elaborate about this guilt, but I assumed it referred to parenting. This is an area where women have suffered grievously, been blamed for causing all manner of illnesses, mental and physical, in their children because they have been the primary caregivers. This has resulted in the loss of a deep instinctual trust in themselves as mothers, which has been replaced by relying too heavily upon external authority. Midlife provides an opportunity to redeem this loss of trust in self.

Susan's response to this fourth question was succinct.

The midlife passage makes you deal with the ultimate questions that must be answered (Who am I? How do I relate to God? How do I relate to my world? How can I make my life worthwhile—to me and those I love?). This can only be done in the theological/philosophical frame. For me it was my separation from the God within and the God without. I need to see my growth as part of a plan.

The need to see one's growth as part of a plan is the need par excellence of the second half of life. The reflective need to find meaning in our lives seems to be uniquely human. Most of us eventually will ask the question, what is the meaning of my life? This inner reflective struggle of self-examination is evident in the following sharings by Lee.

This is an important question at this time, although it is one I have asked throughout my lifetime. However, now more than ever, the question now has to do with me, with the God in me. To say it differently, my life has to have meaning to me, i.e., the quest seems to be what is meaningful about my life now. If my life were to end tomorrow, what would I regret not having done, or been, or said? It's different than having my life have a purpose, or a call. It has more to do with a knowledge that if I pay attention to the God within me, in relationship to that knowledge what does my life mean to me. It's hard to articulate. I am only just beginning to form the question, let alone have any answers. It is unrelated to what the rest of the world might think about me and more to do with what I think about myself. It has to do with experiencing that our life in this form is preciously short.

This is not an easy journey, this midlife transition, this soul's journey into unknown territory. The future does not stretch forth unendingly. Major changes will occur in the familiar life taken for granted. Our bodies begin to tell us that deep shifts are taking place, most of which at age 40 are not yet on the surface. No longer are we so in control. There is a shift from ego consciousness where the self has been identified by learning to "control" our lives. Sometime at midlife we begin to take our first steps toward rebirthing a new self as we face so many changes. The death of the old self and rebirth of the new is not painless, so there is often reluctance, if not resistance, to go in search of our deep self within, often described as the God within. This self often is experienced as pulling us toward the reality of being who we truly are.

Using the words of John 21:18–19, Maureen identified this theme of reluctance to take the journey during the midlife passage:

> The best thematic theological story which related to my experience at that time was the saying of Jesus to Peter in the last chapter of John's Gospel, which suggested that when he was a young man he could go wherever he wanted to go, but when he was older he would be girded with a belt and be led where he didn't want to go.

During her midlife Maureen had many dreams with water symbols which she understood as symbols of death and rebirth. That there is a relationship between identity and spirituality is a realization that often comes through dreams, as Jeanette witnesses:

> Identity and spirituality cannot be separated…graced with the ability to do serious dreamwork—this has been my spiritual path for most of my adult life…I have experienced the power of the Holy Spirit in dream messages and have learned to listen to this inner Self. Some of the most powerful dreams have been the simplest: I am a tree; I have roots, I can stand strong and tall and reach for the sky at the same time; the Tree of Life is in me. I am a kaleidoscope full of color and shapes forever changing and growing while still remaining one whole.

These themes of spiritual growth and the resistance to the pain and rebirth are echoed in Carolyn's description of her midlife issues. There is a sense of awe as if she experienced holy ground:

> I see my issues to be risking fully feeling the pain and loss versus avoidance of pain; accepting myself nonjudgmentally versus seeking perfection; to be vulnerable and more fully human. These are lifetime growth issues—I expect and hope to be processing them still long after "midlife."
>
> These issues are essentially spiritual to me. I cannot really empathize fully unless I've done my own grief work. I resist it—the letting go and I am drawn to it. It's my understanding of the meaning of the cross—to surrender and find freedom after the suffering—the rebirth. I have found that the more attention I give to these life issues of mine…the more frequently I experience those wonderful indescribable moments of Grace! It is both frightening and exciting to me!

The importance of work outside the home in the second half of life for women who have raised children has been stated by several women. Joanne connects this work with her spiritual value of mission. She identifies music as essential not only to her work but also to her very being which she had put aside for many years.

Social work enabled me to feel that I was fulfilling my earlier commitment to some kind of mission: although it is not within the church, I
see serving children and families and the school as a ministry equal to
that in a church, since my support comes from the love of God in Jesus
and I believe I could not do what I do without it. Also, serving at the
same time in some capacity in the church (with children again) gives
me a bridge between work and volunteerism (what I do without pay
for enjoyment) in that both functions help the other. Doing children's
worship has been very nourishing for me...But what keeps me sane
when discouraged is music in a variety of forms, whether singing
with the children, planning for a conference with my husband where
I will do the music, or just going to a community concert or fooling
around with my piano board. This is different from just attending a
concert. I like to be involved with music...I realize more and more
that this will always be a necessary part of my life, having put it aside
for many years.

Women at Midlife and the Church

Question five was concerned about how these women experienced assistance from their church or what would have been helpful during the crossing
of the midlife. The women who responded to the questionnaire were well
educated, intelligent, mothers and wives. They were, also, committed church
members who have had their share of suffering because of the traditional
hierarchical nature of the church. They do not hesitate to say where the church
has helped them and failed them. They have stayed in the church to give and
to receive, which requires the courage to speak their minds and hearts. Susan
joyously and enthusiastically seemed to shout her words:

It did! The church provided counseling—support groups—education—acceptance. But perhaps the #1 thing that the church can do to
begin with is to provide an equal role of women, and equal priority
given to women's problems. Let's hear more about women, beginning in Sunday school!
    Life's passages are inevitable, painful, and exciting. But like any
other adventure, they could be better navigated when you are knowledgeable and informed. The church can help by celebrating women—
period. Let's have women heroes of the Bible. Let's use the religious
myths that involve women more in sermons. Let's organize women's
groups that provide support and education instead of church sup-
pers. Let's ordain more women. Let's have more women counselors.

Joanne, also, mirrored this need for small support groups. She felt a lack
of connection with other women. While she thought that the church does not
need to officially recognize women's midlife passage, there was an implication that there could be unofficial ways to do this so an introvert would be
comfortable.

I don't think the church needs to officially recognize a woman's midlife transition like the biggies, I'd run from that, introvert that I am. But I think the church could help by providing small groups for discussion of where we are going or what we are struggling with…I feel quite a stranger in our church right now, in spite of my involvement with children. Large-group, monthly women's meetings do not appeal to me. But that is my problem. I have so much involvement in my husband's life that it is very full. I think that I am paying the price of a lack of connection with other women, with fewer friends in my later years, but then I will just have to make new ones.

Carolyn's deep appreciation of her church community does not keep her from constructively critiquing it and lifting up two major issues, aging and sexism:

I am profoundly grateful for what my church community has already contributed—opportunities to feel and receive love and acceptance as well as opportunities to give both in many, many ways.

As I leave midlife in the next few years, I think the church needs to address two areas more seriously: Aging and Sexism. Aging—Helping maintain integrity, purpose and meaning as aging occurs with its inevitable related losses. Sexism—the church could (should) be more sensitive to the subtle effects on both men and women of the male-centered language in scripture translation, hymns, standard litanies, and so forth.

Beverly's experience within her church is reminiscent of the concept of liminality, introduced by Gennep in 1909 and expanded on by Victor Turner based on their anthropological studies of rites of passage in "primitive" societies. Rites of passage, according to Gennep, have three phases: separation, transition, and incorporation. Transposing these processes onto the midlife passage, the reality of aging will begin to separate a woman from what and where she was, that is, a young woman in her society. Gennep called the rites of passage during the transitional phase the liminal rites. Liminal derives from the Latin *limen*, meaning threshold. The threshold or liminal time is an in-between time, a time when the woman in transition is not where she was, and is not yet where she will be. She has left the known and entered the unknown. During rites of passage, the liminal time is a time of danger and powerful potential for the woman, with serious consequences for the community. There are only faith and hope that she will arrive on the other side, the incorporation phase, and can take her new place in the community, but it is not certain and there is fear. This could be a description of Beverly's midlife passage, for her arrival on the other side can be heard in her words:

The church-sponsored encounter group led to much personal growth; many retreats of a spiritual nature provided a substitute "family," and finally, a numinous experience of grace which changed my whole inner life. Our church last year sponsored a weekend retreat for people going through a midlife crisis. I think it should be repeated every couple of years. Maybe some older women could lecture to younger women having problems with menopause in an intimate and confidential format.

This is truly a Crone speaking from her wisdom and wanting to share it. Happily, women are beginning to reclaim the ancient and venerable word Crone as one of the rich images of the older self.

Although Maureen and Lee are committed church women of faith, neither of them experienced adequate support from their church community. Maureen found support from women and men at school, and Lee found the deepest sharing, understanding and celebration from a women's dream group. Maureen wrote:

> I received support from women and men at the seminary who were going through that transition and others. It helped to see this experience in a theological perspective.

Thoughtfully, Lee wrote of her experience of her church and found much to admire: the church's willingness to use consensus, its investment in education for lay and clergy, its support of women's ordination and its strivings to promote inclusive language and images. While these were very important, they were not enough. Much of the lived life of her congregation was noted only in the printed word but was not an intrinsic part of the worship service with the community. The nourishment of the soul was missing for Lee:

> I belong to a faith tradition that is simplistic when it comes to liturgy. Communion is served once a month. There are no saints or statues. I continue my alliance with this tradition for several reasons. I value its emphasis on consensual agreement to revise church law and policy. I was raised in this tradition and those early associations are important to my emotional response to the service today. I support the church's emphasis on education for both lay and clergy. The church was one of the first to ordain women, and actively seeks to promote inclusive language and images.
>
> At the same time, there is much missing in its liturgy that is spiritually nourishing. Its small size means limited diversity and richness in terms of global membership...As for transitions, it would be nice for the service to contain some prayer, some liturgy that recognizes the passing of one's parents, or children leaving home or even the end of marriage whether by death or divorce. Elder statesman status is available in leadership roles although not formally recognized. Graduations, deaths, illnesses, wedding anniversaries are noted in the

bulletin or newsletter, or in the congregational news during the service so in that sense these markers are noted. But they are not part of the worship experience, and that is missing.

Despite my church's attempt to be inclusive in language and image, it cannot transcend a predominantly patriarchal culture in which it is embedded. For that reason, the special times unique to women, such as first mensis, menopause, first pregnancy are basically left out of story, myth, images, theology, and liturgy. Women's role as silent servant is still very much alive. Women's experience and style of leadership are still undervalued. Often women themselves, because of the power of socialization, perpetuate these assumptions and omissions. I'm saddened by the realization that basically my church has not been helpful in most of these transitions, with one exception. The conversations that I have with other women around these themes have been useful. These take place in the daily encounters in meetings, after service, or on retreat. Once a year the women of my church go on retreat and it is there that much sharing takes place. But at one retreat where a closing service celebrated women's creation and caring, there was criticism by some as too contemporary or not understandable. It has been a dream group of women, not connected to my church, where the deepest sharing, understanding, and celebration has occurred.

Although the institutional church was the cause of much of Jeanette's pain, she readily acknowledged two concrete ways in which her church had been helpful to her during midlife. The church offered the sacrament of the anointing of the sick and she received money to help pay for her therapy. As part of her spiritual journey toward inner healing, Jeanette several times chose to receive this sacrament within the celebration of Sunday eucharist.

[The sacrament of anointing] graced me with hope and fortitude and real healing-as-a-process.

I truly believe that an important ministry of any church is to recognize adult developmental transitions such as midlife and old age...There is a lot of isolation out there. Most people are not even aware that midlife transition is normal and so is any accompanying crisis. The church can help in several ways. Just recognizing adult transitions as the norm within the church structure by some sacramental sign is a good start. Catechesis belongs with this and includes discussion/support groups for midlife people, in or out of crisis...Also, to have a budget line for counseling assistance is a very realistic ministry...many women in midlife transition are single mothers, in between careers or just finding one, and cannot afford the therapy they need. By helping women actualize themselves, it is not only their lives which are changed for the better, but those of whole families and whomever these people touch and relate to.

The self-actualizing of women who are connected with the church necessarily includes awareness of feminist theology and spirituality. I am not so sure that the institutional church would really wish to engage in such consciousness-raising. It might just put them out of business. Many women have had to empower themselves in this work. But we know that women in midlife transition must connect with their spirituality if they are to actualize growth toward selfhood and become who they were created to be—the image of God. This is genuine soul-crafting. This is what women in midlife do. This is what needs to be voiced by them.

Let Us Celebrate

I celebrate the lives of these women who have contributed anonymously to this chapter by their generous giving of their time, their thoughtful reflections, and their courageous writing of their experience about midlife.

If the church is to be a healing place for women, the church will need to listen to women's stories, and women will need to feel safe in the church. Can the church be open to hearing stories of women in travail and transition? In order not to see women through men's eyes, the church will need to stand on its head and see the world upside down, as the Sufi was instructed to do in his search for God. This is indeed a powerful paradigm shift and can threaten those in power as it did in Jesus' day.

As our population grows older and women live longer, women hope that the church will lead the way in honoring women and age. Midlife challenges our illusions that we stay the same and do not change. The church, too, is challenged to change and to speak to people where they spiritually live. The church needs to celebrate the diversity and complexity of women's lives, images and experiences. Women need to find places where they can celebrate the ripening years of midlife that can prepare them to become wise women. Let us all have the courage to listen to women's voices, both in pain and in joy, and celebrate.

RITUAL FOR WOMEN IN MIDLIFE

"Liturgy is central to the Jewish and Christian traditions, to both sacramental and word traditions. Religious rituals are where people traditionally encounter spirituality."[10]

Can the church liturgically nourish the souls of women or will women have to look elsewhere? The traditional paradigm upon which the institutionalized church has been built over centuries is one of masculine hierarchy and control. In conjunction with the values of our Western culture, objectivity, linearity, autonomy, scientific progress, a very narrow reality has been created where women do not comfortably fit. In general, women see and relate to the world differently than men do. Women do not feel safe in our culture. Women are sexualized, trivialized, ignored, abused, and killed, or idealized as child bearers and nurturers. "Honesty about women's experiences frequently calls forth expressions of lament, grief and rage."[11] Is the church willing to incorporate experiences of rape and incest into their rituals?[12]

Writing about a culture in transition and empathizing with the earth-shaking event of slave sitting down with master in Jesus' time, Priscilla L. Denham concludes her chapter:

> Jesus Christ allowed himself to be challenged by a nontraditional woman from Canaan. He allowed himself to be touched by a woman who was considered unclean. He regularly risked ridicule by speaking with women in public. He kept himself available to those culturally uncomfortable ones who needed his presence and allowed the vision of his ministry to be shaped by them. The effect on him and his early followers was so profound that the role of women in the Christian religion stood out as significantly different from other women in that part of the world.[13]

As is evident in the previous section, there is a hunger for meaningful liturgy and a longing for the church to provide the place for this to happen. Working with both women and men in the field of pastoral counseling, I have noticed over the years that faith, belief and spirituality are harder for most people to talk about than sex. If the church is willing to really listen and incorporate the life events of its members into ritual, worship and ceremony, I believe people will become more conscious of their spiritual journey.

Listening to women, the church will discover the diversity among women. Not all women will be interested in ritual for a variety of reasons. Some women will be interested in creating a personalized ritual, others a more traditional one that could be included appropriately in public worship, and others no ritual at all. Some will prefer a small group of close friends to be present. Some will prefer the church sanctuary, others a backyard. Some will prefer that the minister not be present, others that the minister be the facilitator.

The church needs to remember that there must truly be a choice of whom, when, where and what in constructing a ritual. While the structure of the ritual can be shared with others, the person's story is always respected with the seal of confidentiality. Ritual is created out of personal story, which is why many women's rituals deal with healing of physical, emotional and spiritual wounds, and therefore privacy and confidentiality are necessities in creating and performing rituals.

From the shared stories in the previous section, these women could create rituals of losses: losses of mother, father, husband, children, parts of the body, church home, and the self. Rituals of healing could also be constructed: healing of the physical body, of dissatisfactions, guilt, acceptance of limitations, vulnerability. Obviously, there is overlap among loss, grief, letting go and healing. From these same shared stories rituals of transition into, through and out of the midlife could be created.

Wise Old Woman (The Crone)

"No woman is as devalued by patriarchy as the Crone, which indicates how powerful the Crone really is."[14] The Crone is an archetypal figure which is within the human psyche, even if she is repressed in our culture. The Crone was a title assigned to an older woman once respected and feared for her wisdom, but now we do not need to look far to see the various ways our society devalues, ridicules and dismisses the older woman. In actuality, the power and wisdom of the older woman is needed desperately in our society where worship of youth and stereotypical beauty too often has aborted the inner spiritual journey of midlife.

Midlife is the beginning of a great transformation. Defining when a woman reaches the passage into midlife varies with experience. From the previous chapter we can see it could be when the last child leaves home, when menopause begins, when a woman becomes a grandmother, and/or when a parent dies. The important timing really depends upon when the woman is ready to validate her inner power and wisdom gleaned from half a lifetime. By then she has passed through girlhood, maidenhood, and often motherhood. Every woman loses her biological fertility and this signals a special rite of passage into Wise Old Woman. We cannot be separated from the body and we must not fear our bodies as has been the destructive perspective of the patriarchy.

> For good or ill, much of women's existential life is oriented toward the body and the physical, psychological, emotional and spiritual aspects of reproduction.[15]

The church has an opportunity and an awesome responsibility to empower our young girls, maidens and mothers (whether by birth of a child or of other creativity). Too many of these women have been afraid of their own bodies, have striven to look like the stereotypical perfect body, and have fear of growing old.[16] The implications of releasing the power of the Crone for the good of the person, the community, and the planet Earth are truly awesome.[17]

I would like to offer the following simplified ritual of transition into the life of the wise old woman for the purpose of reclaiming the power of the approaching wise woman, allowing for the fact that some of these women would feel no need for a midlife ritual. As a basic structure I would like to use Gennep's three phases: separation, transition, and incorporation. However, the content of the objects used in the ritual are as varied as people and their experience.[18]

Ritual for Croning

Separation

CALL TO CELEBRATE

The gathering of participants—participants are invited by the honored woman—is a time to focus with a call to celebrate, which states the purpose of gathering. The person of honor, the woman being Croned is separated out, acknowledged as distinct from the others. This is her Croning ceremony which supports and assists her in the transition and her transformation. This can be done by one person or each sentence can be said by a different person. This can be planned or spontaneous. For example: We gather together here in this holy place to perform a sacred ritual, a ritual of Croning. We recognize a new life is beginning. The old is dying and the new is being birthed. We honor her passage into the time of wise woman. We call forth our ancestors, great-grandmothers, grandmothers, mothers and any and all wise women from past ages to be witnesses and to celebrate with us and to help us be midwives together.

The Supportive Community

Participants may introduce themselves by honoring and invoking those Crones in their lives who have been significant and important, whether names are known or unknown. These can be relatives, friends, acquaintances, and even nonacquaintances from the past or present. These also can be historical or fictional women. Sometimes only a name is known and occasionally a name is unknown. Actually, there are many women in history who are unknown and forgotten by the world, but the power of the Spirit can invoke their presence. The purpose is to invite and welcome a company of witnesses to the ceremony who will help in the support of the honored woman. For example:

I am Marie, daughter of Mable Ulrika and granddaughter of Helena Maire and relative to many who came before them. I invite and welcome them to this cere-mony. I also would like to invite my daughters, Gretchen Lee and Helena Marie, and my sister, LeAnn.

Representational Objects

The woman being Croned has brought precious objects which symbolize whatever is important to her about herself and her past journey and future journey. She may or may not desire others to participate by bringing some of their symbols. A table may be used to hold the objects or a blanket on the grass. The woman may ask some of the older women to share the meaning of their symbols.

Candles, water, earth, rocks, shells, incense, music, chimes, story, poem, scripture, prayer, painting, sculpture, an old toy, jewelry and picture may be used and chosen for their meaningfulness to the woman. Perfume, cloths, scarves, special containers, boxes, baskets, bowls, goblets can be used. Color is often important. Pictures of women, of relatives, of friends may be displayed. The list is endless. The important factor is that the woman chooses what representative objects have stirred her soul with meaning and that she would like to share with the community gathered. The woman may choose to share whatever symbols she has chosen to bring as well as the meaningful history behind the symbol. It is important to remember that what has stirred a soul and/or brought meaning to a person is intimately personal, powerful, and precious and requires the deepest respect.

Transition

This is the time of the dangerous crossing, the threshold of passage into wise old woman. To assist this process, chanting, drumming, silence, meditation, prayer of imagination, or dramatic action may be used. A litany may be used recounting the important events, accomplishments, experiences, attachments in the past which are no longer. The woman may sit or stand in the center of a circle. At some point those Crones present may invite her into their circle of wisdom by forming a circle around her. Holding hands may be done. When it is time, the laying on of hands may be used to consecrate the passage. She may be given a gift to symbolize her safe crossing.

The following poem, untitled, by Patricia J. Lesch echoes something of this middle.

I find myself in the middle of something.

What happened to the beginning?
It's as if I hadn't been around for the beginning.
Was I asleep?
Was I given only the middle pages of the script?

As if there were no beginning.

My nervous talk stops me short.
What am I trying to do?
Work backward from the middle
 to construct some beginning by my words?
Can't do it.

The beginning was there, all right,
Just not all linear and discursive,
Built of blocks, one by one.

But there, nonetheless,
Amid daring leaps and spectacular catches.

Ah, in the middle:
Barefoot dancers on holy ground.

Incorporation

The woman is welcomed back to the community as a Crone. She may have a particular older woman present introduce her new status. The woman may want to thank all present and especially those special women who have helped her arrive at this point in her life. Those present may give to her symbolic or concrete gifts of affirmation of her strengths. There is joyous celebration because she made it safely through the holy ground of the liminal time, and now she is a Crone.

---

[1] I asked for their responses to eight questions:

1. Are you approaching, in (the middle), at the end, or through the midlife transition period?
2. Did any event signal your entry into this time period? Or looking back on it, do you identify an event (external/internal)?
3. What are/have been the life issues for you during this time, or what do you expect if you are approaching this time frame?

4. How would you define these issues theologically or in relation to God/higher power, etc.?
5. How do you see that your church community did, can, or could have helped you to enter this period, during it, or even leaving it?
6. If you would like to share memory, poem, journal entry, dream, experience, book, or other resource that has been meaningful to you, please do so.
7. Please give your age.
8. What else would you like to add?

[2]Carol Gilligan, "Woman's Place in Man's Life Cycle," *Harvard Educational Review*, Vol. 49, No. 4 (November 1979), 431–46.

[3]Mary Field Belenky, Blythe McVicker Clinchy, Nancy Rule Goldberger, Jill Mattuck Tarule, *Women's Ways of Knowing, The Development of Self, Voice, and Mind* (New York: Basic Books, 1986).

[4]Judith V. Jordan, Alexandra G. Kaplan, Jean Baker Miller, Irene P. Stiver, Janet L. Surrey, *Women's Growth in Connection* (New York: The Guilford Press, 1991).

[5]Nancy Chodorow, *The Reproduction of Mothering* (Berkeley: University of California Press, 1979).

[6]Sarah F. Pearlman, "Late Midlife Astonishment: Disruptions to Identity and Self-Esteem," in Nancy D. Davis, Ellen Cole, Esther D. Rothblum, eds., *Faces of Women and Aging* (New York: The Haworth Press, Inc., 1993).

[7]Betty Friedan, *The Feminine Mystique* (New York: Inc., 1964).

[8]Estella Lauter and Carol Schreier Rupprecht, eds., *Feminist's Archetypal Theory, An Interdisciplinary Re-Vision of Jungian Thought* (Knoxville: The University Press, 1985).

[9]Valerie H. Mantecon, "Where Are the Archetypes? Searching for Symbols of Women's Midlife Passage," in *Faces of Women and Aging*.

[10]Diane New, "Celebration in a Different Key: Feminists Transform Liturgies," *Daughters of Sarah* (November/December 1990), 3.

[11]Marjorie Procter-Smith, "The Marks of Feminist Liturgy," *Proceedings: The North American Academy of Liturgy* (Washington, D.C., 1992), 70.

[12]Cynthia Ellen Elledge, "Healing in the Silence: Assessing and Creating Tools for the Pastoral Care and Liturgy with Rape and Incest Survivors." Thesis submitted for Master of Arts in Theological Studies, School of Theology at Claremont, March 20, 1995.

[13]Priscilla L. Denham, "Life-Styles: A Culture in Transition," in Maxine Glaz and Jeanne Stevenson Moessner, eds., *Women in Travail and Transition, A New Pastoral Care* (Minneapolis: Fortress Press, 1991), 179.

[14]Diane Stein, *Casting the Circle: A Women's Book of Ritual* (Freedom, Calif.: The Crossing Press, 1990), 178.

[15]Mary Cullen Dean, "Woman's Body: Spiritual Needs and Theological Presence," in *Women in Travail and Transition*, 86.

[16]Naomi Wolf, *The Beauty Myth*.

[17]Barbara G. Walker, *The Crone, Women of Age, Wisdom and Power* (San Francisco: Harper & Row, Publishers, 1985), 171–78.

[18]Hallie Iglehart, *Woman Spirit: A Guide to Women's Wisdom* (San Francisco: Harper & Row, 1983).

9
Men at Midlife

William O. Roberts

THE MALE MIDLIFE PASSAGE

It was Christmas week. Life felt more stable than it had in many years. I had left my work and my role as a minister two Christmases ago, and now I was surprisingly settled and fulfilled in a new career. I had separated from my wife and children four years ago, and now I was part of the family again. The boys were home from college. We were at a video store looking for a movie that we could watch as a family when I saw one called *Middle Aged Crazy.*

When no one was looking, I rented it. When no one was home, I watched it. The story was so familiar as to be hackneyed. It begins at a birthday party, a fortieth birthday party for a man who has everything—a beautiful wife (played by many a man's fantasy woman, Ann-Margret) who has just arrived at her sexual maturity and has "multiple bingos" every time they make love, a highly lucrative career as an architect, a gracious home, two healthy parents, a seemingly well-adjusted son, a fine complement of friends, and a nagging uneasiness that somehow there is something missing.

As the story unfolds, his father dies, his well-adjusted son cannot adjust to college and returns home with a pregnant girlfriend, his wife decides to play bingo with a young policeman, and he goes through what is called his midlife crisis.

The nagging uneasiness is probed to full-bloom neurosis by a question from his sister as they drive to their father's funeral. "You still driving this same old car?" (He rightly hears that as "You still living this same old life?") Within days he is at the new car dealer trying to buy a new life for himself.

He trades in his old Oldsmobile for a Porsche, replaces his wing tips and three-piece suits with cowboy boots and a metallic blue shirt, compromises his career by missing appointments with his biggest client and shucking his reputation for reliability and thoroughness, and, of course, he spies the girl of his dreams and pursues her to her bedroom. In this case, she is a Dallas Cowboy Cheerleader who just happens to be an interior decorator who would do anything to have a meaningful relationship with a successful architect who can help her with her career. (True to form, her own life journey has little to do with intimacy and sex, which seem to be easy for her, but rather with identity and making a name for herself.)

The story ends happily but tragically. It is happy, I guess, in that by the closing scene he is "back to his old self," which means back in his hot tub with

Ann-Margret. It's tragic in that the poor man has no idea what happened to him. He, like so many of us, is simply embarrassed to be Middle-Aged Crazy.

This tragedy, that so many men never know why they become crazy at midlife, should be addressed by the church. There is a body of literature on adult development. There are numerous biblical precedents of men passing through midlife. And there is a possibility that the church could create a rite of passage to assist midlife men.

This chapter is offered in the hope that the church will seize that opportunity. In the first section I will summarize the major developmental tasks—soul tasks—of men in midlife. In the second section I will make suggestions on creating a rite of passage for men at midlife.

Dan Levinson and Gail Sheehy

In 1978 Daniel Levinson and four colleagues at Yale published *Seasons of a Man's Life*, the result of a ten-year in-depth study of forty men at midlife. Their work was preceded in 1974 by Gail Sheehy's best-seller *Passages: Predictable Crises of Adult Life*, which relied heavily on Levinson's work.

At the center of Levinson's thought is the concept of the individual life structure. "The concept of life structure—the basic pattern or design of a person's life at a given time—gives us a way of looking at the engagements of the individual in society. It requires us to consider both self and world, and the relationships between them."[1]

An individual life structure can have various components—occupation, marriage and family, friendships and peer relationships, ethnic identity, religious affiliation, hobbies and avocational pursuits, personal values, fantasies, character traits, and so on. But, Levinson found "...that occupation and marriage-family are usually the most central components...Work and family are universal features of human life."[2] This reminds us of that classic comment from Sigmund Freud. When he was asked what he thought a normal person should be able to do well, Freud is reported to have said: *Lieben und arbeiten* (to love and to work).

Levinson observed that life structures shift and change in a predictable manner. There are stable (structure-building) periods and there are transitional periods.

> The basic task of every stable period is to build a life structure. The way people do this is through making certain key choices, usually relating to career, marriage, family and the like. They then form a life structure around these choices and pursue goals and values within this structure....The primary tasks of these transitional periods are to question and reappraise the existing structure, 'to explore possibilities for change in self and world, and to move toward commitment to the crucial choices that form the basis for a new life structure in the ensuing stable period.'[3]

Levinson said these transitional periods were times of crisis. He also argued that there were *predictable* crises in adult life, to use Sheehy's phrase, or *seasons* of a man's life, to use his. The seasons can be graphically portrayed as follows:[4]

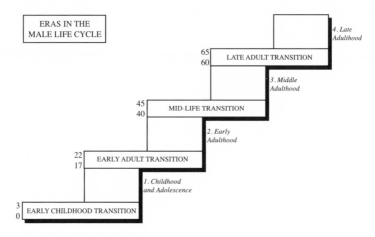

Even as Levinson offers this model, he does not mean to suggest this template must be followed by every man. Each life must discover its own variations on this theme.

Although Levinson's book is thoroughly clinical and seems to avoid making explicit value judgments of its data, it implies that the midlife crisis is not only predictable, but even necessary and can be a valuable part of men's development. His feeling on this is made explicit in an interview with Gail Sheehy. "If a man goes through a relatively bland period when midlife transition is going on, it will limit his growth. Many men who don't have a crisis at 40 become weighted and lose the vitality they need to continue development in the rest of the adult stages."[5]

Erik Erikson and Variations of His Eight Ages of Man

In 1950 Erik Erikson, then a professor at Harvard, published his first book, entitled *Childhood and Society*. The book included an essay on the "Eight Ages of Man" which identifies eight developmental stages, each with its own psychosocial tasks.

Basic Trust vs. Mistrust	Birth to One Year
Autonomy vs. Shame, Doubt	1–6
Initiative vs. Guilt	6–10
Industry vs. Inferiority	10–14
Identity vs. Role Confusion	Adolescence: 14–20
Intimacy vs. Isolation	Early Adulthood: 20–40
Generativity vs. Stagnation	Middle Adulthood: 40–65
Ego Integrity vs. Despair	Later Adulthood: 65+

Erikson, in a remarkably pithy way, explains each of these eight ages. Since our focus is on adult development, I will limit myself to the last four stages with a brief quote from Erikson followed by a comment of my own.

> *Identity.* "The sense of ego identity…is the accrued confidence that the inner sameness and continuity prepared in the past are matched by the sameness and continuity of one's meaning for others."[6] Identity is "a unity of personality now felt by the individual and recognized by others as having a consistency in time…a sense of inner self-sameness and continuity."[7]

The individual and society negotiate identity. The individual, by words and actions, says, "This is who I am…" If he is successful in establishing his identity, he will hear deep within himself, society's affirmation, "Yes, that is who you are." The better one does at establishing an identity, the more likely he will become the victim of his success and eventually feel himself unduly restricted by the very identity he has worked so hard to achieve.

> *Intimacy.* "Intimacy (is) the capacity to commit himself to concrete affiliations and partnerships and to develop the ethical strength to abide by such commitments, even though they may call for significant sacrifices and compromises."[8] True intimacy, to Erikson, involves genitality.[9]

My own understanding of intimacy derives from the word's etymology. The Latin word *intimatus* means inmost or innermost, as in "Thou knowest the innermost secrets of my heart." I do not believe intimacy necessarily involves genitality. On the contrary, I feel that the connection of intimacy with genital sexuality is what keeps so many men from experiencing true intimacy with other men or with women. We do not wish to risk genital involvement. But we do want to know and to be known at the level of the innermost secrets of our hearts.

> *Generativity.* "Generativity…is primarily the concern in establishing and guiding the next generation, although there are individuals who, through misfortune or because of special and genuine gifts in other directions, do not apply this drive to their own offspring."[10]

> *Ego Integrity.* "This state of mind…is the ego's accrued assurance of its proclivity for order and meaning. It is a post-narcissistic love of the human ego—not of the self—as an experience which conveys some world order and spiritual sense, no matter how dearly paid for. It is the acceptance of one's one and only life cycle as something that had to be and that, by necessity, permitted of no substitutions…Although aware of the relativity of all the various lifestyles which have given meaning to human striving, the possessor of integrity is ready to defend the dignity of his own life-style against all physical and economic threats…In such final consolidation, death loses its sting."[11]

This final age is entered when one is 65. I have not yet reached that age, but I still feel that Erikson does not state the psychosocial task in sufficient depth or breadth. Death can lose its sting, not only because one can accept his life, but also because he is ready "to meet his Maker." This is a spiritual task, a soul-task, better, though still inadequately, expressed by the Jungian notion of encounter with the Self.

Erikson's schema has proven exceedingly helpful to men, but many women have expressed their feeling that it applies less well to women, an assessment with which I agree. In fact, having used Erikson's "Eight Ages" with men and women for more than twenty years, I am persuaded that it makes sense to alter the sequence of the final four stages: (for most males) identity (and intimacy), generativity, intimacy, and ego integrity; (for most women) intimacy (and identity), generativity, identity, and ego integrity. This change in sequence is important and has a major impact on what happens to men and women in midlife.

In adolescence boys, as they become men, are primarily concerned about identity and only secondarily about intimacy. For girls becoming women, the reverse is true. Their primary concern is intimacy, a deep connection with other human beings, perhaps; their secondary concern is negotiating an identity, making a name for themselves.

Then, in early adulthood, men and women meet together to share the tasks related to generativity—child bearing and rearing, creating a home, making money, becoming an economic unit.

As midlife sets in, men and women go back to the secondary task of adolescence. Women rightly want to be taken seriously on their own, not as someone's mother or spouse. If not yet accomplished, they are determined to establish an identity. At this time in our culture's history, women have the women's movement, which encourages them in their quest. Many men, and I count myself as one of them, are sufficiently feminist in our inclinations to want to help our sisters, including our wives, to find their own distinctive and distinguished identities.

Men in the meantime are trying to deal with the old adolescent task of establishing intimacy. Most of us do not know how to do it. The issue is confused in our minds with sexuality and homosexuality and genitality and marital fidelity. And there is only the beginning of a men's movement to encourage us in *our* quest. Few women, and rarely our wives, can be expected to encourage us in our search for intimacy.

Too often, there is a great deal of hostility between men and women in midlife, perhaps because, as adolescent boys and girls, we had different priorities.

Carl Gustav Jung and the Jungians

Jung is so important to my thinking that much of what he has said will shape the last section of this chapter in which I try to tell my own tale as I have come to understand it. In this section, I will give a brief summary of his thought and indicate his strong feeling that a midlife crisis of some sort is a necessary prerequisite for vitality in the second half of life. But before I do that, I want to tell you about Jung's own midlife journey.

Almost everyone knows that Jung was a Swiss psychiatrist whose ways of thinking about the unconscious have greatly influenced Western thought in the last part of this century. Few, however, know that Carl Gustav Jung suffered a midlife crisis that was of the magnitude of Job's. Jung's biographers generally date the onset of the crisis during 1912 and see it lasting for ten years.

In order to understand what occurred, let us look first at the external manifestation of the inner turmoil by going back to 1911. Jung was 36 years old. He was happily married to Emma Jung, daughter of a wealthy industrialist. They had one child. Jung was professionally established with a flourishing private practice. He was lecturer at the University of Zurich, President of the International Psychoanalytic Association, and heir apparent to Sigmund Freud himself. In short, it looked, in 1911, as if Carl Gustav Jung had it all.[12]

Within a few years all those signs of success would be gone. The stable life structure he had worked so hard and so effectively to create in the first half of his life would be shattered. Specifically: in 1912 he wrote a paper that took issue with Freud, causing that central relationship to become strained and then broken; he lost his capacity for professional work, cutting his private practice back to the bare minimum and resigning his position at the University of Zurich; he fell in love with one of his patients, the then twenty-three-year-old Antonia Wolf. Needless to say, this relationship put severe pressure on his previously stable marriage, especially when he insisted on bringing his lover to Sunday dinner. Even though incredibly stressed, the marriage did not break. Emma and Carl Jung were married "until death did them part," and the relationship with Toni Wolf lasted for more than fifty years.

Those were some of the external signs that things were falling apart. What was far more important for Jung, however, were the internal dynamics. As the shell that had provided shape and meaning for his life cracked, the unconscious was loosed upon him with unbelievable fury. He experienced immense self-doubt as he began to question the most fundamental values to which he had given his life. A terrifying encounter with what he came to call the Shadow—the dark, hidden side of the psyche, which he found filled with images of death and corpses and demons of all sorts—scared him to the core, made him become more private, fearing that if he shared any of his experiences, he would be misinterpreted and looked upon as insane. In addition, as if the above were not enough to overwhelm him, he experienced an utterly confusing relationship with what he came to call the *Anima*. No doubt this relationship was activated and shaped by his affair with Toni Wolf, whom he called his *soror mystica* (soul sister), but it was clear that his Anima was more than and different from Toni Wolf, even though she was in some fashion a manifestation of it.

Through all this turmoil, Jung battled to hold the center. "My enduring these storms was a question of brute strength," he wrote, but he became persuaded that he was driven to survive "these assaults of the unconscious," because he was "obeying a higher will."[13] He had a mission. "I was committing myself to a dangerous enterprise not for myself alone, but for the sake of my patients . . . It was then that I ceased to belong to myself alone, for there were things in the images which concerned not only myself but many others also . . . I myself had to undergo the original experience, and then try to plant the results of my experience in the soil of reality."[14]

What did Jung's great midlife struggle yield to those of us for whom he believed he was suffering? As his writings have indicated, it was a greater knowledge of the Persona, the Shadow, and the Anima, all of which we are likely to encounter in our own midlife passages. But far more important, Jung set out the task for the second half of life, namely, to establish a dialogue between the ego and the Self. Perhaps a quote from one of his most articulate disciples will help explain.

> There is in the unconscious a transpersonal center of latent consciousness and obscure intentionality. The discovery of this center, which Jung called the Self, is like the discovery of extraterrestrial intelligence. Man is now no longer alone in the psyche and in the cosmos. The vicissitudes of life take on new and enlarged meaning. Dreams, fantasies, illness, accident and coincidence become potential messages from the unseen Partner with whom we share our life.[15]

Jung argued that in order to realize the goal of establishing a dialogue with the Self, one's ego, as the center of consciousness, and one's Self, as the center of the psychic totality (both conscious and unconscious), must serve one another. Of course, the Self can inform the ego, constantly providing more material from the unconscious with which to make conscious life more comprehensible and secure. It is also true that the ego can serve the Self.

Robert Bly, to whom we will turn in a moment, says it more simply. "Our work, then, as men and women is not only to free ourselves from family cages and collective mind-sets, but to release transcendent beings from imprisonment and trance."[16]

Before I leave Jung, I want to share the best summary of Jung's understanding of the midlife tasks. The summary comes from Murray Stein's excellent book *In Midlife*. Stein is a Presbyterian minister and a Jungian analyst.

> What Jung describes is the breakdown of the *persona*, a psychological structure that is the approximate equivalent of what Erik Erikson calls the psychosocial *identity*, accompanied by the release of two hitherto repressed and otherwise unconscious elements of the personality: the rejected and the inferior persons one has always fought becoming (the *shadow*), and behind that the contra sexual "other" whose power one has always, for good reason, denied and evaded (the *animus* for a woman, the *anima* for a man).

The threat created by this degree of intense internal restructuring, Jung observed, can produce a defensive "reconstitution of the persona," a retrenchment and retreat into former patterns of identity and their defenses. On the other hand, this era of change can create movement into depth, into unknown and threatening psychological territory. A prolonged psychological journey of this kind, Jung felt, could lead a person to discover the core of his being, the Self. This discovery of the Self, and the gradual stabilization of its felt presence and guidance within conscious life, would become the foundation for a new experience of identity and integrity based on an internal center, the Self, rather than rooted in externals...What one can gain from going all the way *through* the midlife transition, then, is a sense of an internal non-egoistic Self and the feeling of integrity and wholeness that results from living in conscious contact with it...The midlife transition and crisis, then, involve making this crucial shift from a persona-orientation to a Self-orientation.[17]

This quote from Murray Stein serves as such a fine summary of the tasks of midlife that I want to underscore its most salient points:

(1) The breakdown of the Persona is accompanied by the release of two hitherto repressed and otherwise unconscious elements of the personality—the Shadow and the Anima.

(2) The threat created by this degree of internal restructuring can, and I would add, often does, create a defensive "reconstitution of the Persona." So often men become terrified by their Anima and their Shadow and beat a hasty retreat back to the old structures. They become what I call "the conspicuously virtuous" and "the zealously monogamous," constantly drawing attention to their reformed state.

(3) But those courageous souls who do not retreat from the threat of the Shadow or the Anima, who stay with the "prolonged psychological journey," could be led to discover the core of their being—the Self.

(4) The midlife transition and crisis, then, involves making this crucial shift from a Persona-orientation to a Self-orientation.

Robert Bly and Gatherings of Men

Robert Bly is a poet, storyteller, translator, and the prime mover of the men's movement. He is also a phenomenon of our times. His book *Iron John* was a best-seller. His PBS specials with Bill Moyers have been a source of courage and inspiration to men who yearn to feel comfortable about their maleness.

Bly is clearly versed in Jungian thought. His own retelling of a nineteenth-century Grimm Brothers' story called "Iron Hans" or "Iron John" has a definite Jungian slant to it, but his lyrical poetic style makes the midlife task sound much more appealing. He talks about the Loss of the Golden Ball (the breakdown of the persona), Taking the Road of Ashes (the encounter with the shadow), the Woman with the Golden Hair, and Delicious Confusion (in place of that abstraction, the Anima). Because Bly does use such compelling imagery, I will make extensive use of him shortly when I attempt to synthesize Levinson, Erikson, and Jung. But I want to cite two other contributions that come from Robert Bly—his sensitivity to ritual and his courage in providing *communitas* for men by gathering them into groups.

When Bly talks about the midlife journey he uses a powerful image. "Every man and every woman on this planet is on the road from the Law to the Legends.....The Legends stand for the moist, the swampish, the wild, the untamed. The Legends are watery when compared with the dryness of the Law. It takes twenty years to understand the Laws, and then a whole lifetime to get from there to the Legends."[18]

To get from one state of existence, that of the Laws, to something so radically different as that of the Legends, we need to pass through some type of transformation. "Change or transformation (of this magnitude) can happen only when a man or a woman is in ritual space…Human beings enter and leave ritual space over a ceremonial threshold, or *'limen'*: Such ritual space can also be called *liminal* space…Entering, one first needs to step over a threshold, by some sort of ceremony; and second, the space itself needs to be 'heated.' A man or woman remains inside this heated space…for a relatively brief time, and then returns to ordinary consciousness, to one's own sloppiness or dullness."[19]

I wrote about this liminal condition fifteen years ago. Allow me to quote my first book:

> We begin a journey, a passage. We cross a threshold, enter a state of liminality. (The word *liminality* is derived from the Latin word *limen,* which means threshold.) Once in this liminal state, we can no longer be identified in terms of our past involvements and projects; we have passed out of the familiar, with its known points of reference and safety. We are at sea with ourselves and our world.
>
> This is a time of crisis. The etymology of the word takes us back to the Greek work *krises,* which means decision. The dictionary definition tells us that crisis "is a stage in a sequence of events at which the trend of all future events, especially for better or worse, is determined." The Chinese word for crisis combines two symbols. If taken alone, the one symbol means opportunity; the other, danger.
>
> Life's passages are times of decisive change, with possibilities for better and for worse. They are times of great opportunity—and of great danger.[20]

This talk of danger and opportunity brings me to Robert Bly's greatest contribution to our search for a rite of passage for men at midlife. The dangers are too great and the opportunities too full of promise to risk this journey alone.

Yet many men are embarrassed by what their wives and their children and their parents and their peers might think of them. Many men, most men, go through the perilous journey of midlife alone. Alone.

Consider this tale out of my own life's journey. I had a friend. His name was Jon. We went to college together and toured Mexico twice with our college choir. And then my friend went off and made a name for himself, quite a name. Even though he was an Anglo-American, Jon learned to sing the music of South India. Once I was told by someone who did not know of my friendship with Jon that he was the Pavarotti of Indian music. That's quite a name. Or to say it another way, that's a powerful persona.

However, once when Jon came back from a concert tour in India, when he was once again lauded, there was a little crack in the shell of that persona. He told me about it on a visit to our home on Cape Cod, and that night he did not sleep well. In fact, he did not sleep at all. And he did not sleep well in the weeks and months that followed, because he had begun the journey of midlife. For him it would be a demanding journey.

He used to call me, sometimes very late at night, and ask if he could come over to talk. He did talk, but he also yelled and screamed, ranted and raved, and I, because I was his brother, would do my best to calm him.

When he settled down, he then began to thank me, profusely, for being with him. I would say, "Don't thank me, Jon. My turn's coming, and when it comes, promise me that you'll be there for me, because you're going through it before me." Jon would promise, and I know he would have been there had he not been killed by a drunk driver a year later.

I am certain that his death contributed to the onset of my midlife crisis. But even more significantly, I am sure that the loss of this friend, who had already made the journey, made my passage much more perilous. Somehow, when the nights came, there were no men with whom to talk. There seemed to be women, single women, all the time. There were married men whom I saw over lunch, but by evening those men were home with their wives and children. I was alone.

Robert Bly has done us all a great service by creating communities of men, by reminding us of the need for ritual, and by writing poems and telling tales that help men find their way from the Laws to the Legends, from the stable structures they create for themselves in the first half of life, through the chaos of midlife, to the appropriate purposes for the second half of life.

Synthesis: The Four Soul-Tasks

Midlife happens. Not in the same exact way and certainly not with the same intensity for everybody. Yet I believe it happens even to those persons who, sadly, refuse to give it conscious attention. To underscore the sadness of this, I share a comment from Murray Stein.

For years I have wondered what it takes to become "psychological." What brings a person to attend the psyche, to respect its force, and to honor its gifts?…One way, I have concluded, is through psychological "crisis." When you are thrown into a psychological emergency, you cannot avoid seeing the soul at work. When things are going by plan, the soul sleeps, its realm as faded and vague as moon and stars in the brightness of the sun…But in the dark night of psychological crisis, when the light of day is eclipsed, the figures of the psyche stand out and assume another magnitude…

By the time that midlife comes, a person has usually settled into familiar psychological patterns and is ensconced in work and family. And then, suddenly, a crisis; you wake up one day and you are unexpectedly out of gas; the atmosphere of personal ownership stinks; the sweet milk of achievement is sour; the old patterns of coping and acting pinch your feet. The ability to prize your favorite objects…has been stolen, and you are left wondering what happened.[21]

I consider midlife to be a time when persons are going through a fundamental shift in their alignment with life and with the world, and this shift has psychological and religious meaning beyond the interpersonal and social dimensions. Midlife is a crisis of the spirit. In this crisis, old selves are lost and new ones come into being.[22]

The opportunity for growth at midlife comes knocking in many different ways. Sometimes you hear the tapping from the outside, from events exterior to you and beyond your control—the death of a child or a parent, divorce, job termination or career collapse. Or perhaps less dramatic but equally perplexing changes—your children leave home, your wife strikes out on her own career quest and search for identity, you lose your hair, or your physical stamina, or that sense that you are still young and vital. Or perhaps the strange call to midlife opportunity starts knocking deep within you—unexplained moodiness, sleeplessness, lethargy, anxiety, fear or denial of death. Sometimes, of course, probably most times, it is a combination of many of these knocks.

In my own case it was a combination. The earliest knockings were so gentle that they were easy to ignore, rationalize away, or project onto someone else. But the knocks kept getting stronger, and I became more confused and restless. I finally felt myself ready to begin this journey of midlife about which I had heard so much.

I spent a lot of time wondering through those early sleepless nights. I yearned for sleep, but I still resisted drugs (sleeping pills) or anything else that would take me away from what I called "my night work."

Just as I resolved to get some real help by beginning therapy I had a dream. It is an unusual dream in that it is the only dream I have ever recorded that did not include people. It was nothing but arrows (forces) interacting with one another.

Somehow two, then four, arrows present themselves. The arrows are in exact counterpoint to one another like this.

The system is static. There is no movement. But then a small arrow enters the system and gently nudges one arrow slightly off center, which then puts pressure on the next arrow, which does likewise to the rest. The whole system begins to move. Slowly at first, but it keeps going faster and faster.

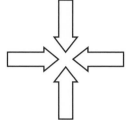

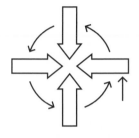

At that time I did not know that four is often seen as the number representing wholeness. Nor did I know that I would eventually be writing about the four soul-tasks of midlife, or what I had done with that gentle nudge of a static system, or that one can grow by going around in circles (Jung called it *circulatio*).

Several years later, as my life was spinning out of control, I had a follow-up dream to "the Four Arrows." In this one, I was a young boy walking with an older man to a square of some old Mexican Indian village. He told me, "There is a great waterfall in the center of the square. It has all the energy in the world. It gives off a spray and a great deal of noise. We will be in a fog. You will not be able to see me, except dimly through the fog, and you will not be able to hear me. For that matter you will not be able to hear yourself think. But if you can get all the way around the square and back to this road, all the energy of the waterfall will be yours."

And then he went on. "There are four roads that enter the square, which, you will soon see, is really more of a circle. It would be best if you started out to your right. But you may find that you have to go against the traffic. No matter what, I will be with you, but you will not see me or hear me."

I am staggered by the wisdom of that dream. I used to record my dreams without having any idea what they might mean. Now, years later, looking at life from a very different perspective, I believe I can see the meaning more clearly. This is how I see it. (See illustration at top of page 148.)

You enter this ancient town on the same road which you will take when you leave. There is someone bringing you down the road, someone who is older and wiser than you. There is a great, dynamic energy here. There are three roads that are lost in the fog and the din. It would be best (that is to say, safest, most helpful) to begin with the road to your right and learn its lessons before moving to the others, but you cannot control the sequence. You may have to go against the traffic. You will not be alone.

For the rest of this chapter, I will walk with you around the square/circle, which is actually a mandala, the ancient symbol of wholeness. I will begin in

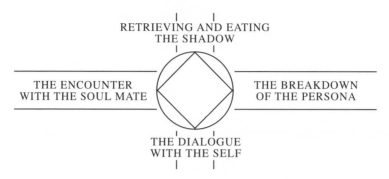

RETRIEVING AND EATING
THE SHADOW

THE ENCOUNTER
WITH THE SOUL MATE

THE BREAKDOWN
OF THE PERSONA

THE DIALOGUE
WITH THE SELF

the way I now wish I could have begun, with the road that teaches us about our Individual Life Structure, our Identity, our Persona.

The First Soul-Task: The Breakdown of the Persona

In midlife, we find ourselves at odds with ourselves. Somehow we do not fit anymore. We have spent a lot of time and energy negotiating a place with our society. Levinson calls that our Individual Life Structure. Erikson calls it our Identity. Jung calls it our Persona. I often call it our lobster shell.

Again and again the lobster sheds its shell in order to grow.

In the early years this can happen several times a year. When the lobster becomes an adult, it happens less frequently. But if the process ever stops, the lobster not only ceases to grow; it ceases to live.

Any of us who has ever chosen a lobster for dinner knows that its identity is expressed through that hard exterior shell. So to live without that shell involves a complete loss of identity. But that is not all. To live without that shell involves a frightening loss of security. The lobster without its shell is in the midst of a period of incalculable risks.

I use this image when I work with persons going through career transitions, which generally means loss of job and concomitant loss of self-worth, self-acceptance, and self-definition. I never make light of those losses, but I try to help them see that they really are free to grow without that shell.

In early adulthood our task is to develop an identity. We take on a social role, or more correctly, a combination of complementary social roles. We might be a struggling writer or musician, banker, doctor, minister, professor, plumber, realtor, businessman. In addition we can become father, husband, and citizen. Jung maintained that all those social roles or masks that we wear to play our various parts in the drama of life are aspects of the collective psyche. On one hand they are social identities, and on the other they are ideal images. A particular person is not being described by them; no one doctor or father or banker is being distinguished from any other.[23]

Paradoxically, these social roles or personae give us a frame of reference in which to grow, but they also limit our growth. In early adulthood we are more aware of the positive aspects of our identity. In midlife we become aware of the restrictive aspects. It is important to know two things about this paradox:

1. Some personae are more restrictive than others. The more distinctive the role and more significant the role in the social scheme of things, the more likely that role will eventually restrict growth.

2. This is true especially if you fill the role well. This is crucial. The more successful you are at being this being you have "chosen" to be, the more likely you are to build up a shell that is so restrictive that you must break it…but so thick that you cannot.

I know some of this struggle out of my own life. I was a minister for more than twenty years. Even though I always struggled with the role (never wore a collar, never was called Reverend or Pastor or anything except Bill), I worked hard and genuinely cared about people. Slowly but very surely over twenty years my success created a shell, an identity, I just could not break. That was a terrible shell. But I loved it. I *needed* it to keep my sanity—or, at least, my respectability. Even as the chaos of my midlife journey was tearing me apart, I could still put on my role, go to work, listen to people, preach the Word, administer the sacraments, and pretend to know what was happening. No one seemed to complain.

However, some strange voice within me did complain in a major way. The voice spoke through a dream.

> I have been charged with some crime. I am in a white-tiled room, deep underground. Someone comes in to prepare me for my death. He seems very nice. He asks me a few questions about what happened. I answer. He then says that there is no reason for me to die, because I have been unjustly charged. "You should just file a countersuit." He takes me out to see a judge. It is in a town square where the judge has his place. Suddenly I protest, "No. That's not fair. Melissa (my wife) is not the reason I am in prison." But then they will not release me.

That dream came to me at a time when I was separated from my wife and family and had thrown myself all the more fully into my work at the church. I chanced to share the dream with a friend. She responded with a few words, "The dream speaks the truth. Melissa is not the reason you are in prison. Your prison is your job."

She was right. Going all the way back to Freud's comment about what one had to do to live a successful life—love and work—well, when I had trouble with my love life, I threw myself into my work life. It became a veritable prison. When I dared to leave it, I was astounded at how thoroughly the chains not only held me, but had actually worked their way into the fibre of my being so that I couldn't even see them. I had created such a persona that people in both church and community would not let me abandon it. They refused to believe that I would leave. They pleaded. They bargained. They got angry with me. In some perverse way, I needed it all. I needed them to tell me that I was trusted, because I knew I was not worthy of that trust. I needed them to tell me that I was indispensable, because I feared I was worthless. I needed them to keep on believing in that nice fit between Bill Roberts and his shell, because without that shell, I would be nothing. The shell protected me from my own worst fears.

The Second Soul-Task: Retrieving and Eating the Shadow

Robert Bly explains our relationship to the Shadow in the best way that I know.

> When a person moves into the black, that process amounts to bringing all the shadow material, which has been for years projected out there on the faces of bad men and women, communists, witches, and tyrants, back inside. That process could be called retrieving and eating the shadow.[24]

For any of a number of reasons, including that the shell of the Persona cracks, shadow material, all that stuff we have repressed over all those years since birth—and before—is there to be dealt with. We drop lower and lower, become baser and baser, darker and darker, until we are one with our own Black Hole, barely alive.

One night I walked with another old college friend. He had left his life—wife, family, job, identity. He had gone through all that effort to project his dark stuff onto others. He was now in that lifeless state that precedes new life. We walked for a long time, a very long time, without speaking. It was very quiet and very dark. Then we walked under a street light and he broke the silence. "See my shadow?" he asked. And I could see it, very faintly through the fallen leaves. "That's proof that I'm still alive. But it's the only proof I have."

Too many men run from the dark silence of the Shadow. They put all their energies into projecting the contents of it onto others, "bad men and women, communists, witches, and tyrants," as Robert Bly says, or good men and women, friends, wives, and colleagues. It is natural to project, but it surely would help if we knew what was going on.

> Projection is a psychic mechanism that occurs whenever a vital aspect of our personality of which we are unaware is activated. When something is projected, we see it outside of us, as though it belongs to someone else and has nothing to do with us. Projection is an unconscious mechanism. We do not decide to project something, it happens automatically. If we decided to project something it would be conscious to us that then, precisely because it is conscious to us, it could

not be projected. Only unconscious contents are projected; once something has become conscious, projection ceases.[25]

Projection is not necessarily a bad thing. When we project onto something we can see it. My friend projected his shadow on the ground and then saw it. We project an unaccepted part of ourselves onto another, and, if we are wise enough to realize that the projection comes from us, not the other (and if the other does not accept the projection—an unhealthy psychological process known as projection identification), then we just might know ourselves better through our projections.

Jesus warned about the negative aspects of projection. "Judge not that you be not judged." Another way of saying it: "When you point an accusing finger at another, three fingers are pointing back at you." We need to use projection not to blame or hurt another, but to know ourselves, especially those unacceptable parts of ourselves that are lost in the darkness. "Retrieve and eat the shadow."

My own midlife passage involved a lot of wrestling with the Shadow. Seeing it, first through the glass darkly, then more clearly, then retrieving it and eating it. I will never forget the day I ate more Shadow than I could handle. I gagged, but I will remember the experience forever.

It was a holiday. I was very much alone. Holidays are awful times if you are alone and do not wish to be: awful and also awesome. In that sense, holidays can actually be holy days.

On this particular holy day, when I could not stand my loneliness any longer, I called a friend and asked if I might come by. It was inconvenient. To be honest, I had depended on this friend through so much sadness that it had reached the point at which my requests to get together always seemed like an inconvenience. However, after checking with his wife and family, he realized that he could spare about ten minutes later in the afternoon. I went. We walked. He talked. He had heard enough of my melancholy that he really did not want to hear any more. He tried his best to humor me for these few minutes that we had together.

"We gotta paint lines on our parking lot." (My friend is a psychotherapist.) "We've noticed that our patients are parking according to their diagnoses: Schizophrenics take up two spaces; obsessives park so close to the next car they can't open the door; paranoids always back in."

As he continued to talk, I asked, "What's my diagnosis?"

"You don't want to know."

"No, I really do want to know."

"Not now."

"C'mon, you're supposed to be my friend. Tell me the truth."

"O.K....You're narcissistic."

"What does that mean...in my case?"

"Narcissists spend their lives trying to get people to mirror back approval.

They will do anything to get approval, even adoration. The good ones can actually construct whole environments that will feed them approval. (And I thought of my relationship with the congregation.) Narcissists have thousands of tentacles that can pick up signals from their worlds. And on each tentacle, thousands of sensors. And all these sensors are constantly working to pick up signs of approval."

"What do you do to cure narcissism?"

"I don't think you can finally cure it. It comes from a wound, probably very early in life. You just have to know that you have that wound and become conscious of how you try to fill the wound with mirrored approval. Try to live on the edge of the wound rather than going into it all the time. Oh by the way, I know about this because we share this diagnosis. I'm a narcissist, too."

"And what did you do?"

"Well, I went to this counselor in Hartford. He said a few things that cut right to the core of me. He was very helpful."

Within a day I called that counselor, made an appointment, checked out books on narcissism, and began what I imagine will be a lifelong struggle to understand another aspect of my self. It is not easy or pleasant, but it is important. After a certain period of time "eating and retrieving the Shadow," which means eating large quantities of "humble pie," I actually felt as if I had eaten enough for a while. It was a gentle dream that told me I had worked long enough.

There were bears. Lots of bears. Big, powerful black bears. And a few rather feeble white bears. The black bears could clobber the white bears and they seemed to take sadistic pleasure in doing just that. Finally, because they were exhausted and it was winter, all the bears lay down to sleep. When they woke up, they were a panda.

The Third Soul-Task: The Encounter with the Soul Mate

We now move three quarters of the way around our square/circle, the mandala, and come face-to-face with the most troublesome and mysterious aspect of the midlife passage—the Anima.

For many men this is the only part of the midlife passage they will ever know. Somehow the Anima gets activated within their souls, and immediately it is projected out onto women. Often the negative aspects of the feminine are projected onto the wife; the positive, onto the dream woman. Without having any idea what is going on inside him, the man resolves to solve the problem with divorce of one and marriage to the other.

So common is this at midlife that most people think it is the whole story. Talk shows dedicate hours to "Surviving Your Husband's Midlife Crisis," and everyone seems to know that they are really talking about his midlife affair.

The situation is not as simple as that. And every time you see it being treated at that simplistic level, start asking questions, such as:

What happens when we fall in love?

Why are some men attracted to certain women and not others?

Why does it not last?

What is the relationship between love and marriage?

What is the Anima anyway?

Is the Anima a flesh and blood woman? Or just a figment of the imagination? Or both?

Why does this Anima thing, whatever it is, get activated at midlife?

And can anything good come from the encounter with one's soul mate?

I know the questions better than I know the answers, but I am going to try to deal with them, using my own terms and experience as well as Robert Bly's and Carl Gustav Jung's.

The word Anima comes from the Latin word *anima* (soul) or *animare* (to animate, to enliven, to bring to life). Its masculine form is animus. According to Jung, a man has an Anima while a woman has an Animus. "Anima and Animus remain somewhat borderline concepts, verifiable in experience, useful in therapy, practical when we apply them to ourselves, but at the same time not capable of being precisely defined."[26]

It seems that a certain notion of the feminine is somehow pre-configured in our unconscious or soul. No one knows where these notions come from. Perhaps, says Bly, it is "some template in our genetic memory."[27] You can know that the Anima is activated when you see a woman who fits that template and you find yourself not being yourself, and saying, almost unconsciously, such phrases as:

I feel as if I've known her all my life.

If I were a woman, she's what I'd be like.

If only I could just touch her, I would feel wonderful.

If only I could hold her, I would have all that energy within me.

She reminds me so much of myself when I was beginning (my career).

She's perfect.

But maybe you do not say anything. Maybe you just discover more spring in your walk, more energy in your life, more volume in your laugh, more of a desire to be at those places where she is likely to 'e. Or maybe you are just nicer to your dog.

Probably now you are asking: "Is the Anima a flesh and blood woman?" The answer is YES and NO, but mostly NO. Robert Bly has a wonderful line on this. "Another mistake the Jungians make is to adopt that hideous word *Anima*, and to regard every good-looking woman you meet as your Anima...When a man says to a woman, 'You are my Anima,' she should quickly scream and run out of the room."[28]

Gail Sheehy and John Sanford, who has written one of the best books on the Anima, introduce two powerful and powerfully conflicting images in their respective presentations of the Anima. Sheehy talks about the *Testimonial Woman*.

Enter a figure who can offer the man a convenient lift out of his knot: the Testimonial Woman. Because the transition from the twenties to the thirties is often characterized by first infidelities, she is not hard to find. She is behind the secretary's desk, in the junior copywriter pool, in the casting call lineup, in the next lab coat. The root of the word *testimonial* is *testis* (plural *testes*). I read somewhere that when one aboriginal man bumped into another, he cupped the sexual parts of his tribesman in greeting. It was a "testimonial to manhood" and the original basis for the handshake. Whether or not it's true, the Testimonial Woman offers the same service: She fortifies his masculinity.[29]

If one is truly to understand the Anima, this modern Testimonial Woman must merge with a more ancient figure, the *Tutelary Spirit*:

> The shaman, the primitive healer or "medicine man," often has a tutelary spirit who assists him in the work of healing and teaches and instructs him in the healing arts. In the case of a male shaman, this tutelary spirit is female and acts like a spirit wife to him. In the case of the shamaness, the tutelary spirit is male, and is her spirit husband…A shaman spirit wife says to her shaman husband, "I love you, I have no husband now, you will be my husband and I shall be a wife unto you. I shall give you assistant spirits. You are to heal with their aid, and I shall teach and help you myself." The shaman comments, "She has been coming to me ever since, and I sleep with her as with my own wife."[30]

By now you should be sufficiently confused to ask some of those other questions. Why does this Anima get so animated when men are at midlife? What is the relationship of the Anima and the love she seems to inspire to marriage? And can anything good come from this encounter with the Anima?

Bly seems to address the first question—why does this happen at midlife?— by saying that we do not have enough consciousness before then to be affected by the encounter.[31] At midlife, however, as that which has been pushed into the unconscious begins to emerge, the Anima becomes more active, and as she does, men begin a life-wrenching experience of questioning the merits of their marriages.

Robert Johnson, in his helpful little book, *We: Understanding the Psychology of Romantic Love*, tries to sort out our midlife confusion by talking about the finite and the infinite.

> When a man tries to live his soul within infinite marriage with a woman, his soul puffs up and distorts his view of both wife and marriage. His soul keeps trying to pull the relationship toward the infinite, make it into an allegory of love, death, and paradise lost, convert this human marriage into a huge, sweeping, archetypal drama. That drama goes on inside him, anyway, all the time—at the fantasy level. If he could learn to keep it there, to see it as symbol and experience it as symbol, then he could live correctly with his soul. He could follow

his soul in his inner life toward the infinite but stay within the limits of the finite in his relationship with his wife.[32]

When we ask our wives to join our cosmic drama, we are always disappointed, because our wives must live their own dramas, not play a supporting role in ours. And in that disappointment, we often reach out to an Anima-Approximate, who, especially if she is younger and has not reached a level of psychological maturity, will become the Testimonial Woman to our Mentor and accept a supporting role in our drama. If we leave our marriage and enter a new marriage with an Anima-Approximate, we will eventually have to deal with that discrepancy between the finite and the infinite.

It would be my hope for men who divorce at midlife and remarry, that they would learn to deal with those two worlds and not let their partners accept supporting roles. It would be my hope for those who stay married that they would know the agony and the ecstasy of that finite relationship expressed most eloquently in a book called *Marriage: Dead or Alive*.

> The life-long dialectical encounter between two partners, the bond of man and woman until death, can be understood as a special path for discovering the soul, as a special form of individuation…a soteriological (salvation) pathway…
>
> For those who are gifted for the soteriological pathway of marriage, it like every such pathway, naturally offers not only trouble, work, and suffering, but the deepest kind of existential satisfaction. Dante did not get to Heaven without traversing Hell. And so also there seldom exist "happy marriages."[33]

We can live and love in a variety of ways, but we must remember that the finite and the infinite, though related, are not the same. We can fall in love. Even more, in falling in love we can experience "a fantasy of ultimate peace and wholeness," but we need to understand that fantasy as a statement of what we can achieve within ourselves. Robert Johnson, once again:

> But usually he will project his image of paradise on a woman, unconsciously asking her to fulfill it, to bring it into some physical actuality, to deliver it to him. In that instant he creates the illusion; he sees "through a glass, darkly." He no longer sees his external wife as she is, and he doesn't yet see his inner vision as the reality that it is. Both worlds are mingled; both worlds are dishonored.[34]

Truly creative people keep these worlds separate. The life story of Dante, one of the most creative men of all time, tells it best. His masterpiece, *The Divine Comedy*, begins with these words about the midlife passage:

> Midway upon the journey of our life
> I found myself within a forest dark,
> For the straightforward pathway had been lost.[35]

When Dante is in the dark wood of midlife, he is sustained by a most unusual relationship with a woman named Beatrice. He met her when he was nine years old. She was also nine. Instantly, he fell in love with her. (Note: when we fall in love with someone instantly, we can be sure that a projection is involved, for how could we love someone whom we do not yet know?) Here is how Dante, writing some years later, described his nine-year-old love:

> Her dress on that day was of a most noble color, a subdued and goodly crimson, girdled and adorned in such sort as suited with her very tender age. At that moment I say most truly that the spirit of life, which hath its dwelling in the secretest chamber of the heart, began to tremble so violently that the least pulses of my body shook therewith; and in trembling it said these words: *Edde Deus Fortior Me, Qui Veniens Dominabitur Mibi* (Being a deity stronger than I, who, coming, will rule me)…From that time forward Love quite governed my soul.'[36]

Nine years later, when Dante was eighteen, he saw her again. After his second meeting he wrote of her:

> It happened that the same wonderful lady appeared to me dressed all in pure white. And passing through a street, she turned her eyes thither where I stood sorely abashed: and by her unspeakable courtesy…she saluted me with so virtuous a bearing that I seemed then and there to behold the very limits of blessedness…I parted thence as one intoxicated.'[37]

That was the last time he actually saw his Beatrice. At age twenty-three she married someone else and died shortly thereafter. Dante also married someone else. But Beatrice was with him all through his life, and especially at midlife, when he was lost in that dark wood. He wandered for years through his Inferno. And then Beatrice reappeared. She was his guide through Paradise. She showed him the way to heaven.

The Final Soul-Task: Initiating the Dialogue with the Self

The final soul-task of midlife passage is to initiate the dialogue with the Self. The dialogue should continue throughout the rest of life and beyond. But for most, it begins in midlife.

In order to help us know how to begin this encounter, let me make sure that there is sufficient mystery and confusion about the nature of the Self. I do so with another guide from the Jungian tradition, Edwin Edinger:

> The term "Self" is used by Jung to designate the transpersonal center and totality of the psyche. It constitutes the greater, objective personality, whereas the ego is the lesser, subjective personality. Empirically the Self cannot be distinguished from the God-image. Encounter with it is a *mysterium tremendum.*[38]

As noted earlier, Edinger emphasizes that while encountering the Self results in the ego's defeat, "light is born from the darkness. One meets the 'Immortal One' who wounds and heals…"[39]

Finally, I will share two moments from my own journey. The first has to do with my deep fear, once I began to know just a bit about my Shadow, that I would be found out and condemned by this all-powerful Self/God/Christ. I was surprisingly worried about this, when I happened to sit in on a presentation by a friend on a Jungian way of reading the Gospels. He was talking about the story of Zacchaeus, the tax collector who was short and therefore had to climb a tree to see Jesus when he passed that way, determined that he would be able to see the Master if only from a distance. As so often happens when I deal with scripture, I was relating empathetically to Zacchaeus. I am short. I knew that my own character was much more despicable than that of a mere tax collector, and I was sure that I wanted to keep a safe distance from this Christ. Those feelings caused me to be shocked by my friend's words: "Notice that Jesus comes toward Zacchaeus, tells him that he wants to come to his house. The fact is that the Christ wants to be with us, even, especially, when we're not so good. In order for God to be with us, to be Immanuel, God has to become one with all the dark stuff of our lives." Then, following a long pause: "In fact, God, in order to be truly God, needs to be freed from goodness."

It was in that moment that I could understand Robert Bly. As quoted earlier:

> Our work then as men and women is not only to free ourselves from family cages and collective mind-sets, but to release transcendent beings from imprisonment and trance.

It was also in that moment that I could appreciate the deep wisdom of Yeats's midlife poem that I had memorized as a college student:

> But now I know
> Than twenty centuries of stony sleep
> Were vexed to nightmare by a rocking cradle,
> And what rough beast, its hour come round at last,
> Slouches towards Bethlehem to be born?[40]

God will merge with our Shadow. God will emerge out of our Shadow. God will be present where we least expect the Presence.

Equally important, God may well come to us through the Anima. My most powerful encounter with God was given me by my Anima.

Years ago, I spent eight days in silence in a discipline known as the Spiritual Exercises of Ignatius Loyola. Each day, three times a day, I would pray for hours—an hour in preparation, an hour in meditation, and an hour in reflection. On the first several days those prayer times felt like an eternity, but as the days passed and I became more comfortable with what I called "the pyrotechnics of the unconscious," the hours passed like minutes.

It was, I believe, the seventh day when I was to meditate on a passage from Philippians:

Rejoice in the Lord always; again I will say, Rejoice…
And the peace of God, which surpasses all understanding,
will guard your hearts and your minds in Christ Jesus (Philippians 4: 4, 7).

I began my preparation at my desk in the corner of this barren cell which had become my world, but Something invited me to lie down on the floor. Almost instantly something changed the floor into a green pasture—a lush green pasture in the midst of a wooded glen, beside a stream that bubbled along quietly, experienced as gentle, still waters. Then Something—no, Someone—came to me and caressed me, anointing not only my head, but every part of my body, my being—loving me and entering me. I moved this way and that, and it felt nice. My soul was restored. She spoke: "Just say peace; just feel peace. No other word, no other thought, just relaxed, easy peace." Then She left quietly.

Within a matter of hours my wise old Jesuit guide came to my cell. I quickly told him, as best I could, what had happened. He smiled, I think, a slight smile and gave me a poem from a twelfth-century mystic.

What is that sweet thing
that comes sometimes to touch me
at the thought of God?
It affects me with such vehemence and sweetness
that I begin wholly to go out of myself
and be lifted up, whither I know not.
Suddenly I am renewed and changed;
it is a state of inexpressible well-being.....
I grasp something interiorly
as with the embrace of love.
I do not know what it is,
and yet I strive with all my strength to embrace forever,
and I exult with ineffable intensity,
as if I had at last found the goal of my desires.
Is it my Beloved?
Yes, it is truly thy Beloved who visits thee.[41]

A RITE OF PASSAGE FOR MEN AT MIDLIFE

Preliminary Issues

As far as I can determine, there is no rite of passage for men at midllife in our churches, or in our society, or, for that matter, in primitive societies. Therefore, we will have to create our own, using the classic pattern and our understanding of the soul-tasks of midlife.

The pattern for all rites of passage is: separation, transition (journey, passage, trial), and reincorporation. The soul-tasks are the four described in the previous section.

Even with the shape and content of our rite given, however, two very basic problems must still be addressed. The first is a problem of the heart: How can the church be expected to have the wisdom and *courage* to recognize the male midlife passage and honor it with a rite of passage? The second is a problem of the mind: the male midlife passage comes in an infinite number of variations. Some are very short; some are endless. Some begin at thirty; some do not start until fifty. Some are little wrinkles in life's fabric, while others tear the fabric to pieces—and so on and so forth. So how can a single rite of passage represent all that variety?

Recognizing that each of these problems is monumental, the church may well choose not (or, more likely, not choose) to deal with the male midlife rite of passage. One or the other or both of these problems may persuade the church to continue to avoid the passage altogether.

Frankly, the church is much more comfortable in the world of the Laws, as described in the preceding section, than that of the Legends. Most preaching frightens persons away from the Shadow and the Soul-mate and the Journey. As one preacher after another falls prey to the crisis, there is always a self-righteous one to take over the abandoned pulpit and make light of "just another midlife crisis." So there is a good chance that the church will avoid the risk. But this author cannot give up the hope that somewhere in this thing called Christendom there is a wise and courageous and humble congregation that is up to the challenge.

The second problem focuses on how any rite of passage can represent a passage so varied and complex as midlife. The answer, of course, is that the creators of the rite have to be both arbitrary and flexible—arbitrary in making choices and creating a structure that has evident shape and content, and flexible in allowing the spirit to move within that structure to give it individual vitality and meaning.

One of the primary issues has to do with time. When would this rite be offered? At what age is a man eligible? How long should the rite last?

Midlife, like adolescence, does not start or end on cue. We do not imagine that our initiation rite for adolescents, our rite of passage to adulthood, makes someone an adult. At best, it *helps* someone become a responsible adult and allows society to acknowledge the change. But change is a process rather than an event. The changes characterized by adolescence go on for years; the changes characterized by midlife also go on for years. The initiation rite is a series of events that empower the process of adolescence, making it safer, steadier, deeper, and allowing both the initiates and their world—family, friends, church and community—to come together and say something has really happened. The child has become and is becoming an adult. The initiation rite of passage, in my view, can be offered at any time from early adolescence until the mid-twenties and still be valid.

The same issues pertain to the midlife rite of passage. As long as the rite of passage is not mistakenly equated with the *passage* itself, then the rite can be offered to men who are at least thirty-five years old. Each man may choose for himself when he is ready for the rite.

Finally, there is the question of how long this rite should last. There is no right answer to that. It could be a weekend retreat, a series of retreats, or a journey that lasts several years. I have arbitrarily decided to design a rite that lasts nine months—one month of preparation leading up to the rite of separation, followed by two months for each of the four soul-tasks.

The Preparation

Over the years I have found that it is best to form groups with a time-limited commitment at the outset. During this time, which I would suggest be three or four weeks, the leader can set out purposes of the group experience, and the potential members can begin to know one another and the likely character of the group.

In the early 1970s, I convened twenty adolescents for a three-week introduction to initiation; at the end of that brief period, those who wished made a two-year commitment to become the first initiation group. Since then, hundreds of adolescents have followed their example. In the early 1980s, I invited a group of men to share lunch and Bible study for six sessions. At the end of these six weeks, those men became the Jacob Group. A decade later they are still having lunch with Jacob as they study scripture, ponder their lives, and support one another through life's journey.

I would propose the same pattern here. Gather a group. Members are to talk about their lives, using stories, poetry, movies, and scripture. Give them some introduction to the soul-tasks of midlife and try to agree upon a reasonable commitment of time for the rite of passage (I would recommend weekly meetings with bimonthly special events such as retreats or extended sessions for the mystery rites discussed below). At the end of this period of preparation, each man should decide whether he wants to continue. Those who so choose are ready for the rite of separation.

The Rite of Separation

Every classic rite of passage begins with a rite of separation. In midlife, what is it that we are separating from? Let us be clear. It is not our wives or families. It is not our jobs or careers. It may turn out that we do require that physical and psychological separation, but that is by no means a prerequisite and by no means the intention of the rite of separation.

Rather, what we are marking in this rite of separation is our willingness to separate a part of ourselves out of our "mundane" life to do some serious soul work. We are also saying that we are willing to be open to separating our lives into two halves—the first half is coming to an end; the second half is about to begin—and that we are ready for the second half.

Although the content of the rite of separation will vary from situation to situation, the underlying tone should be the same everywhere. This is, first and foremost, a time of penitence.

I recall Jung's classic statement about neurosis and individuation, which I am quite certain was made in reference to the midlife transition in general and to his own midlife transition in particular.

> The man with a neurosis who knows that he is neurotic is more individuated than the man without consciousness. The man who is a damned nuisance to his surroundings and knows it is more individuated than the man who is blissfully unconscious of his nature.[42]

The phrase that jumps out at me is "the man who is a damned nuisance to his surroundings." Now remember that the author of those words is a man who had the audacity to bring his lover home for Sunday dinner, and I will bet he made his wife shine up the good silver for the feast! Such a man is more than "a damned nuisance to his surroundings." He is an extreme menace to society!

I believe that most men in midlife are somewhere on that continuum from damned nuisance to extreme menace. Therefore, when we present ourselves in church about ready to start out on the journey, we need to come in a penitential mode.

The finest penitential psalm is written by one of our brothers, David, after he spied Bathsheba bathing on her roof, instantly fell in love with her, arranged the death of her husband Uriah, and was confronted with the truth by the courageous prophet Nathan. David wrote the 51st Psalm:

> Have mercy on me, O God, according to thy steadfast love;
>> according to thy abundant mercy blot out my transgressions.
> Wash me thoroughly from my iniquity,
>> and cleanse me from my sin!…
>
> Create in me a clean heart, O God,
>> and put a new and right spirit within me.
> Cast me not away from thy presence,
>> and take not thy holy Spirit from me.
> Restore to me the joy of thy salvation,
>> and uphold me with a willing spirit…
>
> O Lord, open thou my lips
>> and my mouth shall show forth thy praise
> For thou has no delight in sacrifice;
>> were I to give a burnt offering, thou wouldst not be pleased.
> The sacrifice acceptable to God is a broken spirit;
>> a broken and contrite heart, O God, thou wilt not despise.
>> (Psalm 51:1–2, 10–12, 15–17, RSV)

At the rite of separation for men at midlife, that psalm should be spoken. Even better, it should be sung. For some, it should be memorized. We must confess that in the course of our passage we have and will hurt people, especially women.

Even as we confess, we must also be willing to ask openly for support and for as much understanding as possible. For far too long many men at midlife have tried to hide from others as they have tried to hide from themselves and from their God. At the rite of separation, we will say, paradoxically, that even though we need some special time apart with our brothers and ourselves, we will not be in hiding. Rather, we will be searching.

It is appropriate that there be scriptures and singing at this rite because both can give us courage for the journey. There are so many biblical passages that speak to our passage that I will not try to list any. There are also hymnals filled with great hymns of pilgrimage. Almost any of them will help, but there are two little-known hymns that I do want to mention.

I Sought the Lord, and Afterward I Knew

I sought the Lord, and afterward I knew
He moved my soul to seek him, seeking me;
It was not I that found, O Savior true;
No, I was found of thee.

Thou didst reach forth thy hand and mine enfold:
 I walked and sank not on the storm-vexed sea;
'Twas not so much that I on thee took hold
As thou, dear Lord, on me.

I find, I walk, I love, but O the whole
Of love is but my answer, Lord, to thee!
For thou wert long beforehand with my soul;
Always thou lovedst me.[43]

I Was There to Hear Your Borning Cry

I was there to hear your borning cry,
I'll be there when you are old.
I rejoiced the day you were baptized,
To see your life unfold.

I was there when you were but a child,
With a faith to suit you well:
In a blaze of light you wandered off
To find where demons dwell...

In the middle ages of your life,
Not too old, no longer young,
I'll be there to guide you through the night,
Complete what I've begun.

When the evening gently closes in
And you shut your weary eyes,
I'll be there as I have always been
With just one more surprise.[44]

Both hymns are important for the beginning of this journey because both underscore the end, the goal of the journey. The goal is to avoid being stuck with the Persona, the Shadow, or even the Anima, and to get all the way around the Square/Circle, all the way around the Mandala of Wholeness to the point where the Self, that is to say, our God, can be discovered in dialogue and invited to share control of our lives.

The first hymn speaks volumes about the nature of dialogue. "He moved my soul to seek him, seeking me." The second is remarkable in that the subject of the poem, the singer of the song, is God. "I was there to hear your borning cry, I'll be there when you are old...In the middle ages of your life...I'll be there to guide you through the night, complete what I've begun." What an incredible statement to be proclaimed as we head out on the perilous midlife journey. God will be with us. "In the middle ages of your life," sings God, "I'll be there to guide you through the night, complete what *I've* begun!"

The First Soul-Task:
The Breakdown of the Persona, Our Brother Abraham

Nearly forty years ago, in the early 1960s, a group of committed Christians founded the East Harlem Protestant Parish. They served the people of that downtrodden part of New York, and they also served the rest of the church. One of the services that I have appreciated most through the years has been their style of studying scripture. They have recommended a four-part process:

(1) Read the text in several translations. This not only gives you nuances of meaning, but the repetition allows the story to enter you from many different angles.

(2) Look at unusual or significant words. This involves some preparation by the leader, who needs to preview the text and engage in some research.

(3) Close the book and have someone tell, as accurately as possible, what the story actually says. Try not to bring your own meanings to the story yet.

(4) Now you are ready to ask what the story means for you...and the meanings are endless.

When we gather for Bible study, as we will each week during the Midlife Rite of Passage, we follow this discipline. It is our way of keeping the original shape of the story while we intentionally fill it with our own understandings. Generally, each of our four soul-tasks will be expressed by a central story out of the life of a central biblical character. Read the central event first. Then, in following weeks, pick up other moments out of that life, returning at the end of the unit to the original story.

Abraham is our first traveling companion. He is the best example of the breakdown of the Persona. I am not going to comment on each of the stories of his life in detail. They will offer their own meanings if you follow the East Harlem discipline. You do not need to be an expert. In fact, you do not want to be an expert. The stories speak more clearly if you do not fill your mind with lots of information, and simply allow yourself to wonder about the meaning of it all.

> Now the Lord said to Abram, "Go from your country and your kin-dred and your father's house to a land that I will show you. I will make of you a great nation, and I will bless you, and make your name great, so that you will be a blessing" (Genesis 12:1–2).

Let us start the wondering. Wonder what, where, and how Abraham heard that voice. Why was he asked to give up everything—"Your country, your kindred, your father's house"? Why was he not told where he was going? What did Sarah think? And what about his colleagues and neighbors? Is this man Middle-Aged Crazy or what?

What about me? How do I hear God's voice? What are dreams? What might I be asked to leave behind if I really heard a voice and risked a journey, a faith journey of this sort? Where does one get the courage? How could I live without a protective shell and wander aimlessly through the desert? What *was* Abraham's first half of life? What did he become in the second? What have I come to be in the first half of my life? And what will I be in the second?

Once the questions start flowing it is hard to stop them, and, please, do not imagine that they have to have answers. Most of the time you just live the questions until they present their own personalized answers. Remember, life is not a set of problems to be solved. It is a mystery to be lived. Brother Abraham is a living mystery from the day he got that call to leave it all behind until the very end.

The study of Abraham's life can provide understanding and courage for modern man to go searching for his soul by actually allowing the breakdown of the Persona. There are some rituals that can help as well. Rituals need to be created in each local setting in order to have integrity and vitality. I am always saddened by the painstaking work of "liturgical commissions," which almost always produce dust-dry documents that appear to belong more to the Laws than the Legends. Much better that each tribe discover its own rituals. They are more likely to be moist, swampish, and life-giving.

It is important to use rituals—we will call them mystery rites—in the midlife rite of passage. By so doing, we create threshold or liminal space and time. We recommend fasting and quiet as a way of preparing for each mystery rite. We enter that other time through silencing, centering ourselves, and stepping over the threshold where we willingly relinquish control over our lives, including our consciousness. In every mystery rite we invite the Source of all mystery to take over.

The first mystery rite is a variation on an ancient custom. It is called the masking ritual. I have explained this ritual in detail elsewhere,[45] so I will comment primarily on the shape of the exercise for men at midlife. Its purpose, in brief, is to invite the Self, not the Persona, to inform our lives.

The Shape of the Mystery Rite

(1) A PERIOD OF PREPARATION

Fasting, prayer, and reflection on our human-divine nature—perhaps by considering the wisdom of Psalm 139:

> O Lord, thou hast searched me and known me!
> Thou knowest when I sit down and when I rise up;
> thou discernest my thoughts from afar...
> Even before a word is on my tongue,
> lo, O Lord, thou knowest it altogether.
> Thou dost beset me behind and before,
> and layest thy hand upon me.
> Such knowledge is too wonderful for me;
> it is high, I cannot attain it.
>
> For thou didst form my inward parts,
> thou didst knit me together in my mother's womb.
> I praise thee, for thou art fearful and wonderful.
> Wonderful are thy works!
> Thou knowest me right well;
> my frame was not hidden from thee,
> When I was being made in secret,
> intricately wrought in the depths of the earth.
>
> (Psalm 139:1–2, 4–6, 13–15, RSV)

(2) THE CREATION OF A MASK FOR OURSELVES

Each man has his own bag—a plain, ordinary grocery bag. Each man has access to ingredients with which he can create his work—arts and crafts supplies, magazine pictures, anything. Each man creates a mask for the world to see, and, on the inside, he puts some of the secrets of his innermost heart, which he may or may not wish to share with the others.

(3) THE VOICE OF MYSTERY

When the masks are complete, we move closer to the mystery—we actually move to a campfire. We then enter into our masks and speak to one another and ourselves from our center. No longer are we merely describing the mask we have created. We are now speaking as the one who works in secret, as in the mother's womb. The response: We listen carefully and prayerfully to one another and ourselves.

(4) THE RETURN FROM THE MYSTERY

It is very important that we deliberately step back across the threshold into the here and now. It is necessary, especially if the time with the mask became somewhat heated, as it usually does, to cool down. We generally share a meal.

You will not learn all you can from this mystery rite on the night when it occurs. It is designed to activate a process in your soul. The voice that spoke from the center of the mask will continue to speak.

Furthermore, we recommend that the mask ritual be repeated at the end of the rite of passage, when we are seeking to initiate the dialogue with the self, so that a dialogue, as we have said repeatedly, goes on throughout the rest of life.

Before this unit is over, it would be well to balance the story of Abraham's life with one statement from Jesus of Nazareth: "Whoever loses his life will preserve it" (Luke 17:33, RSV). Spend a session pondering *that* wisdom!

The Second Soul-Task:
Retrieving and Eating the Shadow, Our Brother Jacob

That same night he arose and took his two wives, his two maids, and his eleven children, and crossed the ford of the Jabbok. He took them and sent them across the stream, and likewise everything that he had. And Jacob was left alone; and a man wrestled with him until the breaking of the day. When the man saw that he did not prevail against Jacob, he touched the hollow of his thigh; and Jacob's thigh was put out of joint as he wrestled with him. Then he said, 'Let me go, for the day is breaking.' But Jacob said, 'I will not let you go, unless you bless me.' And he said to him, 'What is your name?' And he said, 'Jacob.' Then he said, 'Your name shall no more be called Jacob, but Israel, for you have striven with God and with men, and have prevailed.' Then Jacob asked him, 'Tell me, I pray, your name?' But he said, 'Why is it that you ask my name?' And there he blessed him. So Jacob called the name of the place Penuel, saying, 'For I have seen God face to face, and yet my life is preserved.' The sun rose upon him as he passed Penuel, limping because of his thigh. (Genesis 32:22–31, RSV)

Jacob is our companion for this part of the journey. He is a bonafide scoundrel: tricked his brother Esau into giving him the birthright, scandalously duped his father into giving him a blessing, cheated his father-in-law out of all the good sheep, and most important, all through the first half of his life, deceived himself and shaped an identity around that non-name, Jacob—the Usurper, the Trickster, the Devious One.

Only at Penuel, that dark night of the soul, when Jacob wrestled with whatever — a demon, a man, a God, an angel, a devil — only then was Jacob broken, so Israel could come to life.

Let us look at Penuel and wonder about our brother Jacob and, of course, ourselves. Why did he leave his two wives, and two maids, and eleven children on one side of the Jabbok? What happened when he stepped into the stream and then stepped out into that other world? Surely this is liminality, but is it subliminal or supraliminal? Can we know that level of the unconscious consciously?

What is this shadowy figure who met him that night? Man? God? God-man? A power? A demon? A personal dynamism? Why can we not see the face? And what would we see if we could see the face? What are our deepest fears about that face? No, the *deepest* ones! Is there any hope for us if we see the face and are seen face-to-face?

What about that wound? A broken hip, it says. A lifelong limp. He is an invalid! In-valid! Not valid!

What about the name change? How does Jacob become Israel? How do any of us devious men ever get a new name? Can we possibly see God face-to-face, with God's knowing all of our dark underside and still have our lives preserved?

Remember there are no general answers to these questions. Just mysteries. There is much mystery lost in that dark night at Penuel. But this mystery is so central to our quest that we have designed a mystery rite. It is very basic. We call it Crossing the Jabbok.

(1) It begins with preparation, a long and intense preparation. We leave everything behind and approach the stream.

(2) One of us, on behalf of all of us, will go across and meet the Force, wrestle with it, and try to turn it over and see the face, thereby risking being pinned, defeated, destroyed. And as we watch, we will all know that moment when the Power touches the hollow of the thigh and puts it out of joint.

(3) At the moment each of us will go to that wound and go into that wound, that black hole that is every one of our souls, and explore it. We will let the wisdom of the wound speak to us. (We men are conditioned to be strong, to deny our woundedness, and, therefore, we never learn the meanings, the wisdoms, of our wounds.)

(4) We stay with our wound as long as we need to, and then we come back for the blessing. If appropriate, we also participate in a renaming. No longer will we deny—to the world or to ourselves—that we are Devious Deceivers. Now, having acknowledged that, we can open ourselves to God. "We have striven with God and men, and have, at least so far, prevailed."

(5) Finally, we must cool down. It is hot at Penuel, hot as hell, and moist, damp, and full of potential for new life. But we still have to go back across the Jabbok, out of our liminal space and time, to see our wives and maids and children whom we left on the other side of the stream.

The Third Soul-Task:
The Encounter with the Anima, Our Brother David

> It happened, late one afternoon, when David arose from his couch and was walking upon the roof of the king's house, that he saw from the roof a woman bathing; and the woman was very beautiful. And David sent and inquired about the woman. And one said, 'Is not this Bathsheba, the daughter of Eliam, the wife of Uriah the Hittite?' So David sent messengers, and took her; and she came to him, and David lay with her. Then she returned to her house. And the woman conceived; and she sent and told David, 'I am with child.' (2 Samuel 11: 2–5)

What a hell of a thing! Here he is, David, the great king of Israel, the greatest king of Israel, the one from whose loins the Messiah will come. And here is our Bible saying for all the world to see: It Happened! The man should be a disgrace to humankind. Yet he is the epitome of manhood. Plumb that mystery!

As you plumb it, read the whole story of David, which includes the victory over Goliath, that beautiful love relationship with Jonathan, the confusing and troubling relationship with Saul, the military victories with all their brutality, and the harp and the poetry. Make sure you follow him all the way to the end. Note the weakness and the impotence, the one last futile attempt to get it up with Abishag.

> Now King David was old and advanced in years; and although they covered him with clothes, he could not get warm. Therefore, his servants said to him, "Let a young maiden be sought for my lord the king, and let her wait upon the king, and let her lie in your bosom, that my lord the king may be warm." So they sought for a beautiful maiden throughout all the territory of Israel, and found Abishai the Shunammite, and brought her to the king. The maiden was very beautiful; and she became the king's nurse and ministered to him; but the king knew her not. (1 Kings 1:1–4, RSV)

When you have read the whole story, from glorious beginning to final frustration, return to that warm spring afternoon when It Happened. Start asking questions.

What happened? How can any sane man merely see a woman, even a beautiful woman, even a beautiful woman who is bathing (we assume naked or near naked, right?) on her roof so the king could see, and fall in love so suddenly, so totally, so desperately? And wait: What was Bathsheba doing on that roof in the middle of the afternoon naked? And then: How did David get that power just to demand that she come to him and lie with him? Is that only for kings and presidents? Or do the rest of us have that power too?

Then, oh my God, she is pregnant. What does he do? He schemes, of course. He tries to work something out. And he does in Uriah.

Now stop and ask yourself: Who is this man, this David? Is he merely "a damned nuisance to his surroundings"? Or is he an extreme menace to society? Ask others what they think. Ask Joab. Ask Uriah. Ask Bathsheba. Ask yourself. And then, ask Nathan the prophet.

Hear all the answers and then go on with your life, determined to learn from your brother David's experience, so that when you are old and worn out and cannot get warm, you will not still believe that you need a beautiful young woman to nurse you. You will have learned to take care of yourself.

To help you, to help us, it is important that we look to woman to teach us about the mystery of our sexuality. Fortunately, the scriptures give two such women. The first is the writer of the Song of Songs. (Those songs were not all written by women, but the best ones were!) Listen to her wisdom.

> Upon my bed at night
>   I sought him whom my soul loves;
> I sought him, but found him not;
>   I called him, but he gave no answer.
> "I will rise now and go about the city,
>   in the streets and in the squares;
> I will seek him whom my soul loves."
>   I sought him, but found him not.
> The sentinals found me,
>   as they went about in the city.
>   "Have you seen him whom my soul loves?"
>
> Scarcely had I passed them,
>   when I found him whom my soul loves.
> I held him, and would not let him go
>   until I had brought him into my mother's house,
>   and into the chamber of her that conceived me.
>
> I adjure you, O daughters of Jerusalem,
> by the gazelles or the wild does:
>   do not stir up or awaken
> love until it is ready! (Song of Songs 3:1–5)

The second woman is the woman with the ointment, who bathed Christ's feet with her tears and dried them with her hair. She is such a mysterious figure that we cannot hope to meet her unless we cross the threshold into her space. We call this part of the journey the rite of the ointment, or, more simply, the anointing.

(1) Begin with preparation. This time it is crucial to read the text.

One of the Pharisees asked him to eat with him, and he went into the Pharisee's house, and sat at table. And behold, a woman of the city, who was a sinner, when she learned that he was sitting at table in the Pharisee's house, brought an alabaster flask of ointment, and standing behind him at his feet, weeping, she began to wet his feet with her tears, and wiped them with the hair of her head, and kissed his feet, and anointed them with ointment . . . (Luke 7:36–38)

(2) Make sure you know who those Pharisees are. They are the people of the Laws. They are not very open to the Legends. In fact, they are not at all open to the Legends. They are all around us, and they are well established within us. They control most of us.

(3) Also make sure you know who this Woman is. She certainly is no saint. *Au contraire,* she is, according to that society, a sinner. All she has are tears, and hair, and some ointment.

(4) And make sure you know what ointment is. It is perfumed oil. It is sweet. It is sensuous. It is expensive. It is the stuff that makes us the Anointed One. The Hebrew word for Anointed One is Messiah. The Greek word is Christ. Jung's word is Self.

(5) Now we are prepared to cross the threshold for our Anointing. The place belongs to the Pharisees. Every place of Anointing originally belongs to a Pharisee. Listen to them recite the Laws, those Laws you have been hearing since you were a little boy. "Don't play with yourself. It's dirty." "If I catch you masturbating…" "You know you can go blind, or lose the gray matter, or your hair will fall out later." "You're just like your father. You men are so helpless." "It's a sacred thing, this sex. You shouldn't do it until you're *much* older." "Your body is a temple. Don't profane it." "No sex before marriage." "No sex outside marriage." "No sex, period." "Keep it in your knickers." "And for goodness' sake don't even *think* of touching another man."

(6) As the litany of the Laws drones on, notice the Woman. Notice the hair, the shape of her body, her feet, her eyes, her tears, her person, her depth, her love. Let her open her alabaster flask of ointment, and slowly, go to your feet, tears dropping, hair falling down, with her ointment ready to make you Messiah.

(7) As she begins to anoint you, ask her to tell you about her Self, her Womanly, Feminine Self. Ask her all the questions you ever wanted to know but were afraid to ask. Ask her, and listen deeply, very deeply. It would even be wise to write down what she has to tell you, because eventually you are going to leave this place and you surely will not want to forget her.

(8) When the time comes and you must leave, be warned that, as you leave, the Pharisees, the men of the Laws, will attack you. Try to keep yourself centered, difficult as that is, as you talk to them about sin and forgiveness. By the way, I would strongly encourage you not "to judge" these Pharisees. Remember: "Judge not that you be not judged." "One finger pointing out and three pointing back." The Pharisees you need to

fear are not outside you—that would be projection. The really fearsome Pharisees are deep within us.

(9) As a final act, before you step back across the threshold, thank the woman; bid her to go in peace.

(10) Be sure to *cool off* before you go home.

The Fourth Soul-Task:
Initiating the Dialogue with the Self, Our Brother Job

The terrifying journey around the square/circle, the mandala, now brings us back to where we began, but we are different. No longer imprisoned in the shells of our Personae, no longer denying the Shadow, no longer avoiding the Anima, we are now ready to begin the second half of life. The soul-task of all soul-tasks awaits us—the encounter with the Self.

Since this soul-task is only initiated in midlife, we will touch on it only lightly as part of our rite of passage. We touch it lightly ("brush it lightly with the wing tips of our mind," to use Robert Bly's phrase) by being introduced to Job. There is enough wisdom in Job to last us a lifetime, so we just read some sections from the beginning, when Job was mostly Persona, a very fine Persona.

> There was once a man in the land of Uz whose name was Job. That man was blameless and upright, one who feared God and turned away from evil. There were born to him seven sons and three daughters. He had seven thousand sheep, three thousand camels, five hundred yoke of oxen, five hundred donkeys, and very many servants; so that this man was the greatest of all the people of the east. (Job 1:1–3)

You would think that such a man would be content to live out his days with as little personal turmoil as possible—just enjoy his blessings.

However, just like that poor forty-year-old Middle-Aged Crazy guy who should have been content with his life with Ann-Margret, there was something going on deep within Job that began to work upon him. The Bible calls that something Satan. Satan means Adversary in Hebrew, a counterpoint. We think of Satan as evil and God as good: good and evil, God and Satan. Some say we need these contrapuntal forces to be at work within us if we are to stay alive.

The poet William Blake was one who believed in "contraries":

> Without Contraries there is no progression. Attraction and Repulsion, Reason and Energy, Love and Hate, are necessary to human existence.
>
> From these Contraries spring what the religious call Good and Evil. Good is the passive that obeys Reason. Evil is the active springing from Energy.
>
> Good is Heaven, Evil is Hell.[46]

Job, who created the best possible Persona of all time, who is the greatest of all the people of the east, who enshrouded himself in an aura of goodness, is dead by his fortieth birthday party. But, thank God, there is something that calls him out on the journey from the Laws to the Legends. Messenger after messenger comes from nowhere with the news.

The first step is, as you no doubt have guessed, the breakdown of the Persona.

> "The oxen and the asses...and all servants with them have been killed...and I alone escaped to tell you."
>
> "The sheep and their shepherds have been consumed by fire...and I alone escaped to tell you."
>
> "The camels and their camel drivers have been slain...and I alone escaped to tell you."
>
> "Your sons and daughters were killed by a mighty wind...and I alone escaped to tell you." (Job 1:14–19, RSV)

The Persona is cracking, badly, but Job is determined to cling to his familiar ways of responding.

> Then Job arose, and rent his robe, and shaved his head, and fell upon the ground, and worshiped. "Naked I came from my mother's womb, and naked shall I return; the Lord gave and the Lord has taken away; blessed be the name of the Lord." In all this Job did not sin or charge God with wrong. (Job 1:20–22, RSV)

But the Adversary will not give up. Satan and God, evil and good meet again, and it is determined that there is still more Persona to be broken. Job has so internalized all of this virtue that it will be necessary to strike his very person. Sores cover his body, and his long-suffering wife, who is happily an extension of his person, begins to doubt. Then and only then does Job begin to feel his depression, his Shadow, his depth. He curses the day when he was born.

> "Let the day perish in which I was born,
>   and the night that said, 'A man-child is conceived.'
> Let that day be darkness!
>   May God above not seek it, or light shine upon it.
> Let gloom and deep darkness claim it.
>   Let clouds settle upon it; let the blackness of the day terrify it.
> That night—let thick darkness seize it!
>   let it not rejoice among the days of the year;
>   let it not come into the number of the months.
> Yes, let that night be barren;
>   let no joyful cry be heard in it." (Job 3:3–7)

This reminds me of a stunning poem quoted several times by Robert Bly.

> Well, on the day I was born,
> God was sick. . .
> They all know that I'm alive,

that I chew my food . . . and they don't know
why harsh winds whistle in my poems,
the narrow uneasiness of a coffin,
winds untangled from the sphinx
who holds the desert for routine questioning. . .

On the day I was born,
God was sick,
gravely. (Caesar Vallejo)

For most of us, maybe really all of us, God was sick on the day we were born. Yet God was still there, singing that song.

I was there to hear your borning cry,
    I'll be there when you are old.
I rejoiced the day you were baptized
    To see your life unfold.

God is probably just as sick forty years later when that struggle between good and evil is getting animated in our souls, but God is still singing that song.

In the middle ages of your life,
    Not too old, no longer young,
I'll be there to guide you through the night,
    Complete what I've begun.

The process that God activates at midlife within us and within Job *must be completed*. Only if we see it through will it be worthwhile.

This, in fact, is the central theme of the book of Job. Almost all of the poem is a dialogue with three friends, three advisors, who plead with him, for his own sake, to just confess his sins, give up his battle, tuck his tail between his legs, and run back to his former life. Murray Stein calls that the "reconstitution of the Persona."

Job will not do it, and *that* is what makes Job a hero. That unwillingness to give up the struggle until he has learned its meaning is why Job is our brother for this final soul-task of midlife. He dares to dialogue with both good and evil, both God and Satan, until God actually speaks to him.

From the whirlwind or the waterfall or whatever, God will speak to us from the very center of the square/circle, the center of the mandala, the center of the universe. And when God speaks, God elevates Job for the dialogue.

Who is this that darkens counsel
    by words without knowledge?
Gird up your loins like a man,
    I will question you, and you shall declare to me.
Where were you when I laid the foundation of the earth?
    Tell me, if you have understanding.

Who determined its measurements—surely you know!
Or who stretched the line upon it? (Job 38:2–5)

Carl Gustave Jung comments upon this moment:

Job is challenged as though he himself were a god...The conflict becomes acute for Yahweh as a result of a new factor...The new factor is
something that never occurred before in the history of the world, the
unheard-of fact that, without knowing it or wanting it, a mortal man
is raised by his moral behavior above the stars in heaven, from which
position of advantage he can behold the back of Yahweh.[47]

Edwin Edinger then makes additional comment on Jung's observation.

We might ask what does Jung mean by Job's "moral behavior"? I
think he refers to Job's refusal to accept responsibility for events that
he knows he did not cause. Job's intellectual honesty, his loyalty to his
own perception of reality, his integrity in maintaining the distinction
between subject and object, between man and God—all these go to
make up Job's moral behavior, which has forced God to reveal himself.[48]

The midlife passage, so utterly demeaned by our culture, has a moral
purpose! It is in midlife when we are man enough to gird up our loins and
begin the dialogue with God. The dialogue goes on for the rest of our days and
then beyond, when we will hear God still singing that song.

In the middle ages of your life,
Not too old, no longer young,
I'll be there to guide you through the night,
Complete what I've begun.

When the evening gently closes in
And you shut your weary eyes,
I'll be there as I have always been
With just one more surprise.

The last steps of our midlife rite of passage could include a final mystery
rite. I recommend repeating the masking ritual. The rite certainly should include a look ahead to the second half of life, during which we now expect to
be fully alive. Here, once again, our brother Job can help us know what it will
be like. Look at what happened to him.

And the LORD restored the fortunes of Job...and the LORD gave Job
twice as much as he had before...And the Lord blessed the latter days
of Job more than the beginning; and he had fourteen thousand sheep,
six thousand camels, a thousand yoke of oxen, and a thousand she-
asses. He had also seven sons and three daughters. And he called the
name of the first Turtledove; the second, Cassia; and the third, Mas-
cara. And in all the land there were no women so fair as Job's daughters;

and their father gave them inheritance among their brothers. And after this Job lived a hundred and forty years, and saw his sons, and his sons' sons, four generations. And Job died, an old man, and full of days. (Job 42:10, 12–17, RSV, alt.)

This is truly remarkable. In a culture that is patently anti-feminine, Job's daughters are honored in the second half of his life. They have names of their own. They will receive their portion of his inheritance. They are beautiful. The feminine is finally honored. And this good man dies an old man, full of days.

The Rite of Reincorporation

Every rite of passage begins with a rite of separation, follows a journey, and ends with a rite of incorporation. The passage does not end, but the rite of passage must.

I know of no better way to mark the end of the journey than with a hymn sing. Make sure there is a time for penitence and a time for thanksgiving. But mostly, just sing hymns, old ones and new ones, and do not forget the one God sings.

I was there to hear your borning cry,
    I'll be there when you are old.
I rejoiced the day you were baptized,
    To see your life unfold.

I was there when you were but a child,
    With a faith to suit you well;
In a blaze of light you wandered off
    To find where demons dwell.

When you heard the wonder of the word
    I was there to cheer you on;
You were raised to praise the living Lord,
    To whom you now belong.

When you find someone to share your time
    And you join your hearts as one,
I'll be there to make your verses rhyme
    From dusk til rising sun.

In the middle ages of your life,
    Not too old, no longer young,
I'll be there to guide you through the night,
    Complete what I've begun.

When the evening gently closes in
    And you shut your weary eyes,
I'll be there as I have always been
    With just one more surprise.

I was there to hear your borning cry,
    I'll be there when you are old.
I rejoiced the day you were baptized,
    To see your life unfold.

---

[1]Daniel J. Levinson et al., *The Seasons of a Man's Life* (New York: Ballantine Books, 1978), 41–42.

[2]Levinson, 44–45.

[3]John-Raphael Staude, *The Adult Development of C.G. Jung* (Boston: Routledge and Kegan Paul, 1981), 9–10

[4]Levinson, 20.

[5]Gail Sheehy, *Passages: Predictable Crises of Adult Life* (New York: E. P. Dutton, 1974), 251.

[6]Erik Erikson, *Childhood and Society* (New York: W.W. Norton, 1950), 261–62.

[7]Erik Erikson, *Youth: Challenge and Change* (New York: Basic Books, 1963), 11.

[8]Erikson, *Childhood,* 263.

[9]Ibid., 266.

[10]Ibid., 267.

[11]Ibid., 268.

[12]See Staude, 44–68.

[13]C. G. Jung, *Memories, Dreams and Reflections* (New York: Pantheon Books, 1961), 177.

[14]Jung, 177, 179, 192.

[15]Edwin Edinger, *Encounter with the Self: A Jungian Commentary on William Blake's Illustrations of the Book of Job* (Toronto: Inner City Books, 1986), 7.

[16]Robert Bly, *Iron John* (New York: Addison-Wesley, 1990), 233.

[17]Murry Stein, *In Midlife: A Jungian Perspective* (Dallas: Spring, 1983), 26–27.

[18]Bly, 140.

[19]Ibid., 194.

[20]William O. Roberts, Jr., *Initiation to Adulthood: An Ancient Rite of Passage in Contemporary Form* (New York: Pilgrim, 1982), 19.

[21]Stein, 3–4.

[22]Ibid., 3.

[23]Cf. Sharp, 41.

[24]Bly, 206.

[25]John Sanford, *The Invisible Partners* (New York: Paulist, 1980), 10.

[26]Sanford, 111.

[27]Bly, 135.

[28]Bly, 137.

[29]Sheehy, 144.

[30]Sanford, 5.

[31]Cf. Bly, 126.

[32]Robert Johnson, *We: Understanding the Psychology of Romantic Love* (San Francisco: Harper and Row, 1983), 161–62.

[33]Adolf Guggenbuhl-Craig, *Marriage—Dead or Alive* (Zurich: Spring, 1977), 9–10.

[34]Johnson, 159–60.

[35]Dante Alighieri, *The Divine Comedy,* trans. by Henry Wadsworth Longfellow and ed. by Charles Welsh (Davos, New York, 1909), 15.

[36]Sanford, 21.

[37]Ibid., 20–21.

[38]Edinger, *Encounter,* 7.

[39]Ibid., 9.

[40]W. B. Yeats, "The Second Coming," in *The Collected Poems of W. B. Yeats* (New York: McMillan, 1933), 185.

[41]Hugh of St. Victor (1096–1141), (Source Untraced).

[42]C. G. Jung, *Letters*, quoted in Daryl Sharp, *The Survival Papers: Anatomy of a Midlife Crisis* (Toronto: Inner City Books, 1988), 11.

[43]"I Sought the Lord, and Afterward I Knew," *The Pilgrim Hymnal* (Pilgrim, New York, 1986), 578.

[44]John Ylvisaker, "I Was There to Hear Your Borning Cry," *Chalice Hymnal* (St. Louis: Chalice Press, 1995), #75.

[45]Roberts, 39 and 144–49.

[46]William Blake, *The Poetry and Prose of William Blake*, ed. David Erdman (Garden City, N.Y.: Anchor Books, 1979), 34.

[47]Jung, *Answer to Job*, quoted in Edwin Edinger, *Encounter with the Self: A Jungian Commentary of William Blake's Illustrations of the Book of Job* (Toronto: Inner City Books, 1986), 49–50.

[48]Edinger, *Encounter*, 50.

10
Later Maturity

Paul B. Maves

CELEBRATING THE TRANSITIONS OF
LATER MATURITY

Through the years we experience a succession of changes. Some of these changes are made necessary by the environment. Some of these changes in ourselves, in our relationships, in what we do or where we live are chosen, either to escape from less than satisfactory situations or in the hope that a new situation will be more satisfying to us.

This chapter will explore some of the changes that tend to be typical of the later years. It will make a case for communal rituals which can enable persons to face, assimilate, and cope with these changes.

By later maturity I refer to the years after fifty-five. Fifty-five is an arbitrary number and has no magic about it. Some persons retire earlier. But typically as persons come into the late fifties, their children are grown and gone from home, they are beginning to think about retirement, they are becoming aware of physical changes which affect what they can or want to do, and they may have experienced the death of one or both of their parents.

This group of persons may span two generations. Many persons who have retired have parents who are still living. In this period of twenty to thirty years many changes can take place. Some will retire more than once. Some will lose a spouse, remarry, and lose another spouse. Some will undergo a period of extreme disability and then recover to resume a life of activity.

The Meaning of Change

As Marris[1] has pointed out, some of these changes are incremental. These are changes that take place fairly gradually over a period of time. They are part of a process, and usually along with them the necessary accommodations are made without a great deal of consciousness. The farmer or the lawyer or the physician who gradually tapers off in terms of hours and difficulty of work are examples of this. What is thought of as retirement hardly occurs. However, at times, refusal to recognize and come to grips with the changes can lead to an explosive break. Changes in the relationship between spouses which erupt in divorce are an illustration. The behavior of a parent which finally becomes intolerable to a child and may lead to some kind of break in the relationship is another example.

Some changes can be characterized as growthful or benign. These are sought out, planned for and even engineered. If they come unexpectedly, they are hailed and celebrated. Receiving an unanticipated inheritance which relieves worries about money, going back to school and studying what could not have been studied earlier, finding a new love and marrying again are illustrations of growthful changes which can be encountered in the later years.

However, some changes come suddenly and are catastrophic in their impact. An unwanted early retirement due to depression or change in company policy is one example. The death of a spouse is another example. The death of a child or a grandchild can be very traumatic. Tornadoes, floods, fires and the loss of life savings in the collapse of financial institutions are other examples.

Both the growthful and the catastrophic changes represent major turning points in life. Catastrophic changes sweep away most of the centers of meanings and the support structures we depend upon. They take away that which gives direction and meaning to life. They destroy habitual ways of acting.

All change entails some loss. Change demands that something has to be given up or left behind. Old ways of doing things have to be surrendered. So these turning points in life are followed by periods of transition in which life has to be reorganized, new centers of meaning found, new relationships developed, and new skills developed. Transitions require the output of additional energy. They arouse greater consciousness of the environment. They demand the making of an unusual number of decisions. Therefore, they face persons with greater risks. Transitions are times of disequilibrium. They result in anxiety and heightened emotionality. Transitions are challenges to courage and to faith.

Here it has to be said that not all persons experience the same number of turning points or experience them in the same way. A study by Kelley, Steinkamp and Kelley,[2] who interviewed persons in Peoria, revealed that about 40 percent of the respondents had lived fairly uneventful lives with a pattern of development called "straight arrow." Twenty-three percent had experienced some major turning points. But the lives of 37 percent could be characterized as "zigzag."

The concept of stages which are experienced by all persons at the same time in a similar way may be useful as a heuristic device, but the infinite variety of lives has to be kept in mind. Neither the "empty nest" nor retirement, nor moving, nor loss of a spouse, for example, come to all persons at the same time. Transitions have to be dealt with when they come in terms of the particular meaning they have for those who go through them.

Some persons cope much more effectively with change than others. Generally, persons who possess what Antonovsky[3] has called a sense of coherence, cope more effectively than those who have a weak or nonexistent sense of coherence. Those who have this sense believe that existence can be understood, that they have the resources to cope with what they face, and that it is worth making the effort to cope. This last is another way of naming "Hope." This sense of coherence is acquired through experience and education.

Also, those who have built their lives on a broad base of relationships, interests, and values are not as devastated by catastrophic events as those who have narrow bases. This underscores the obvious point that some persons have more resources than others to draw upon when faced with transitions.

Against this background, let me consider two of the turning points most frequently experienced by persons in the later years: retirement and moving to a new community.

Work and Retirement

In every society persons have had to expend energy to secure and prepare food, provide shelter, care for the disabled, rear children, and defend against external threats as a matter of personal and social survival. So preparation for work and work itself, or "making a living," are central activities in the lives of human beings, so much so that work sometimes takes on a value of its own apart from its main purpose. More important, throughout the ages, work has been invested with religious significance as commanded by God. In our time this has almost made work an idol, corrupted even further into the goal of "making money." But whatever value is placed upon work, it still is a major arena within which most persons find meaning and purpose in their lives.

Work not only enables persons to secure the resources to live, but also structures time. Work defines when they get up, where they go, when they rest. Work provides the worker with an identity and a status or position in the group. To be without a position and deprived of a title is the source of discomfort to many after they retire, particularly white collar workers. Persons tend to know who they are by what they do. Work gives persons something to look forward to, something to talk about in retrospect. Work provides the occasion for goals to be aimed for and achievements to be celebrated. Work provides opportunities to interact with others, to develop friendships, and to experience camaraderie. Even more basic, as Erikson[4] has pointed out, work links the worker to the long history of the culture. So it is from work that persons receive confirmation of worth and anchorage for their self-image.

Human beings seem to need projects which give meaning to life. These projects can be thought of as commitments to value. Frankl,[5] as a result of his experience in concentration camps, came to appreciate the place of a commitment to values in giving meaning to life. Finding meaning in the experience of the concentration camp not only enhanced life but also made survival more likely. He avers that meaning is the result of choice and that meaning can be found in any situation.

Projects need not be defined as work to be meaningful. Nor do they need to be remunerative to be meaningful. Frequently, the process is as rewarding as the product. Projects can be focused on productive or creative values, such as serving the community, growing flowers, making a quilt for grandchildren, painting, metal sculpturing, or writing poetry. They can be focused on experiential values, such as learning to listen to music, traveling to study other cultures, cultivating relationships with family, or studying birds. They can be focused on attitudinal values, in which a person determines what kind of a person one wants to be, or on spiritual formation.

However, for a value to be meaningful, it has to be a value not only for the one committed to it but also for others who recognize and support or celebrate it, whether an "invisible choir," or God, or those with whom one is most closely associated. A religious congregation is by nature a group of persons committed to similar values anchored in symbols, myths, and liturgies. A congregation's greatest contribution to aging persons may be to assist them to redefine the values which they base their lives upon.

Here it needs to be noted that activity per se can become an opiate, an escape from facing the transition necessitated by retirement or other major loss. Frenetic involvement in community service, laudable on the surface, or constant traveling and sightseeing, which offers creative possibilities, may be frantic and futile efforts to fill the emptiness left by retirement.

Another way to look at retirement is to conceive of it as a *sabbath*, a time to rest from labor, to pray, write letters, meditate, get one's act together, think deeply, not only about life's meaning, but also about the meaning of death. It may be conceived of as a *sabbatical* which allows a time of enrichment in preparation for a new career, by securing more training, by deepening knowledge and obtaining new ways of looking at things, and by deepening relationships with family.

Retirement, as we know it, either as mandatory or as an expectation, has come into being only within the last hundred years. So we have developed a social policy and practice which removes the structuring of time, the opportunity for companionship, a significant social role and a respected status within a group, and one means of anchoring identity. Retirement confers the benefit of a large block of discretionary time which may be experienced as empty, wasted, killed, or invested. It requires the deliberate reorganization of life.

One theological issue raised by retirement is that of vocation. What does God intend for us to do with our time, our lives, our energy in these later years? What values does God intend for us to pursue? What projects will realize those values? In short, what on earth are old persons good for anyway?

What gives persons worth and entitles them to respect? What properties are possessed by the elderly that make them valuable to society as a whole? Does the current value of the old rest simply upon what they have done in the past? Within the Judeo-Christian tradition, persons are of worth because they are children of God and bearers of the image of God. Persons are called to love God and to love their neighbors. Vocation, then, is not simply earning a living or achieving success. Our vocation, our calling, is to work with God in creating community. Religious communities have developed disciplines which structure time, which bring persons together in service, and which point to ends that fulfill life.

The biblical story of the man who amassed many goods and built larger barns to house them is significant here. The man then said to himself, "Soul, you have much goods. Enough to last for the rest of your life. Take it easy now. Eat, drink, and have fun." God said to the man, "You fool! This night you will lose your soul!" While this may be read in several ways, the passage may be interpreted to mean that without a commitment to anything but consumption the man had no life. He had died as a spirit (Luke 12:16).

A study commissioned by the Religious Education Association[6] uncovered the fact that the time of greatest spiritual growth took place in the subjects during periods of doubt and disequilibrium. Unfortunately, these subjects also disclosed that at such times they were unable to turn to their religious communities and share their problems. The reason given was that they feared rejection and scorn.

Persons in transition need support and are open to learning. Religious communities will do well, to become aware of not only the need to support persons in crisis, but also of the opportunity to enable them to enhance their lives and deepen their spiritual commitments as they reorganize their lives.

Relocation

A second transition faced by many persons is that of moving from one community to another or from one location to another. This transition may come before retirement with changes related to occupation. It may come at the time of retirement. It may come sometime after retirement, perhaps occasioned by the loss of functional capacity or by the death of a spouse or companion. One man, whose wife had died and whose strength was no longer sufficient to maintain the residence in which he had lived for forty years, and who was moving to a retirement community, called it "breaking up the home." Some may live all their lives in one place. Others may have moved as many as fifteen or twenty times.

Health care workers often refer to "relocation shock" when a person has to enter a nursing home. But this is simply one critical event which may have been experienced a number of times, although this may be seen as the most traumatic by the one who has to move, made more so by the foreboding of the nearness of death, and exacerbated by the negative attitudes of society toward sickness and the nursing home. Of course, it is most traumatic for those who may be relocating for the first time or who have had no experience with nursing homes.

The meaning of an accustomed place has to do with the familiarity of routines associated with it, with the memories that are evoked by it, and all the relationships that have been established around it. "This is where we raised our children." "This is where our children were married." "This is where our family has lived for three generations." Even a single article of furniture can acquire symbolic as well as functional significance.

My wife and I have lived in fourteen different places since we were married. For us it is our dining room table that has acquired special meaning because of the persons we have entertained at dinner parties and the significant events we have celebrated around it. We have even had to select houses with dining space large enough to fit the table.

To move any distance at all means that deep and meaningful relationships are broken. Persons who have to enter a nursing home often need to be able to take along a few choice articles with them as anchors to their past and symbols of identity.

This is poignantly illustrated by the story of Jacob's break with his father-in-law and the sudden departure with his wives and flocks (Genesis 31:17). As they left, Rachel purloined her father's sacred objects or household gods. When her father, Laban, overtook them, Rachel hid the objects in the camel's saddle-bags and sat on the objects so she could be sure of keeping them. Moving is fraught with the grief of breaking close relationships, the rupture of routines, the anxiety aroused by the need to make choices in establishing new relationships in the midst of strangers, and the expenditure of an unusual amount of energy in getting reoriented.

The theological issue raised by moving from one place to another, especially one community to another, is that of finding stability and permanence underlying contingency, flux, and change. The Judeo-Christian tradition is rooted in the experience of migration, nomadism, exile, and Diaspora. The unchanging character of God and the awareness that "underneath are the everlasting arms," places the temporal in the context of the eternal, the contingent in the context of the constant.

The fact that congregations of religious communities are found around the world and that the liturgies are similar to those found everywhere else offers the comfort of familiarity to the stranger and the traveler. In the past, in nomadic cultures, the entire community moved together. In our nomadic culture, we have to find communities which transcend distance and within which we can move more securely. Liturgies which support persons in moving from one place or one community to another have to enable separation on one end and initiation and receptivity on the other end.

Other Transitions

An additional transition is required by the death of a spouse or companion or confidante. The death of a child or grandchild may be exceedingly traumatic. However, religious congregations already have funeral liturgies, although some of them may leave much to be desired. So I will not deal with these liturgies here.

Another difficult transition is experienced by those whose spouse or companion or confidante has experienced severe memory loss and to all intents and purposes has died as a person although he or she is still living in the body. In many cases the one still healthy has to take on a new role as caregiver. Then comes the time when they have to be separated by the need to have the other cared for in a nursing home. The ambiguity of these situations and the accompanying denial characteristic of so many of them makes the development of liturgies other than supportive presence so problematical that I will not deal with these here.

In the next section I shall put forward some possible liturgies focused upon the transitions of retirement and of moving from one community to another. A liturgy for leaving a home is treated in a separate chapter.

RITUALS FOR THE TRANSITIONS OF LATER MATURITY

The liturgies in this chapter are tentative and experimental. They are designed to stimulate additional work. They may serve as the basis for making adaptations which are more appropriate to a specific situation.

Principles of Liturgy Creation

In developing these rituals the following principles were kept in mind:

1. In the broadest sense, liturgy, as the work of the people and the worship of God, involves the total life of the congregation. Rituals and ceremonies have meaning when they articulate understandings, values and visions held by the members of the congregation collectively. Therefore, rituals which have the most meaning will be rooted in the experience of the congregation and in the interpretation of that experience in light of the gospel. They will have been prepared for by preaching, instruction, and counseling which have dealt with the themes of change, aging, loss, vocation, and death.

These rituals represent climactic moments in the process of what has been called anticipatory socialization, or rehearsing in advance the actions and behavior that might be called for in the new situation. Persons will have been enabled to become somewhat comfortable in confronting the issues posed by these changes and will have some notion of the place of community rituals in supporting transitions.

2. These rituals will need to be grounded in understandings developed through particular attention to the meaning of the aging process in the context of the life span, including death at the end. Old age is both a personal and a social phenomenon. It is defined by the norms and expectations of the society and culture within which we live. The attitudes persons have toward the transitions demanded by the aging process tend to be established by their own experience and by the way in which they are socialized by the community. Therefore, the congregation which uses the rituals suggested here will face the values its members live by and the attitudes they have toward life in general. These concerns will be allowed into and dealt with within the normal services of worship. They will be articulated by appropriate scripture, hymns, poetry and drama.

3. It follows from this that, ideally, the central participants in these rituals will have been consulted and prepared for their participation by pastoral conferences. This is in line with what congregations do to prepare persons for baptism, entrance into membership, and marriage. In this process the participants themselves may wish to modify or add to the rituals proposed below. In one congregation in which we worshiped, where many members moved frequently, the pastor tried to develop some kind of brief recognition of the leaving in the Sunday morning service of worship. Most of the persons refused because they said they could not deal with the emotional trauma of leaving. I believe that a careful program of education and personal consultation might have obviated some of this reluctance.

4. The rituals proposed recognize the central importance of life review and reminiscence in the search for meaning, especially in the later years. Remembering, recollecting, and relating what has happened thus far enable persons to begin to fashion the ending to the story of their lives. Therefore, it is assumed that in these rituals it is important to recall the past, to celebrate what is good, and to experience forgiveness for what has not been good. It is assumed that business left unfinished from earlier times of life will accumulate to complicate coping in the later years. In this process persons will be helped to discover and to affirm their strengths and to gain confidence in their capacity to cope.

5. The liturgies put forth here have to do with leaving, with departure, with setting forth, and then finally with arriving as a stranger and being received into a new setting and a new community. In the long tradition of the human community eating together has been a central experience and rite. The child's first experience of being nurtured and loved comes from suckling at the breast. It is not accidental that times of celebration include ceremonial meals in the midst of communal gatherings. It is significant that, in the parable of the waiting father told by Jesus, the prodigal son is welcomed home with a feast. Therefore the eucharist can be a central element in these rituals of transition. But at the same time receptions at which refreshments are provided and dinners served can be an important part of the celebration.

Traditionally funerals have been times of family gatherings, often in the context of congregational gatherings, and the communal meal has been a part of this. The same can be said of first communion and of weddings. The food which neighbors carry in when persons are ill or when strangers are moving into the neighborhood has symbolic as well as practical significance.

Various branches of the Christian movement have differing approaches to liturgy. In recognition of the different liturgical traditions, the rituals suggested below represent outlines and hints which may be changed, adapted, and built upon. They may become the occasions for creating alternative rituals.

Rituals around Retirement

In the past, when persons spent a lifetime working at one place or for one organization or at one occupation, retirement was a major, once-in-a-lifetime event. This may still be true for some. More and more, however, retirement probably will be a time of change of occupations, a time for the reassignment and redirecting of life. In any event, it probably will include these experiences: (1) a breaking off of relations with a particular social system, and (2) a change in the place where activities occur. To illustrate from my own experience, at age fifty-four I resigned from the faculty of a university to assume another position but continued to live in the community. My colleagues on the faculty sent us off with a farewell dinner and a gift. This was the last time I was to gather with them as part of a working social system. The next time, I resigned in order to take a position halfway across the country. My colleagues where I worked had a farewell dinner and gave us a gift. The same thing was to happen a few years later when I moved again. In other words, I left a work setting three times in the ten years before I retired. When, at the age of sixty-five, I formally retired and started collecting my pension benefits, we were given a dinner and a gift once again. At this time I accepted a part-time position which entailed a major relocation. Eight years later, in response to new opportunities, we moved again. At that time, we were given a farewell reception by our church, a farewell party by colleagues in the organization for which I worked, and a farewell reception by the volunteer organization in which my wife and I had been active. These were all very meaningful and helpful in enabling us to cope with the grief of leaving and putting the past behind us. Here it must be said that it is important to involve spouses and other family members because they too are affected by the redirection occasioned by retirement.

What did not happen was a liturgy of sending forth and of commissioning for the new activities and new commitments in new places by the congregations in which we were active, either within the context of worship services or socially, although at our last move the congregation held a farewell reception for us after the Sunday service which we deeply appreciated and found very supportive.

Also, what did not happen on the occasion of our coming into a new community was the same kind of deeply meaningful reception into the new congregation. Admittedly, it would be hard to invest initiation with the same depth of feeling as that engendered by leaving a social system. However, it must be noted that the new congregation did better on the reception than on the sending forth since they did have a ritual for the receiving of new members by transfer.

What has been said so far implies for the most part that retirement and relocation tend to come together. This also implies that often the ritual dealing with retirement has to be coupled with a ritual for departure from the congregation. But in cases where this is not true, there still is a need for a ritual which recognizes a major vocational redirecting.

What I am pleading for, then, is a ritual enacted by the social system from which a person is retiring, followed by a ritual of reception and initiation by the social system into which a person is entering. Pastors and congregations may be able to alert their members to these needs and even assist them by suggesting outlines for such rituals.

In the rituals suggested below retirement is conceived to be a passing of a milestone, an entry into a time of transition, a shift in focus, a redirection and a reorganization of life. The transition itself may extend over a number of months. The transition may be from one kind and place of work to another, although the new occupation may be part-time and may not always be remunerative. Or the transition may be from work to a sabbatical or even to a late-life sabbath. The sabbatical may include such commitments as going back to school and completing an education that was diverted or interrupted. It may include a time of exploration, study and travel plus relaxation. It may represent a shift from focus on productive values to experiential values. A sabbath may include a commitment to get affairs in order, to write one's autobiography, to meditate upon the meaning of one's existence, or to devote one's life to prayer and contemplation.

The date of retirement from work comes at almost any time of the year. Most congregations will have a number of members who retire at various times of the year. Thus, it may be most appropriate and convenient to recognize these times of entry into a transition within the regular service of worship close to the actual time of retirement.

With this in mind, the following is suggested as a brief liturgy to be inserted in the service. Those congregations that open the service with an ingathering period in which concerns and announcements are shared and visitors welcomed, might include this ritual in that part of the service. Others might want to insert it following the offering, which is a symbol of commitment. I strongly advocate that liturgies celebrating retirement be observed within the gathering of the total congregation as would be true of baptism, although in some cases families and friends might want to have a special service focusing upon the retirement of a particular person, as is the case with most weddings and almost all funerals.

Recognition of a Retirement
(to be used within the context of a regular service)

STATEMENT OF PURPOSE
Today we recognize and celebrate the passing of a milestone in the career of *name* and *spouse's name* as he/she has retired from *occupation/job* as of *date*.

READING OF THE WORK HISTORY OF THE RETIREE
At this point fellow workers and friends might want to share some memories of the retiree's career. The retiree may want to comment upon the meaning of the work.

SHARING OF FUTURE PLANS
These may be read by the liturgist, or the retiree may want to tell about any plans, even if tentative. In some cases all the retiree can do is to say he/she is open to the future and may want to indicate grief or confusion and solicit prayers.

A PRAYER OF THANKSGIVING FOR THE PAST AND A COMMISSION FOR THE FUTURE
Gracious God, you who have been at work from the beginning creating your world and who have given us the privilege of working with you in the creation of the world, we thank you for the contributions which workers like *name* have made to all of us through *his/her* labor. Grant unto this your servant a continuing source of satisfaction from *his/her* endeavors in the days ahead, as *he/she* seeks to do your will in all things and to be faithful to your call to love you and to love our neighbors. Amen.

A Service of Worship Celebrating Work and Retirement

This might be observed at a separate time, most convenient to all, when members of the congregation as well as family and friends might be invited to participate. It also might be used as the basis for an annual service to be held on the Sunday nearest Labor Day. Labor Day is not a religious festival, but it is observed in many places as a paid holiday and as a secular celebration of labor. This might be an occasion when the theme of Christian vocation is emphasized, when the meaning of work is explored, or ethical issues arising out of the marketplace are discussed. All those who have retired during the preceding year could be memorialized by having their names read. They could be invited to be liturgists for the service.

STATEMENT OF PURPOSE AND CALL TO WORSHIP

We gather here at this time to celebrate the contributions which all those who work make to our common life, and to recognize the careers of those who have retired from a particular occupation during this year. Hear these words from the Epistle of the apostle Paul to the Romans (8:28–30).

"We know that all things work together for good for those who love God, who are called according to his purpose. For those whom he foreknew he also predestined to be conformed to the image of his Son, in order that he might be the first born within a large family. And those whom he predestined he also called; and those whom he called he also justified; and those whom he justified he also glorified."

PRAISE AND THANKSGIVING

A hymn may be sung here such as "For the Fruit of All Creation."[7]
A Psalm may be read here such as Psalm 112.

CONFESSION AND ABSOLUTION

Gracious God, unto whom all desires are known and from whom no secrets are hidden, we confess that we have not always loved as we ought to have loved, we have not always been as forgiving as we need to be forgiven, we have not always worked as we have been called to do, and at times we have done less than we wanted to.

Forgive us the failures we have experienced, the shortcuts we have taken, times we could not see where our duty lay, and the less than noble ends we sometimes pursued. Cleanse us of any unrighteousness, make us whole again, and enable us to live by your commandments in each and all of our relationships. Amen.

Now hear the good news: Christ died for us while we were yet sinners. In the name of Jesus Christ you are forgiven.

HYMN

SCRIPTURE

Genesis 2:4b–15; Romans 12: 1–8; Matthew 16: 21–8

HOMILY

Here a homily upon the meaning of work and vocation could be given.

A Recognition of the Occupations
Various categories of occupations could be read and persons invited to stand. Significant achievements by members of the congregation during the year could be noted.

A Recognition of Those Who Changed Careers during the Year
One or more persons may be invited to share what their careers meant to them; they may share also what they are now doing that is meaningful to them.

Reaffirmation of Commitment to God's Vocation

Hymn
"The Gift of Love"[8] would be appropriate.

The Benediction and Sending Forth
We have been commanded to be caretakers of the garden created by God, to love God with all our being and our neighbor as ourselves, to go into all the world and spread the good news of God's redeeming love.

Go forth now to work with God in the fulfillment of the purposes God intends. Amen.

Liturgies for Relocation
It is my belief that when members of a congregation are leaving to move to another community, too far away to keep on returning to participate in the life of their "home" congregation, it is more important to emphasize the sending forth than the leaving. Of course, it is important to recall what their membership has meant to a particular congregation and to celebrate that. It is important to assure them that they will be missed and to acknowledge the pain of parting as well as the anxiety of going into a strange environment among strange people.

A Service of Sending Forth
(to be observed when persons are leaving the congregation)

Statement of Purpose
Read Acts 13:1–3.

Brothers and sisters, from the very beginning of the Christian movement congregations have been sending out representatives commissioned to bear witness to the love of God in Christ Jesus.

Today we are sending out *name(s)* who *is/are* moving to *location*.

Review, Recognition and Appreciation of Service
We are grateful for what you have been and what you have done as members of this congregation. We shall miss you. We remind you that going out to a new place has long been a common experience. We urge you to see in this the leading of the Holy Spirit. Hear these words from Hebrews 11:8–10.

You do not go alone. Our God goes with you.

Psalm 139 *(may be read responsively)*

THE COMMISSIONING
If it seems appropriate, the persons who are leaving may come forward and appropriate persons may lay their hands upon their heads.

Go forth now, carrying with you all our love and prayers, knowing that your lives and your work will witness to your faith. (*If the congregation to which they go is known, the following may be said:* We commend you to the care and keeping of *name[s]*. In the name of the Father, the Son and the Holy Spirit. Amen.)

A Liturgy of Welcome to Newcomers to the Community

When persons move into a new community it has to be acknowledged that many of them take time to shop around before they make up their minds to affiliate with one particular congregation. Also, every congregation has a ritual and a way of receiving new members by transfer from other congregations. However, this may be done only periodically until a class of what is deemed sufficient size has been built up. In order to be most helpful to persons who have moved, some service of reception is most meaningful when done soon after the move and when they feel comfortable in being singled out for this kind of recognition.

A brief service of welcome to the community without implying that there is an obligation to transfer formally their membership to this congregation is suggested. Some congregations still may prefer to retain this as a part of formal transfer of membership.

WELCOMING
Name(s) has/have recently moved here from *location* where *he/she/they* were (a) member(s) of *church name*. We want you to know that we are glad you are living in this community. We want you to know that our doors are open to you and our friendship is extended to you, for in the Letter to the Ephesians it is written, "He came and proclaimed peace to you who were far off and peace to those who were near; for through him both of us have access in one Spirit to the Father. So then you are no longer strangers and aliens, but you are citizens with the saints and also members of the household of God."

---

[1]Peter Marris, *Loss and Change* (New York: Pantheon, 1974).

[2]J. R. Kelley, M. W. Steinkamp, and Janice Kelley. "Later Life Leisure: How They Play in Peoria," *The Gerontologist* (October 1986), no. 26: (5) 531ff.

[3]Aaron Antonovsky, *Unraveling the Mystery of Health: How People Manage Stress and Stay Well* (San Francisco: Jossey-Bass Publishers, 1987).

[4]Erik Erikson, "Identity and the Life Cycle," *Psychological Issues,* no. 1 (1959).

[5]Viktor Frankl, *Man's Search for Meaning*(Boston: Beacon Press, 1962).

[6]*Faith Development in the Adult Life Cycle: Report of a Research Project* (Religious Education Association, 9709 Rich Road, Minneapolis, MN 55437, 1987).

[7]By Fred Pratt Green (1970). See *Chalice Hymnal* (St. Louis, Chalice Press, 1995), 714.

[8]By Hal H. Hopson (1972). See *Chalice Hymnal,* 526.

11
Upon Leaving a Home

Bryan J. Cannon

SAYING GOOD-BYE TO A DWELLING PLACE

In a cartoon that I ran across recently, a salesman is showing a middle-aged couple a little travel trailer: "Nothing like a well-built home to give you a feeling of permanence and stability, folks!...In addition, it's ready to roll!" Eighteen to 21 percent of Americans are on the move every year. As George Pierson observes, "to live is to move. We cannot live without moving."[1]

America has always been on the move. Our country was born out of the necessity of the need to move wedded to adventure. The Pilgrims were hardy folks whose lives were ruptured by their circumstances. Political winds in Europe blowing primarily against them necessitated their pulling up stakes and sallying forth in the face of an awesome challenge: traversing thousands of miles of ocean, facing the terrible odds of weather conditions and health hazards, and settling a wilderness with meager provisions. Yet they went, leaving their homes and all that was familiar. The new land was given birth by pioneers who knew what it was to leave a home. For years the frontier was settled by that same spirit.

Among the pioneers were those who wanted adventure, who were tired of the familiar. Hawthorne recognized even a deeper revelation: the desire to explore. "Why should he make himself a prisoner for life in brick, and stone, in old worm-eaten timbers, when he may just as easily dwell, in one sense, nowhere—in a better sense wherever the fit and beautiful shall offer him a home."[2]

Traditionally, men have been the warriors and wanderers and women the keepers of the nest. The investment women have had in a stable home has been intensely focused with the care of children falling primarily on them. Wrenching a family from its familiar surroundings often has had different implications for women than for men, namely, striving to maintain a stable environment for the family. Contemplating a move often has had a different set of considerations for men. In the past, when men were the primary bread-winners, their considerations focused around their work and providing for their family.

While one of the major reasons for people moving today is still change of employment, families and the roles of spouses are far more diverse. Fewer families are traditional in pattern. There is an increasing number in which both parents are employed, and almost 50 percent of households now have a single parent head. When a move is being contemplated due to a loss of job, a company transfer and/or advancement, or the desire to find new or different employment, it will entail different issues for nontraditional than for traditional families. For the latter, the mother might resist relocation while her husband emphasizes all the benefits of the change. She must leave security and familiarity of her home as well as seek out new doctors, dentists and places to shop. Her husband may be focused on income, possibilities for advancement and recreational advantages. For the nontraditional families, while some of the above concerns may be present, far more at issue may be employment possibilities for both spouses or replacing good child-care providers and/or facilities.

Of course, people move for many other reasons. At least a quarter of all moves are linked in some way with other family motives such as marriage, divorce, separation, death and rejoining relatives.[3] People also change locations to improve opportunities, for schooling for themselves or their children, or at retirement. Some simply want a change in environment or the experience of what a new place has to offer.

Pierson points out that family patterns have changed so that we no longer have grandparents or maiden aunts living with us, and the children are gone all too soon. (While numbers of parents complain about the empty-nest syndrome, others object to adult children moving back home.) The house crammed with gadgets has been stripped of ancestral memories and often deprived of its family character. Pierson sees what people own as often being drained of much of its human feelings and associations. Yet, most Americans still need to belong, and as Pierson expresses it, "a house is a place to belong in."[4]

The Importance of Place

The place in which we live represents more than what one might imagine on first thought. "It takes a heap o' living in a house," observed Edgar A. Guest, "t' make it a home." The house is more than shelter. There we may be birthed, nurtured, instructed, loved, wounded and sometimes abused, impacted and imprinted with behavior and memories.

A house represents a fixed asset that means security, emotionally as well as financially. As persons grow older, their reluctance to move often increases. In a study by Prasad and Johnson, it was found that for retiring persons only 3 percent of those owning houses moved in contrast to 15 percent of those who rented. Home ownership reduces mobility.

The place where we live also represents more than what occurs within. Our friends, family, and nearby recreation possibilities influence how we feel about our home. The climate, our feeling about the change in seasons, our health, and those subtleties of spiritual attunement to an area all contribute to the emotions impacting leaving a home. And for most, we must leave that home at some time.

Saying Good-bye to a House

How do you say good-bye to a dwelling place that has been the location of joys, comfort, safety and growth? Even the anticipation of a new home and the adventure of the future do not compensate for the sadness of leaving one's house. Sorting, discarding, packing and planning use great amounts of energy and distract us from the moment when we look around and see the house empty that once was filled with people and activities. There is almost a sense of the space murmuring its feeling of abandonment. There the house stands, stripped naked, bare, exposed to the glances of everyone. Defenseless, it seemingly has as much difficulty saying good-bye to us as we do in gathering our feelings and expressing them.

Closure is important. That place that provided so much living for us must open itself to welcome new residents and to make a home for them just as a new home awaits to greet us and take us in.

We do not want sorrow or grief, the residue of anger or unsettled problems, lingering there. We must be as tidy in cleaning those up in confession and healing as we are in sweeping the place clean and removing unwanted material debris.

Every person, from those who are by circumstances confined to the most avid wanderer, must concede that life is movement and change. From our mother's womb to our final transition into the eternal, we are in journey. No place is ours; no home is permanent. We receive for a while and then release it to others. Can it be that we are afraid of the unknown tomorrow, or even more deeply, that the fear of death underlies our tendency to place so much security in a "nest"?

While some philosophers condemn the thought as an inadequate dualism, still it is true: Christians understand themselves as living in two kingdoms. However much we cherish and assume responsibility in this world with the use of our five senses, there is another realm. Given all the emotional and material investment we make in a place to ground our security and stabilize some small portion of our life in this physical world, leaving a home for many symbolizes life's transitory nature.

Jesus challenged us to keep our priorities straight. "Do not store up for yourselves treasures on earth, where moth and rust consume and where thieves break in and steal; but store up for yourselves treasures in heaven" (Matthew 7: 19, 20). Two worlds, one temporal and passing away, the other eternal, held out to us as our blessed and ultimate home.

How important is this? Is this wishful thinking or a mere intangible so far removed that it cannot touch the feelings we struggle with in the realities of transition and change? Hardly so. We live a breath away at any moment from the reality of that other world. At any time any one of us might be saying good-bye permanently to our present places. Remembering that our ultimate and permanent home is with God helps us maintain perspective. Then we dwell less on our loss. We put less emotional investment in that to which we will say good-bye at some future date. We will be freer to celebrate the temporal and let it go, moving on in our journey.

I am a part of all that I have met,
Yet all experience is an arch wherethro'

Gleams that untravell'd world whose margin fades
Forever and forever when I move.[5]

Then God will be more of a participant in process living, more a friend and trusted companion in the change that continues to occur.

The Beloved Community's Role

We need to say a word about the role of the church in leaving a home and a community. Far too often we have seen the church playing an important role only in processing and providing ritual and symbol for birth, confirmation, marriage, and death. There were times in the past when the church gathered to bless a home. More than once I have participated in such a significant service expressing a couple's belief that not only all they had was a gift from God, but also that God's Spirit would fill their new home and guide their life together as they entered there to dwell.

We live so privately in our impersonal, modern world on the move. The church is usually not the intimate family where all our high-impact experiences are shared. No one is to blame but ourselves, for we are the church, responsible for its behavior and ethos. We will be the benefactors if we have expectations of the church, invest in it, call forth from it, and share with it our times of joy and sorrow, change and transition, as when we leave a house. We are creatures who need symbols and ceremonies. The church can be a beloved community providing emotional support and help through the grief of saying goodbye.

Naturally there are those within a congregation with whom we have close ties and natural affinity. We can invite them to share with our family as we leave this familiar place. They can represent the whole church. "Where two or three are gathered…" The time comes to depart, and the community of faith should be the natural bearers of burden and confession, the reservoir of grace, and the assurance of the ongoing presence of the God who travels with us to establish us and protect us. We ought to call on the church to share in the ritual upon leaving a home.

A Ritual upon Leaving a Home

There are many memories, sad and joyous, connected with our dwelling places, all part of our history. Unprocessed grief and unexpressed thanksgiving burden our departure and encumber our future. When we are older and we must give up our home for a retirement center or nursing facility, or we go to live with children, the anxiety or grief can be heavy.

So before leaving the house with all of its memories and meanings, let family members, friends and/or those important to us from the church fellowship, gather to worship God. Different members may lead in parts of the service so that all share in the ritual of leave-taking.

Opening Sentences[6]
Lord, you have been our dwelling place in all generations.

Before the mountains were brought forth, or even you had formed the earth and the world, from everlasting to everlasting you are God.

Satisfy us in the morning with your steadfast love, that we may rejoice and be glad all our days.

Let the favor of the Lord our God be upon us, and establish the work of our hands upon us, yea, the work of our hands establish it.

Open to me the gates of righteousness, that I may enter through them and give thanks to the Lord.

This is the gate of the Lord; the righteous shall enter through it.

This is the day which the Lord has made; let us rejoice and be glad in it.

Save us, we beseech you, O Lord! O Lord, we beseech you, give us success!

Trust in the Lord with all your heart, and do not rely on your own insight.

In all your ways acknowledge him, and he will make straight your paths.

The Invocation (*in unison*)
Almighty God, Lord of all places and people, Master of all times and situations, Divine Healer and Keeper of Memories, Lord of the future and of all hope, we take these moments to acknowledge our gratitude to you for this dwelling place which has held so much meaning. We are creatures of territory, finding a home, security and safety. We need your merciful help in processing transition to another place. Make these moments redemptive, healing the memories of pain and sadness, and blessing those of joy and happiness. Grant us insight from this time, that we might leave this place wiser, grounded more in trusting you, rather than geography, as our true dwelling place. For you alone are our hope of a final resting place. We are on a sacred journey. So grant us freedom to leave and move on, in the name of Jesus, our friend and traveling companion, we pray. Amen.

Acknowledging and Celebrating Memories
This is a time to recall good memories, struggles, victories and simple pleasures. Be in touch with feelings and mental pictures and share them. Let everyone reminisce. Celebrate with laughter and tears!

A Responsive Litany of Affirmation[7]
I will praise you, Lord, with all my heart; I will tell of all the wonderful things you have done.

We praise you, Lord.

I will sing with joy because of you. I will sing praise to you, Almighty God.

We praise you, Lord.

Whoever goes to the Lord for safety, whoever remains under the protection of the Almighty, can say to him, "You are my defender and protector. You are my God, in you I trust."

We trust in you, O God.

He will keep you safe from all hidden dangers and from all deadly diseases. He will cover you with his wings; you will be safe in his care; his faithfulness will protect and defend you.

We trust in you, O God.

You need not fear any dangers at night, or sudden attacks during the day. You have made the Lord your defender, the Most High your protector.

We trust in you, O God.

So no disaster will strike you, no violence will come near your home. God will put his angels in charge of you to protect you wherever you go.

In **your confidence, we have peace, O God.**

The Lord will keep your going out and your coming in from this time forth, and forever more.

 Blessed be the name of the Lord!

A Prayer of Thanksgiving and Trust (*in unison*)

Our Divine and Holy Parent, in a world where so many do not have any place to lay their heads, no place to call home, we thank you for provisions of this dwelling. Now, Lord, we commit to those who would follow here, this house that has known so much of our living. Establish securely with us the good memories that have been part of living here. Heal all the wounded thoughts, erase all the painful pictures of the past, disengage us from entangling regrets of what should and could have been. Now turn the remembrance of struggles into wisdom and maturity for the future. We celebrate all that has been that is good, and with expectation that comes from trusting you as the Lord of new beginnings and as the Great Companion of our journey, we give leave of this place, through Jesus Christ our Lord. Amen.

Hymn (*a parting hymn or the Doxology may be sung*)

The Benediction (*in unison*)

Now may the Lord bless us and keep us; may the Lord cause his face to shine upon us and be gracious to us; May the Lord lift up his countenance upon us and give us his peace, now and forever more. Amen.

---

[1]George W. Pierson, *The Moving American* (New York: Alfred A. Knopf, 1973), foreword.

[2]Nathaniel Hawthorne, *The House of the Seven Gables* (Danbury: Grolier, 1985).

[3]Clifford J. Hansen, *Readings in the Sociology of Migration* (New York: Pergamon, 1970), 22.

[4]George W. Pierson, *The Moving American*, foreword.

[5]"Ulysses," Alfred, Lord Tennyson, *Complete Poetical Works of Tennyson* (Boston, Mass.: Houghton Mifflin, 1898).

[6]From Psalm 90:1–2, 14, 17; Psalm 118:19–20, 24–25; Proverbs 3:5–6.

[7]From Psalm 9:1–2; Proverbs 91:1–6, 9–11.

12
Dying

William E. Phipps

DEATH: THE FULFILLMENT OF LIFE

In religious literature, both *life* and *death* have double meaning. The creation account treasured by Jews, Christians, and Muslims well illustrates the dual connotation. The garden of Eden story refers, first of all, to physical life and physical death which is a part of the immediate awareness of all—irreligious and religious alike. The opening chapters of Genesis affirm that living humans and animals are distinguished from inanimate clay figurines by breath. After respiring creatures expire (literally, "breathe out"), they return to "dust." When that dry earth is mixed with water, it can be reconstituted into some other organism in a "dust to dust" cycle.

In addition to an explanation of the start and finish of physical life, the Eden story holds a more subtle meaning of life and death. The announcement of the punishment for eating forbidden fruit displays this: "In the day that you eat of it you shall die" (Genesis 2:17). The first mention of death cannot refer to physical death because the humans who ate the forbidden fruit continued to breathe for many days afterwards. The writer of this simple but profound story is referring to a kind of spiritual suicide by which men and women cut themselves off from companionship with God. The mythological account concludes by asserting that had they not stolen fruit, they would have been permitted to partake of the "tree of life" fruit. This tree symbolized the "life forever" (Genesis 3:22) which would have resulted for Adam and Eve had they not been alienated from their Creator.

The primeval Eden story introduces the concept of everlasting life that is prominent in subsequent religious literature. Beliefs about everlasting life can be divided into two major classifications: conditional and unconditional. The conditional theories have this form: if something is done by or for you, then you will attain life after death. Immortality is not guaranteed for everyone because humans—like all other organic species—are inherently mortal. Death is the final end if nothing is done to keep one's spirit alive.

Throughout history the most widespread form of conditional immortality has been rooted in reproduction. If one raises a family, one's genes are transmitted, and if there are unceasing generations of offspring, then portions of the biologically constituted person live forever. The transcontinental appeal of this type of immortality can be found in an African saying: "An ancestor lives on as long as there are children who remember." Abraham the Hebrew was also strongly motivated to have offspring so that his name would be great in the future. A cultural as well as a physical inheritance is implanted in one's progeny. Living on through children and grandchildren is still a prominent reason for human procreation.

Both those who do and those who do not multiply are entitled to an immortality of influence. If someone does something that has social impact, she or he will live on. It is said that Abraham Lincoln and other national heroes are as alive as ever because they live in the hearts of their countrymen. The revolutionary ideas of Susan B. Anthony, Martin Luther King, Jr., Thomas Jefferson, and other famous people affect us even as they did their contemporaries, so their deaths remain in some sense unreal.

Social immortality has interested the irreligious at least as much as the religious. Frederick Engels concluded his funeral speech for Karl Marx with this prophecy: "His name will live through centuries and so will his work."[1] At the center of the capital of China is a memorial to the Communist Revolution. On it is inscribed a slogan of Mao Zedong: "The people's heroes are immortal."

Although Mary Ann Evans died more than a century ago in England, she continues to live by means of the acclaimed literary works of her pseudonym George Eliot. She expressed her yearning in these lines:

O may I join the choir invisible
Of those immortal dead who live again
In minds made better by their presence…
So to live is heaven:
To make undying music in the world…
May I…be to other souls
The cup of strength in some great agony,
Enkindle generous ardor, feed pure love,
Beget the smiles that have no cruelty.[2]

The immortality of influence is not limited to those associated with government or those who have international notoriety. Someone who produces crafts or recipes which continue to be used, or someone who originates ideas preserved in libraries will live on as long as her or his contribution is recognized as significant.

One need not have a good reputation to attain this type of immortality. For thousands of years Pontius Pilate's name has been, and will continue to be, remembered by millions every week because they recite from the Apostles' Creed that he was the ruler who permitted Jesus' crucifixion. Because of the atrocities for which he was responsible, Adolf Hitler's name will no doubt live in infamy longer than the thousand years he had hoped the Third Reich would last.

A theological variety of conditional life after death recognizes that all organic things are mortal and presumes that God alone is naturally immortal or deathless. Death is the natural final end of mice and men. God, the possessor of infinite immortality, shares the divine quality with those found to be acceptable. Humans are immort-able inasmuch as each has a deathless potential that becomes actual if positive response is made to God's offer. For humans immortality is a privilege, not an inalienable right. Each has the option of "passing on" or of passing out of existence. Those who devote themselves to spiritual growth during their physical lives will be given the opportunity for further development after physical death. Life after death is seen as a continuance of the eternal or spiritual life which one began to enjoy during his or her mortal life.

The corollary of this immortality theory is that self-destruction is the result of not being united with God. Those who do not become infused with the immortal Spirit of God and who do not accept the ensuing responsibilities of that relationship have nothing within them capable of surviving biological death. If they are on the sensate level of animals, they share the ultimate destiny of subhuman animals.

Some biblical writers accepted a conditional doctrine of everlasting life. The garden of Eden story declares that humans lose spiritual life forever when they separate themselves from God. There is nothing in their future but dusty death. Paul, the writer of about half the New Testament books, held a doctrine of conditional immortality. For him, as R. H. Charles comments, the immortal life "is the privilege only of those who are spiritually one with Christ."[3] Paul states that "the gift of God is eternal life" (Romans 6:23) and that death is the final end for those whom God finds unacceptable.

The biological, social, and theological types of conditional immortality are not mutually exclusive. It would not be inconsistent to think of someone achieving all varieties. For example, Abigail Adams, the wife of one United States president and the mother of another, a noted feminist writer, and a woman of religious devotion, would seem to fulfill the conditions for three kinds of conditional immortality.

The theory of unconditional life after death affirms that all humans are endowed with permanently deathless spirits. This unique spirit, or soul, is given to each person by the Creator, and is believed to continue forever in a spiritual realm after death. The doctrine of unconditional everlasting life was developed by Jews during the last years of the Old Testament era. The book of Daniel contains this forecast: "Many of those who sleep in the dust of the earth shall awake, some to everlasting life, and some...to everlasting contempt" (Daniel 12:2). This verse is the only one in the entire Jewish Bible which states clearly the individual life-after-death doctrine that was to become normative in the Jewish and Christian religions.

The apostle Paul was the earliest and remains the most authoritative Christian theologian. He declared that the living body should be venerated as "a temple of the Holy Spirit" (1 Corinthians 6:19), but he did not find the dead body of sacred value. Like the assemblage of materials used in a temple's construction, the building might as well be leveled or disassembled and used in other structures if there is no more divine worship going on within. Paul viewed his worn-out body as a transient "earthly tent," soon to be demolished. He wrote about looking forward to the replacement of his precarious mortal dwelling by a permanent immortal life (2 Corinthians 5:1–8). As a tentmaker, how might Paul have disposed of dilapidated tents? Is it not likely that he would salvage any reusable parts and then destroy by fire the remaining organic stuff?

Paul's fullest discussion of life after death is in 1 Corinthians 15, where he frankly and plainly states that "flesh and blood cannot inherit the kingdom of God, nor does the perishable inherit the imperishable" (v. 50). He did not believe that the residual dust in a tomb would be the substance of a new heavenly organism. When the apostle writes about "the resurrection of the dead" he does not mean the reassembling and the reanimation of the corpse. The expression "spiritual body" that he uses does not refer to the physical skeleton and the flesh that hangs on it. Rather, in modern terminology, it means the self or the personality. What removed death's sting for Paul was not gazing at a petrified corpse but the good news that mortal nature can "put on immortality."

Some early Christians were burned alive by their persecutors. Church historian Eusebius reports that Polycarp, the Bishop of Smyrna, was the first Christian on record to be cremated. In 155, the aged saint was martyred after he refused to affirm "Caesar is Lord." He presented himself on the pyre as a whole burnt offering and in the midst of the flame his body shone "like a loaf in the oven."[4]

Christians generally rejected cremation, but they realized that the method of corpse disposal was not of fundamental importance. Minucius Felix, a third-century Latin Christian, explains:

> Do you think that anything perishes before God when it is withdrawn from our feeble eyes? Every corpse, whether it is dried into dust, dissolved into moisture, compressed into ashes, or rarefied into smoke, is withdrawn from us, but it is reserved for God who has custody of the elements…We do not fear loss from cremation even though we adopt the ancient and better custom of earth burial.[5]

In the course of Western history, some Christians strayed from the biblical perspective and identified reality with what can be experienced with their five senses: the more tangible, the more real. Church father Tertullian in the third century declared that "nothing exists if it be not a body" and conversely, "nothing is incorporeal except what does not exist."[6] His dictum came from the popular pagan Stoic materialism of his day.[7] Tertullian also consistently held that God, being real, must have corporeality.[8] Unable to conceive of reality in other than a physical manner, he argued that the resurrection has reference to "this flesh, suffused with blood, built up with bones, interwoven with nerves, entwined with veins."[9]

In the twentieth century, Christians with an outlook somewhat similar to Tertullian have called themselves "fundamentalists." Physical resurrection is among their five fundamentals of belief. According to John Murray, one of their theologians, "resurrection cannot be construed otherwise" than "resuscitation of what is laid in the tomb." The resurrected body of Christians, he claims, will have a "physical composition."[10] Harmonious with this doctrine is the anti-cremationist stance of fundamentalists. Fundamentalists seem to believe that the restoring of the soul to the resurrected body is like putting milk in a cleansed old bottle.

Outsiders might find it incongruous that fundamentalists, who stress spiritual intervention in the natural order, would exalt the physical to an eternal realm. But Tertullian and his followers have taught them that the irrationality of such a position should be of no concern, because God specializes in doing what is absurd. As displayed in creationism disputes, fundamentalists do not want to acknowledge our kinship with other animals, and so they declare humans to have little connection with organic development or decay. Since they defiantly reject primates as part of their ancestry, it is understandable that they would not care to admit—as their Bible does—that both animals and humans share earthly elements that do not get transported to heaven.

Materialism, or physicalism as some prefer to call it, has never been accepted by any branch of mainline Christianity. However, many Christians display a metaphysics of naive realism in identifying reality with objects in space and time. Possibly due to an underdeveloped conceptualizing, they have difficulty comprehending the outlook of the earliest and most influential Christian theologian. Paul stated: "Things beyond our seeing, hearing, and imagining are prepared by God for those who love him" (1 Corinthians 2:9). He believed, as has earlier been shown, that it was possible for individual personality to persist after death in a nonphysical manner. Those who likewise believe that human life can continue in radically different conditions after the body expires, plan for funerals suggestive of the new mode. If the holy of holies of a funeral service is a corpse in a box, then the message is this: nothing exists for humans beyond the life that prevails in this realm. Accordingly, devastating grief hits when the lid of the box containing the material body is closed for the last time and the body is placed in a hole.

In recent years, Christian churches have altered their perspective on corpse disposal. Along with most other religious people throughout the globe, Christians are beginning to commend the dignity of cremation. This theological endorsement marks a shift away from the irreligious materialism that has been pervasive in Western civilization. In this regard, Leroy Bowman writes: "The chief significance of cremation" is that it encourages "a more wholesome attitude toward the funeral on the part of the family." It "eliminates the need of embalming, 'restoration,' and lavish expenditures for casket and all funeral 'goods,' but allows for all the social and spiritual aspects of the funeral period."[11]

Presbyterian minister and thanatologist Richard Morgan finds possibilities for funeral reform in cremation. Revering a natural-looking corpse is, he argues, incompatible both with Christian theology and with grief therapy. With cremation, "grief work can begin sooner, since there is no fixation on the dead person." Morgan concludes: "While it is right to grieve over the loss of the person who touched one's life, it seems incongruent to dwell on an empty shell."[12] Ministers are becoming aware that the symbolism of a corpse at the center of the funeral worship runs counter to basic biblical affirmations. The allegedly preserved body is a Promethean rejection of a biblical judgment that "all flesh is grass" which "withers...when the breath of the LORD blows upon it" (Isaiah 40:6–7). The biblical hope for life after death is based on the power of God and has nothing to do with corpse disposal.

The Spirit, declared to be the "giver of life" in the Nicene Creed, is appropriately symbolized by fire. Following the igniting spark, life blazes up restlessly, brightening or transforming what it encounters. After flourishing it less noticeably declines, providing a warm glow before it dies away. Also, the holiest season of the church calendar is associated with fire. Lent traditionally began with ashes on the forehead, a mortality reminder. It ended with lighting a candle during the Easter vigil in recognition of the light of Christ dispelling the world's darkness. Thus, radiant flame has at least as many holy associations as dark earth. Since fire was not repugnant in the Judeo-Christian culture, church leaders have been able to integrate traditional symbolism into cremation. In this context, consider these lines from a familiar hymn:

> Breathe on me, Breath of God, till I am wholly thine,
> until this earthly part of me glows with thy fire divine.[13]

A Service of Joyful Remembrance

Confrontation with our own mortality may be the best way to sharpen one's awareness of what is essential to life. At the University of Wisconsin, Professor Warren Shibles had students in his death education course respond to this question: "What are the most valuable things in your life?" Their answers include friends, love, reasoning ability, inner peace, self-esteem, morality, sight, and family.[14] Money, and things it can purchase, were not listed. Compare those answers with the results of a nationwide, annual college survey. An increasing majority of students rank "being very well-off financially" as "essential" or "very important."[15] These contrasting responses stimulated me to ask my college students about their basic values. In my "Death and Dying" course, I asked: "What qualities make life worth living?" Responses I received have been similar to those Shibles published. But, when I raised the same question in classes where death is not the focal consideration, material possessions were commonly mentioned and often stressed.

Those people who rank life's intangible values higher than things money can buy usually find that reflection on death enhances the quality of life. "To see life, and to value it, from the point of view of death is to see and value it truly," said philosopher George Santayana. "It is far better to live in the light of the tragic fact, rather than to forget or deny it, and build everything on a fundamental lie."[16] To view the whole significance of life, we have to ponder the fact that we are all terminal cases. Brain cells die in us every hour, never to be renewed.

Interest in being closely involved in matters affecting our personal future is on the increase. For example, participants in a wedding are finding it beneficial to work with friends to carry out many of the details even though they may be frowned on by florists, professional photographers, and bridal consultants. Taking a large measure of personal responsibility enables a couple to be more selective of the place, the paraphernalia, and the program. They can calmly balance the promotional pitch of one business against the propaganda of another. Looking at a variety of possible settings, leisurely engaging in comparative shopping, and blending together old and new forms give a personal hallmark to a wedding that enhances memory. As a couple examine possibilities, they may discover that expensive frills correlate little with the affection they have for one another and the potential meaningfulness of the rite.

Planning together when happiness is anticipated comes more easily than planning for unhappy happenings. Even so, some are finding do-it-yourself divorces advantageous to the participants rather than to the lawyers. Also, a realization is dawning that death is more certain than taxes and that planning for its eventuality can translate anxieties into satisfactions. The rapidly developing hospice movement is witness to a widespread interest in caring for the terminally ill in a more personal setting than hospitals can provide. Taking charge of a loved one who has only weeks to live can be a meaningful final act of devotion. Mutual benefits can also result from sharing ideas on body disposal and from helping one another make rational and compassionate decisions about fitting memorialization.

Bereaved families find it bewildering to cope with the many important decisions that need to be made after the death of a loved one. The worst possible time to think creatively about an appropriate funeral is shortly after the death of a loved one. The next-of-kin is then likely to have as little rationality as a drunken person. In such a situation what often happens is that the mortician and the minister are often allowed to do what they think is best. Morticians consequently arrange for public viewing of the embalmed body at the funeral establishment, on the assumption that what best advertises their business is best for the bereaved. Likewise, ministers frequently intone words from their denominational manual, believing that what is easy to prepare is satisfactory for the funeral service. At the time when maximum attention should be given to honoring the dead person in a manner appropriate to his or her lifestyle, a routine and impersonal ritual results.

In my experience as a leader of workshops on personal funeral planning, I have found that almost everyone is somewhat reluctant to look at this painful subject. However, most can be persuaded that there is less anguish for their survivors if they plan for the inevitable. To illustrate the advantage of planning for a liturgy to celebrate a death, let me describe how a former colleague of mine dealt with his death. I assisted in conducting the memorial service for Burr Harrington who, years earlier, had completed the "Personal Funeral Planning" form I have long used in my college death education course.

Throughout his life Burr aimed at fulfilling Jesus' motto, "Not to be served, but to serve." While a student at Princeton he participated in the presidential campaign for Woodrow Wilson, a fellow idealist. Afterward he served in a variety of professions until he was sixty-five, ranging from immigration officer to education professor. For him, to be retired meant to be retreaded, so during most of his last fifteen years he worked vigorously as our church's director of Christian education and as an organizer of West Virginia's senior citizens.

To guarantee that his values would consistently be expressed to the very end, he planned with me and others for the disposition of his body and for his final rites. As a frequent hospital patient in his declining years, he realized he owed much to medical research. Millions die in our nation annually, yet medical schools often find it difficult to obtain the few thousand bodies needed each year to train future physicians and to develop new surgical procedures.

My friend thought of his body as the last earthly thing he could give to help someone. In order to repay his social debt for the many years of health, he completed a form obtained from the Human Gift Registry at the nearest medical school. By this means, he requested that his unembalmed body, after the removal of some organs, be sent promptly to the anatomy department of that school for cadaveral study. Burr thought of dialysis sufferers who might function more normally with his recycled kidneys. Also, he had heard of many who had had their sight restored by cornea transplants, and he longed to become a means for effecting one of these modern miracles. In making his cornea donation he may have reflected that purity of heart, not eyeballs, is needed to "see God." According to Jesus, "the pure in heart" are those who are generous without expecting something in return (Matthew 5:8; Luke 6:35). Also, in the Hebrew Bible, "I was eyes to the blind," is included in the description of a superlatively good person (Job 29:15).

Burr was inspired by the simple dignity of biblical funerals. Except for Jacob and Joseph, whose bodies were mummified for transportation to Palestine as a witness that Egypt was not to be the Israelite homeland, there is no mention in the Bible of corpse preservation, or of burial caskets. Rather, the cloth-covered corpse was buried shortly after tributes of grief were finished. As one who shunned the excesses of capitalism throughout his life, Burr was repulsed by the usual funeral display of conspicuous consumption. He would not have cared for a luxury car if he could have afforded one, so he chuckled over the absurdity of having his carcass carried in a hearse that cost more than his home.

No planning was done with a mortuary because Burr found its services superfluous. He lamented that in the course of his lifetime the funeral business had eclipsed the clergy's traditional role as funeral director. In his childhood the undertaker was commissioned to undertake certain arrangements pertaining to body disposal as requested by the family. But contemporary morticians have usually removed the service from home and church to a "chapel" on their premises. Those places are blandly designed in the hope that they will be inoffensive to customers of all faiths or of no faith, and they feature taped sentimental music.

The mortician increasingly has assumed the role of advising the clergy, telling them when to speak and where to walk. Burr shared the judgment of many Christians that open caskets, which the funeral industry depends on to promote its merchandise and "restoration" skills, are examples of neo-paganism. These materialistic displays become a counterforce to the Christian conviction of the resurrection of the nonphysical body. Ostentatious caskets, lifelike cosmetics, and leakless vaults cannot pull the sting out of death. Those who internalize the courage of Jesus do not need make-believe camouflage to shield them from the tragic facts of existence. Why waste hardwood, metal and land to keep up false appearances? Does not the New Testament assure us that a dead Christian is "absent from the body and present with the Lord?" (2 Corinthians 5:8).

Medical schools provide the option of either cremating the remains or returning them to the family's cemetery. Burr chose the more rapid means for returning the lifeless flesh to its elements. The grateful medical school paid the cost of cadaver transportation and cremation, so thousands of dollars that might have been spent for the average funeral and burial expenses were diverted to more beneficial uses.

Finally, my colleague planned his memorial service. Since it was to be a worship service, he wanted it to be set in the familiar surrounding of our Presbyterian church. He had long thought through his preference that it be corpse-less, for he regarded an allegedly preserved body as a rejection of the biblical affirmation that "all flesh is grass" which "withers when the breath of the LORD blows upon it" (Isaiah 44:6–7).

Burr was frustrated by the impersonal nature of many funeral liturgies, but he realized that it was not altogether the fault of the clergy. Often the minister does not know the deceased well, and the bereaved family is too numbed by its loss to communicate helpful personal information. The minister often has to decide on his own which readings and music would be fitting. Burr provided some literary suggestions from the Bible for whoever would officiate. He requested that Psalm 150 be read. My friend was an accomplished instrumentalist, so it was quite appropriate to conclude his life, as the Psalter is concluded, by a hallelujah from a musical band. Perhaps if he lived farther south, he would have brought in a jazz band to simulate that Hebrew hurrah for Yahweh!

Burr balanced that enthusiastic call to worship with a request that 1 Corinthians 13 be read. By this he testified that praise is no more than "a clashing cymbal" if love is absent. He often said that the gospel is centered on the lonely, the lost, and the loveless. Although it is unusual to hear his biblical selections at a funeral, they were especially meaningful to all who gathered to thank God for the privilege of knowing Burr. They aptly expressed his triumphant and hopeful temperament.

It would have been out of harmony with Burr's lifestyle had the memorial service been lugubrious. So with tears of gladness, we sang "Joyful, Joyful, We Adore Thee" and "More Love to Thee, O Christ." After the celebration in the sanctuary, the congregation met informally in the fellowship hall to visit with his family and to reminisce with one another on this outstanding person. In our pervasively secular culture, it is rare to find a Christian who takes the opportunity to express the central values of the gospel through his or her final requests. But for us, Burr's temporal death gave rich insight into the meaning of his eternal life.

Burr realized decades ago what is now more widely being considered regarding the donation of body parts. Postmortem organ extractions are giving to recipients what may be worth more than the largest monetary legacy. The development of transplant technology now provides the opportunity for repaying a large social indebtedness. Due in part to medical advancements, life expectancy has been extended by many years. Conscientious individuals are beginning to recognize the irresponsible wastefulness of letting organs rot or burn when they could make a critical difference in the lives of handicapped persons.

Burr Harrington shared with Robert Test a yearning that their deathbeds be transformed to beds of life through utilization of them to help others lead fuller lives. From Test's eloquent and oft-reprinted testimony, these items are excerpted:

> Give my sight to the man who has never seen a sunrise, a baby's face or love in the eyes of a woman. Give my heart to a person whose own heart has caused nothing but endless days of pain…Give my kidneys to one who depends on a machine to exist from week to week. Take my bones, every muscle, every fiber and nerve in my body and find a way to make a crippled child walk…Burn what is left of me and scatter the ashes to the winds to help the flowers grow. If you must bury something, let it be my faults, my weaknesses and all prejudice against my fellow man. If, by chance, you wish to remember me, do it with a kind deed or word to someone who needs you.

Had Burr lived a generation later he might have considered some options for the disposal of his cremation remains. Church buildings are once again being used as a repository of remains. Before 1800, notable church members were commonly buried in sanctuaries to remind congregations of "the communion of the saints." Due to lack of space and unhygienic burial conditions, that custom was discontinued. An adaptation of the old tradition is found in churches where columbaria have been constructed. An 8 by 10' closet or area below the main sanctuary can be transformed to an unobtrusive and beautifully crafted columbarium with 320 niches. Some prefer a columbarium within a church because vandalism and other desecration is less likely there. They also find an easily accessible church more conducive to prayer and meditation. New Jersey pastor Ronald Miller writes:

The greatest benefits we have received from our columbarium have been the opportunities to provide significant comfort to those who seek the option of burial space within the church building... Located just inside the main doors of our church building, with a baptismal font nearby, the columbarium expresses our firm belief that baptism is the door of the church militant and that death is the door to the church triumphant.[17]

Some now choose to dispose of cremated remains by scattering them over several square yards of some special soil. The ashes are sterile so they create no pollution, and since they are pulverized, there are no unsightly bone fragments evident. What is disseminated looks like granular chemical fertilizer and performs accordingly in enriching the soil. If seed of a perennial flower—such as forget-me-nots—are spread with the ashes, then the annual blossoms become a reminder of the deceased in subsequent summers. When a shrub is planted in a garden with a memorial plaque nearby, a life is recalled in a decorous manner. A scattering along the deceased favorite hiking trail may stimulate among survivors more positive associations than a cemetery burial. The poetically minded may associate the character of the deceased with that of a memorial tree. The sentiments of a psalmist may be apropos:

He is like a tree planted by the streams of water,
that yields its fruit in its season (Psalm 1:3).

Some image death as returning to the water, the source of all life. The exquisite poem *Crossing the Bar* tells of one who sails after dark into "the boundless deep," hoping to see this "Pilot face to face" on returning home. Those for whom water conveys more significance than earth—especially those who love to sail, fish, and swim—prefer ashes strewn on a sea, lake, or stream. Often a member of the clergy conducts a short service at the place where the remains will rest. An adaptation of a traditional committal follows: For as much as it has pleased God to take into closer communion our loved one here departed, we therefore disperse these remains among the earthly elements—ashes to ashes, dust to dust—in sure and certain hope of the life everlasting. Regarding ways of scattering ashes, Raymond Arvio recommends:

The body's ashes can be distributed among the places and scenes associated with life. Those who have moved in this direction think of it as an incredibly beautiful and sensitive movement when the scattered ashes find their place in the ocean, on a loved mountainside or among flowers and bushes tended so carefully in life. Earth burial, as it is conducted now, with sealed coffins and vaults designed to perpetuate the false image that the body stays in its original condition, does not provide the sense of spiritual connection, of a life joining Life, of returning to the soil from whence we all came.[18]

Requests that an individual makes pertaining to his or her own demise need to be communicated to and accepted by the next-of-kin. Last wills are not the place for this information because they are usually not opened until these decisions have been finalized. Franklin Roosevelt left detailed instructions for his funeral, but he deposited them in his safe without informing anyone. Only after his funeral did his family realize that he explicitly rejected much of what had been done—the embalming, the use of an expensive casket, and the grave-liner or vault. He desired a rapid return of his crippled body to the elements.[19] Thus, one's close relatives must be aware of and sympathetic with one's request for body disposal, because they are the ones who have the legal right to do with the body whatever they please.

A liturgy of joyful remembrance should focus on the well-lived life, not the well-worn body. Multi-sharing rather than solo presentation is usually found more strengthening. Important facets of a person's life are less likely to be overlooked in several short tributes. Both smiles and tears may be evoked by amusing and somber incidents related about the deceased. In contrast to the conventional funeral obituary and rites—where little is said about the deceased other than items that might appear on a formal resume—the memorial service provides a more relaxed occasion for pondering a many-splendored life.

There might have been provided for Burr a variation on his planned celebration of life. I recall one funeral pre-planner saying, with a mixture of poignancy and humor, that she was sorry that she would not be present when her carefully planned memorial service transpired. This caused me to reflect on ways of including the living presence of the person being commemorated. Why not, I thought, have the friends and intimate family engage in a preview of the more public post-mortem celebration. If the dying person is in good mental but extremely frail physical condition—as might be the case in hospice situations—all involved might find it profoundly significant to gather for a celebration of life. Such might well be at a time when gatherings are customary, at a birthday or a holiday.

Several elements might be included. Someone could arrange for brief tributes to be prepared that focus on different shining facets of the jewel-like life. Then, at the designated time, the leader could, in an informal manner, intersperse those treasured memories with literary and/or musical selections that the individual being honored had set down for his or her own funeral service. This might be accompanied by sharing some of the favorite food of that person or, if appropriate, a Christian communion service might be included. What a fine way of displaying to all present that death can be a culmination of life!

---

[1]Frederick Engels, *The Fourteenth of March, 1983* (London: Martin Lawrence Limited, 1933), 13.
[2]F. B. Pinion, ed., *A George Eliot Miscellany* (Totowa, N.J.: Barnes and Noble, 1982), 131.
[3]R. H. Charles, *Eschatology* (New York: Schocken, 1963), 444.
[4]Eusebius, *Church History* 4, 15; 5, 1.
[5]Minucius Felix, *Octavius* 34.

[6]Tertullian, *On the Soul* 7; *On the Flesh of Christ* 11.

[7]A. H. Armstrong and R. A. Markus, *Christian Faith and Greek Psilosophy* (New York: Sheed and Ward, 1960), 60.

[8]Tertullian, *Against Praxeas* 7.

[9]Tertullian, *On the Flesh of Christ* 5.

[10]John Murray, "The Believer's Final Bliss," *Christianity Today* (July 7, 1958), 16.

[11]Leroy Bowman, *The American Funeral* (Westport, Conn.: Greenwood, 1959), 119.

[12]Richard Morgan, "Cremation," *The Christian Ministry* (May 1984), 14.

[13]Edwin Hatch (1878). See *Chalice Hymnal* (St. Louis: Chalice Press), 254.

[14]Warren Shibles, *Death* (Whitewater, Wis.: Language Press, 1974), 13.

[15]*Psychology Today* (May 1987), 54.

[16]George Santayana, *Soliloquies in England* (New York: Scribner's, 1924), 98–99.

[17]From a brochure by Armento Liturgical Arts, Buffalo, N.Y.

[18]Raymond Arvio, *The Cost of Dying* (New York: Harper & Row, 1974), 39.

[19]James Roosevelt and Sidney Shalett, *Affectionately, F.D.R.* (New York: Harcourt, Brace, 1959), 366–69.

About the Authors

Jerome W. Berryman is an Episcopal priest educated at the University of Kansas, Tulsa University School of Law, and Princeton Theological Seminary. His publications include: *Godly Play, Teaching Godly Play,* and *Young Children and Worship* with Sonja Stewart. He also edited and was a contributor to *Life Maps: The Journey of Human Faith* with James W. Fowler and Sam Keen. His lectures and workshops have been presented in Australia, Canada, Denmark, England, Germany, Italy, Mexico, The Netherlands, and the United States.

Bryan J. Cannon is a retired Presbyterian minister with forty years of pastoral counseling and therapy experience. He is a published poet and author who learned to sail when he was fifty-seven, ski when he was sixty, and is now a successful ceramicist living in Houston, Texas with his wife, Phyllis. They have four children and two grandchildren.

Howard Clinebell, who has a doctorate from Columbia University, is Professor Emeritus at the Claremont School of Theology where he taught pastoral psychology and counseling for three decades, served on the Claremont Graduate School faculty, and was Clinical Co-Director of the Pastoral Counseling and Growth Center. He has taught in thirty countries covering all continents except Antarctica, authored sixteen books, and continues to be active as a paradigm-expanding writer, workshop/playshop leader, eco-justice crusader, grandparent, and itinerant teacher in developing countries and the United States.

Paul F. Feiler most recently served as Pastor of St. Philips Presbyterian Church, Houston, Texas, having previously served churches in Minnesota, Massachusetts and New Jersey. He is a graduate of Wheaton College (B.A.), Bethel Theological Seminary (M.Div), and Princeton Theological Seminary (Ph.D.). Paul is the author of numerous anonymous articles and a frequent lecturer to his family and friends.

O. I. Cricket Harrison is Minister of Valley Christian Church, Twin Falls, Idaho. An ordained minister in the Christian Church (Disciples of Christ), she has previously served congregations in Iowa and southern California. She is working toward a Ph.D. in Theology and Personality with an emphasis in Religious Education at the School of Theology at Claremont. Concentrating on the relationship between aesthetic experience and a person's growth in faith, her sermons and liturgical plays have been published in a number of anthologies. She served on the Development

Committee for the *Chalice Hymnal* (the new hymnal for the Disciples) and co-edited a book of worship resources entitled *Chalice Worship*.

Marie Johnson is an ordained minister in the United Church of Christ who presently serves as Clinical Director of the Clinebell Institute. She graduated from Andover Newton Theological School and earned a Doctorate of Education at the University of Rochester. She has served as an adjunct faculty member at the School of Theology at Claremont and the Presbyterian Seminary of the West. She is a licensed marriage, family and child counselor in California, certified as a Fellow in the American Association of Pastoral Counselors, and Clinical Member of the American Association of Marriage and Family Therapy.

Paul B. Maves was a graduate of Nebraska Wesleyan University (A.B./1936), Drew Theological Seminary (B.D./1939), and Drew University (Ph.D./1949). One of the leading churchmen in the field of aging, he was author of numerous articles on the aging process and nine books, including *Older People and the Church* (1949, with Cedarleaf), *Understanding Ourselves as Adults* (1959), and *Faith for the Older Years* (1986). Scholar, teacher (Drew University) and pastor, Paul Maves died September 16, 1994.

William E. Phipps graduated from Davidson College (B.S.), Union Theological Seminary in Virginia (M.Div.), the University of Hawaii (M.A.), and the University of St. Andrews in Scotland (Ph.D.). For most of his career he has been professor of religion and philosophy at Davis and Elkins College in West Virginia. Of his dozen books, two are especially relevant to this study and are still in print: *Death: Confronting the Reality* (John Knox Press, 1987) and *Cremation Concerns* (Thomas Books, 1989).

William O. Roberts, has served as an academic (Assistant Dean of Admissions and Lecturer in Religion at Wesleyan University) and as a United Church of Christ minister of two congregations. After serving as Senior Consultant with KPMG Peat Marwick and as Senior Residential Vice President with Prudential Services and Prudential Connecticut Realty, he began his own consulting firm in 1993. He is author of two books, *Initiation to Adulthood: An Ancient Rite of Passage in Contemporary Form* (1982) and *Crossing the Soul's River: A Rite of Passage for Men* (1998).

Hugh W. Sanborn is a graduate of Muhlenberg College (B.A./1962), Andover Newton Theological School (B.D. and S.T.M./1966 and 1967), and the University of Iowa (Ph.D./1975). He has served as Houston Director of Campus Ministry for United Campus Ministry since 1980, has taught psychology of religion at Rice since 1973, and has been a pastoral therapist serving two churches since 1978. He is author of several articles and a book, *Mental-Spiritual Health Models: An Analysis of the Models of Boisen, Hiltner and Clinebell* (University Press of America,1979).

Laurence Hull Stookey, an ordained United Methodist minister, has been professor of preaching and worship since 1973 at Wesley Theological Seminary, Washington, D.C. He holds degrees from Swarthmore College, Wesley Seminary, and Princeton Theological Seminary. Stookey is author of a trilogy on worship: *Baptism: Christ's Act in the Church; Eucharist: Christ's Feast with the Church*; and *Calendar: Christ's Time for the Church* (Abingdon Press). He served on the committee that produced The United Methodist Hymnal and headed its subcommittee on worship resources.

J. Earl Thompson, Jr., is professor of pastoral psychology and family studies at Andover Newton Theological School, where he has taught since 1964. An ordained minister in the United Church of Christ, Dr. Thompson is also a licensed and practicing marriage and family therapist and a supervisor in the American Association of Marriage and Family Therapists.

Robert Tucker, recently retired, served as senior minister of First Congregational Church of Houston since 1971. Earlier, he taught in Turkey and at the University of Minnesota. He has graduate degrees in theology from the University of Chicago (M.Div.) and Chicago Theological Seminary (B.Div.), a doctorate from United Theological Seminary (D.Min.), and a degree in library science from the University of Minnesota (M.A.).